blue
rider
press

THE BODIES
IN PERSON

THE BODIES IN PERSON

AN ACCOUNT OF CIVILIAN CASUALTIES IN AMERICAN WARS

NICK McDONELL

BLUE RIDER PRESS

New York

blue
rider
press

An imprint of Penguin Random House LLC
375 Hudson Street
New York, New York 10014

Portions of chapter 15, "Record Keeping in the Emergency Room of the Baghdad Teaching Hospital," previously appeared in the *London Review of Books* 38, no. 9 (May 5, 2016).

All photographs are by the author unless noted otherwise. Page 152: Photographer unknown; courtesy the Taha family. Page 157: Photograph by Caecilia Pieri / Fondation Le Corbusier. Page 162: Photographer unknown; photograph provided by Zabiullah Zarifi.

ISBN 9780735211575

Printed in the United States of America
1   3   5   7   9   10   8   6   4   2

Book design by Amy Hill
Maps by Jeffrey Ward

Penguin is committed to publishing works of quality and integrity.
In that spirit, we are proud to offer this book to our readers;
however, the story, the experiences, and the words
are the author's alone.

Contents

THE BODIES
IN PERSON

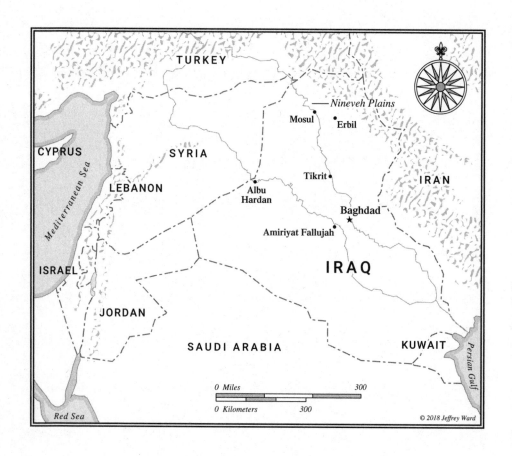

TURKEY

CYPRUS

Mediterranean Sea

SYRIA

Nineveh Plains

Mosul •
• Erbil

LEBANON

Albu
Hardan

Tikrit •

Baghdad
★

IRAN

ISRAEL

Amiriyat Fallujah

IRAQ

JORDAN

SAUDI ARABIA

KUWAIT

Persian Gulf

0 Miles   300

0 Kilometers   300

Red Sea

© 2018 Jeffrey Ward

© 2018 Jeffrey Ward

I.

The Classy Hotel

I didn't always think this way. I'm an American born in 1984, and halfway through my life my country went to war abroad. For a combination of reasons not unusual among young men, I went too. After the initial bloom of romance around working in places where America was at war, hoping to get shot at without getting shot, I believed the best path was to channel local populations in writing and scrub my voice as much as possible from the pages. I've attempted that a few times, tried also to launch projects that move resources faster than words on a screen. But life splinters plans, and ten years into visiting these places and thinking about my own country it's clear to me that some other kind of reckoning is due.

Since autumn of 2001, after nineteen men hijacked and crashed passenger jets into skyscrapers in New York, a military headquarters in Washington, D.C., and an open field bordered by conifers in Pennsylvania, America has been killing civilians in Afghanistan. For nearly as long, and in earlier wars, it has been killing them in Iraq. No one disputes this. The dispute is only over *how many*, *why*, and whether the *why* justifies the killing. Some say America is benevolent, a force for good. Others say it's a brutal empire. Many observe complexity, and many more are not interested in thinking about these questions at all.

———

Like prayer, I'll state here at the beginning that *America, Iraq, Afghanistan,* and all the others represent incomprehensible multitudes,[1] and that the first step away from a person's name is the first step toward killing him without thinking too much about it. So I want to avoid the general, but I also know it to be part of our minds, and a necessary element of progress. In terms of the specific: Endnotes provide sources and additional context, along with some ideas better separated from the rest of the book—but still important to it, and to me. Throughout, *italicized* quotations are taken from my notes and memory; direct quotations are taken from scenes and interviews I recorded in person. Some were beautiful, some awful. When I was daunted, I often looked to the natural world for comfort. Especially on beginning trips of uncertain outcome.[2]

I began several trips like that in the tidy city of Erbil, Kurdistan, northern Iraq. Erbil's not at all like the frantic Hollywood movies about the Middle East. The airport is better than John F. Kennedy International, New York's main airport. The streets are dusty but otherwise clean, people hang out in malls. For a while, most foreign reporters covering the war in Iraq were based in Erbil.

I stayed in the Classy Hotel. The name was funny in a way you never had to explain. There was a short pool in the basement in which I swam laps while a vastly obese Iraqi gentleman watched his son bob on inflatable water wings. The lobby was a popular meeting place for contractors, aid workers, and war profiteers, only a few hours' drive from the fighting by a good road across the Nineveh Plains. The best-known American newspapers kept correspondents in residence. I stayed on a discount rate, courtesy of a friend, a bureau chief at the time.

I was grateful for the discount. Reporting was expensive and the economics of media were, and remain, uncertain. In fact, as I have been writing this book, the company that paid for it—Penguin Random House, majority-owned by the multinational Bertelsmann—has closed down the imprint under whose aegis it was purchased.[3] A lot of people at the Classy were likewise negotiating unstable industries—looking for jobs, doing good work with barely a boss to pitch. A photographer whose business card read "human"; an ex-soldier trying to break into Hollywood; a graduate student trying to break into tenure. You would see them at breakfast, faces to their phones, perhaps a table over from the tattooed mercenaries pouring miniature bottles of whiskey into the morning's coffee. I had a lot of conversations with all of them. Mostly variations on the same conversation, revolving around a handful of questions.

What do you do? Who do you work for?

In my case, according to market research: 60 percent of American book buyers are women, 61 percent are college educated, and 63 percent earn an annual income of $50,000 or more. You could usefully pick a wider variety of numbers to address in this context, but the point, in the conversations, was that any reflection on audience, whatever the job, led to the question of intent, and in turn, resource allocation.

Why are you doing it? Is it effective?

At the time, at the Classy, I hadn't yet come to many conclusions. In anglophone war histories, memoirs, and close anthropologies, such questions are often left up to the reader, *you*, to decipher—though some clear answers have been articulated. In his famous essay "Why I Write," George Orwell provides four: sheer egoism; aesthetic enthusiasm; historical impulse; political purpose. "It can be seen," observes Orwell, "how these various impulses must war against one another, and how they must fluctuate from person to person and from time to time." Orwell explicitly puts aside the question of income:

How do you pay for it?

The answer: one way or another, like everything else. When I signed the contract for this book I was paid $85,000; I'm owed an additional $140,000, to be paid in pieces—on delivery of the manuscript, on publication, and then on its first anniversary. I began the work in August

2015; publication is planned for September 2018. This divides out to $75,000 per year with which to live and cover expenses. I'm fortunate to have this deal, and to have had money saved that I could spend along the way. Without the savings, the reporting would have been more time-consuming, less safe, perhaps impossible. This is part of why a disproportionate number of human rights and conflict researchers come from the middle classes and above. The implications are many. One is that information about innocent death in foreign wars is most accessible to America's cosmopolitan wealthy, even though it's mostly the working classes, domestically and abroad, who become casualties.

There've been quite a few bars like the Classy, over the past century. I suspect those italicized questions have haunted each of them—the Phoenicia in Beirut, the Continental in Saigon, L'Atmosphère in Kabul, the rest. They're important to the American mythology of the wars, stages for personal drama and later television and film, part of the same feedback loop that makes soldiers stick playing cards in their helmet bands because they've seen movie soldiers do it.[4] Violence imitates violence, and so, perversely, unites disparate countries and people. This is how civilians everywhere die for the same reasons, how periphery turns against center, and how, I think, what's best in America's experiment rusts away. Not on account of injustice, which is common to every age, but on account of lies told itself, hollower with repetition. A kind of collective cognitive dissonance.

"We have a very good sense of any civilians that we, our airstrikes, have killed," says the colonel, "and we announce them. . . ."

But I am getting ahead of the story.

High above the rubble, bats were passing in the dusk.

II.

Civil Defense

1.

Attempt to Reach Civilians Trapped in West Mosul

Lieutenant Colonel Rabih Ibrahim Hassan, forty-eight, civil defense, West Mosul. He speaks with the particular rolling accent of that city, as do his six children and wife, in whose company he dons a blue jumpsuit before departing for the station at dawn. It's an abandoned Education Ministry building in the recently liberated neighborhood of Ras al-Jadah, one squat story little furnished or supplied but surrounded by sturdy walls, with enough room for the unit's battered, shining trucks. The men of civil defense haven't been paid in three years. Under Islamic State occupation, they lied to the militants on empty stomachs, misdirected and complied subversively with the letter of command. He and his men were on another call and could not, therefore, come to the aid of the fighters. They could not take up arms against the apostates, as doing so interfered with rescue operations. They were present at the site, digging by hand, expecting the dead but hoping as ever for the living, where were *you*? Rabih is wry, didactic, and exhausted. Faced with a never-ending series of catastrophes, he tends, before delivering his verbose and often shouted orders, to eye closing and lengthy dramatic pause, such as he is now affecting, on the phone, in his makeshift office, while a teary middle-aged couple sits on a ragged sofa opposite, begging that he dig their relatives out from beneath the rubble of yet another American airstrike.

Rabih opens his brown eyes.

"My dear brother," he says into the phone, "I am quite aware of the address you are talking about. I just came back to the base from the middle of Pepsi Road toward the Boursa area. Behind the street directly. We went there, and we assumed there were people alive under the destroyed buildings. We met Colonel Muneer for about fifteen minutes. He didn't let us in, and they were under chemical attack. It is out of hand. When the army claims that there were chemical attacks, how can I go there?"[5]

He listens. It's Sunday. On Friday at about four in the afternoon an airstrike destroyed the house in question, close to the front line in Zanjili. Twenty or more people are reportedly trapped beneath the rubble. This is during the final days of the battle for Mosul in 2017,[6] the largest-scale urban combat the world has seen since World War II. It's a proxy war, fought between ISIS and the combined United States and Iraqi forces, but also the rest of the world's powers, which, in various and shifting configurations, accuse one another of starting the combat intermittently engulfing three thousand miles from Mediterranean to Hindu Kush.[7, 8] The U.S. position is particularly fractured—the American president accuses his predecessor of "founding ISIS."[9] Colonel Rabih doesn't have time to follow the news, though, because he and his men are overwhelmed with bodies.

Rabih's sergeant, Mohammed Shaaban, sits in a corner on a plastic chair adding names to an A4 notebook. On its cover is written MARTYRS' BOOK, MARCH 2017–. The end date is left blank. The rule, to prevent mistakes: No name added unless someone in the unit touches the body. That day, 503 names are in the book, and the official number of civilian casualties caused and acknowledged by the Coalition, over the course of the entire war, all over the country, since June 2014, is 448. And as usual, Mohammed and Rabih have been receiving phone calls all day requesting the retrieval of bodies, or the rescue of relatives trapped beneath airstruck rubble. Often callers ask for the latter, knowing only the former is possible, in the hope that their beloved might receive a timely and so religiously correct burial and passage to heaven. Sergeant Mohammed has forgiving eyes, especially in comparison with Colonel Rabih's, which bug out.

"People," Colonel Rabih massages a temple with his second mobile phone, "you mean . . . alive?"

Sergeant Mohammed goes on writing in the book as Rabih's voice rises.

"Do you have any phone number," Rabih demands, "of one of them, so that I can call them . . . ? The ones you are talking about! Let someone provide me with precise information and the address of the people out there, so that people from the army—including Colonel Muneer!—will provide us an approval to enable us to have our mission there, because the security forces are refusing to let us in. You understand me, my dear brother?"

Before Colonel Rabih sends his men to rescue civilians or excavate bodies, he visits sites himself. He's well known for this, for walking, careful but upright, onto streets resounding with sniper fire. He tried to scout the house in Zanjili earlier in the day, but had been turned away by the army. It's a problematic case, because the trapped family—the Abaji family—is rich and influential, and many connected people are calling to demand their immediate rescue—including the head of Mosul operations for the Iraqi army, Major General Najm al-Jabouri. Some confusion seems to have flowered in the chain of command between al-Jabouri and the men who turned Rabih away.

"I am a high-ranking civil defense officer." Rabih jabs a finger in the air, shouting into the phone. "And there was a provincial council member. Despite that, they didn't let us in. So, then, how can you say that? I tell you it is a dangerous place, and there are snipers over there, also chemical weapons. How can you enter the location . . . from where would *you* enter?"

Rabih hangs up, promptly banishes his deputy and supplicants from the office so that he can take a nap. Mohammed escorts the teary couple away, noting their request.

L ater in the afternoon, several of Rabih's men are detained at a checkpoint. They passed into some army unit's jealously guarded territory without permission. The diverse Iraqi security forces—which officially include Rabih's men—are meant to coordinate, but actually control fiefdoms around the city and often distrust one another. So the detention is not entirely surprising, but it drives Rabih, just awoken, apoplectic. He paces the compound parking lot, shouting into his mobile. The detention, it is clear to him, is not really about being in the wrong territory—it has come down from al-Jabouri! In order to pressure Rabih into rescuing the Abajis!

Rabih suspects everyone in the Abaji house is dead. It's been two days. And he knows of others, trapped elsewhere, recently texting from beneath rubble, who are likely still alive. But Rabih isn't in a position to defy al-Jabouri, the most powerful man in Mosul. And so, stomping through the common room beside his office, where his men are napping through the late-afternoon hunger of Ramadan, Rabih announces that, first thing tomorrow, they'll be setting out for Zanjili.

O vernight, men and women beneath the rubble pray in darkness.

C olonel Rabih is back at the station near dawn. As the sun rises he listens to requests from a small crowd in the shade of his red van. They want bodies collected, want Rabih to sign paperwork certifying their relatives killed and houses destroyed in the battle for Mosul. The government has promised compensation. A trio of middle-aged men in checked keffiyehs tell a long story about four relatives killed, ten days before, and three killed yesterday, some of whom they were able to bury, others not.

"Listen"—Rabih cuts their spokesman off—"you will say this."

"Yeah, yeah."

"They were one family, of seven members, their house was hit by an airstrike, four of them were buried by you, and the three were left for us to get."

"Okay."

"Because if you say those four dead people were killed a long time ago, their rights will be gone forever."

"Yeah."

"No one will take you into consideration if you don't specify exactly when those four people were killed. . . ."

"Right. . . ."

"And since they are related and from one family, we will say four bodies are buried, and three were found now, so all of the seven people will be recorded as dead in one documented case."

"God bless you."

"Once you get into details about which got killed first, it might hurt your case. Am I right, brother?"

"Yes, you're right."

"We aren't gaining anything from doing this," Rabih says, "but this involves people's rights, and this one family got hurt twice in such short time, their case must be documented as one case. Three bodies were just found, and you said the other four bodies aren't in coffins, right?"[10]

"No, they aren't in coffins."

"That's it then. A total of seven were killed from the same family."

The trio in keffiyehs departs.

Rabih works through the crowd until only two men remain. Omer and Ammar are cousins from Zanjili, the neighborhood on the front line. Omer is a nearsighted candy maker in his early thirties, gently mustachioed, glasses pushed high on his nose. Ammar, about ten years younger, is rougher but more stylish, a car painter sporting the close-cropped beard known colloquially as "sexy beard." Two days earlier, they explain, their uncle's house was destroyed by a missile. They believe he's alive but trapped, pinned at the leg, because his youngest son, having escaped, has told them so. Rabih tells them to give their information to Sergeant Mohammed and he will get to their uncle's house as soon as possible. Omer and Ammar, not satisfied, press the case. It turns out their uncle's house is close to where the Abajis are reportedly trapped. Could they just have some tools, maybe a ride?

Absolutely no to tools, for anyone! For the many reasons Rabih has already explained for the benefit of the group. What a question! And the area is too dangerous for Ammar and Omer to attempt a rescue.

But at length, concluding his lecture, Rabih offers the cousins a ride.

It's mid-morning when Colonel Rabih departs in the red van. To his left, his driver, Thanoon, thirty-eight, negotiates the pitted street. The battle for the city has alleviated traffic but made certain areas impassable with stacked, crushed cars, toppled walls, snapped telephone poles, deep craters. Thanoon is a local, however, and a shrewd navigator, most of his adult life spent with civil defense. The past six months have been the most difficult. Burn scarring acquired in a recent car bombing textures the skin beneath his baseball cap. He also recently caught some mortar shrapnel in a leg. Still, Thanoon is a cheerful presence at the wheel. On Rabih's other side sits Ahmed, his handsome bodyguard, Kalashnikov between his legs. Ahmed is twenty-eight and a bit of a brooder. He's the only man in helmet or body armor—his flak vest, which seems a size too small, resembles an oversize bib. In the backseat Ammar and Omer watch one wrecked facade after another pass beyond the dusty windows.

En route to Zanjili, Rabih's short convoy of trucks links up with a cousin unit—Baghdad civil defense, come north to Mosul's aid. All stop some blocks from the front line to discuss an approach. The street where they're staging is awash in brass shell casings, and a soldier sweeps them away with a long-handled broom. The tinkle of the brass is audible over idling engines and irregular *whumpf*s of mortar fire as Rabih consults with Colonel Qusay al-Saadi, commander of the Baghdadis. Qusay is a swaggering bull of a man in a red jumpsuit, about Rabih's age, his mustache black as shoe polish. His deputy, Lieutenant Jabar, is both fierce and playful, with a long face and jaw evoking the statues of Easter Island.[11] Their Baghdad men are more numerous, better fed, and more raucous than Rabih's Muslawis. They are also Shia, where Rabih's men are Sunni. All lean on trucks in the morning heat as their commanders parley.

Rabih and Qusay quickly agree on a route but must wait for the Iraqi army's go-ahead to cross onto Pepsi Road, which separates them from the Abaji house. Pepsi, so called by the locals on account of proximity to a soda bottling plant, is one of the city's "belts," or wide avenues. The next is Boursa, the money changers' avenue, still contested. Belts are connected by streets, which are in turn interconnected by irregular, twisting alleys. Approaching the Old City, all narrow until belts and streets give way to the ancient warren of IED-filled lanes which comprise ISIS's final redoubt, about a kilometer and a half distant. When Rabih visited Pepsi Road the day before, he tells Qusay, the sniper fire from Boursa down the streets made rescue impossible. And anyway, the army wouldn't let him through, though he waited a long time.

Now, as all wait again for permission, Ahmed steps gingerly onto Pepsi Road for a look around. About a block to his right, he sees an ISIS flag flying over the alleys. Immediately to his left, nearly at his feet, the body of an ISIS fighter lies splayed and decomposing in the sunlight. The corpse hardly earns a glance. Ahmed has passed two others en route that morning, seen many besides. ISIS bodies are, as policy, ignored and left to rot. My fixer-interpreter, however, snaps a picture and posts it to his various social media accounts. For some, corpses are a kind of awful currency, proof of a proximity to danger which is often mistaken for access to truth.[12] This particular corpse—he—lies in a stain of blood, arms stretched above his head, jaw open wide as if in scream or song. He's wearing brown track pants with an elastic waistband, and was until recently thinking, speaking, and growing his matted beard according to religious dictate. His leaders urged him to martyrdom, and the Coalition stated it would *eliminate* him, which it did. He must have suspected he would die in Mosul. And so despite rubble, rot, and bloodstain, there is on Pepsi Road a sense of arrangement, of planning. As though the body rots inside a gigantic cathedral, or stadium, some vast carved sarcophagus, the buildings its broken sides, their exposed wires like so much ivy, slowly reclaiming the sturdiest of human works.[13]

A round zips across the road, probably a stray. Ahmed can't detect the source, retreats to safety. Inside a jagged doorway, Omer and Ammar are explaining the location of their uncle's house to Thanoon. After the left onto Pepsi, it's three streets up, between Pepsi and Boursa. The Abaji house is two streets up.

"Is it true they won't let us in?" Ammar is asking.

"They won't allow *you*," Ahmed tells him.

"Man," says Thanoon, "they don't let *us* in sometimes."

Finally, though, the army gives the go-ahead. In their tactical estimation the situation has improved enough, they have pushed ISIS to a safe distance. The men of civil defense are skeptical, but Rabih calls them into the red van, and Thanoon puts it in gear. Behind, Baghdadi fire trucks fall in line and take the turn onto Pepsi. Thanoon gets the van nearly to the Abajis' street, but then it jams to a halt. Something has snagged the undercarriage. He gins the engine, reverses, tries to rock off whatever it is. Tense seconds until it lurches forward, clears, proceeds. A few hundred meters further along. Rabih hops out. He orders the men to wait, then disappears around the corner toward the airstruck house.

A moment later, sustained gunfire sounds across Pepsi Road, like the ripping of a vast canvas. Ahmed, Thanoon, Omer, and Ammar jump from the car and rush through the broken door of an abandoned shop for cover. In flight, they catch sight of one of the fire trucks, a block back. Its right front tire has been shot out, but it's rolling on, just past the first street which, it's now clear, remains under ISIS control. Regular fire sings out, complicating any travel back in that direction.

Inside the wrecked shop, glass glitters and crunches underfoot. Nothing but broken shelves and loose wires, no sign or product to mark what once was sold. Omer, Ahmed, and Thanoon wait against a wall, listening for an ebb in the shooting. Ammar, impatient, sticks his head beyond the door.

"Ammar!" shouts Omer.

Ammar doesn't listen, steps outside. Just as he clears the doorway, an airstrike lands near enough to move earth underfoot, raise the dust into fog. The noise of the explosion lasts two seconds, scaling from high screech to a profound bass that shakes the men's stomachs. Some building on the Boursa side of the block, it seems likely, has been destroyed.

"Ammar! Come down near us."

Ammar, with a not entirely convincing nonchalance, steps back inside. "I'm used to it," he says, rejoining his cousin in the gloom.

"We shouldn't have taken this route here," says Omer, shaking his head, "we should've taken the other one."

When the shooting subsides, Ahmed and Thanoon peek out down the street, then hug walls to where the fire trucks stand, just beyond ISIS's line of fire—or what they hope is ISIS's line of fire. The Baghdadis have carried a wounded driver to the pavement and stand around him in a tight circle, agreeing angrily with one another.

"All those bodies," one shouts, pointing toward the Abajis' street, "don't deserve a single drop of our blood!"

"Fuck their fathers and anyone who supports them!"

The subtext is sectarian. The Abajis, like most Muslawis, are Sunni.

"Back up, everybody, stay calm," shouts Lieutenant Jabar, spreading the circle.

At his feet, the wounded man, Saddam, grimaces. He has been shot through the truck door and is bleeding freely from a hole below his knee. The wound doesn't look serious and a fireman is bandaging the leg, but the crowd is increasingly pissed off, believing, with some justification, that no security forces lie between their flank and the ISIS fighter, or fighters, who shot up the truck. Lieutenant Jabar commiserates for calm.

"They've been putting too much pressure on us since yesterday," he announces. "They're calling for this family because they're with the government."

The Baghdadis load wounded Saddam back into the truck, get in after him, and tear off down the street, leaving Ahmed, Thanoon, and the cousins to return to the red van. Still no sign of Colonel Rabih. Back in the broken shop, the cousins discuss whether to make a run for their uncle's house. It's only one block further.

"Brother," Ahmed interrupts, "it's really dangerous there beyond the alley."

Omer ignores him and looks steadily at Ammar. "What should we do?" he asks.

"We should tell the lieutenant colonel what's happened," says Ammar, without so much of his earlier nerve.

"There's an army!" Thanoon insists. "Tell him," he says to Ammar, but pointing at Omer, "that there is an *army*. Don't go!"

Omer ignores them all, fiddles with his phone, stares into the street. He is the sterner cousin.

"Tell him to call Jabouri," suggests Ahmed, joking.

Omer turns on him.

"Come on, man! What is al-Jabouri, he is nothing!"

"Lieutenant Colonel Rabih will come back and get [the army] to help."

"Yeah," says Ammar, looking less and less like he wants to make another run down the street, "that's possible."

Above, the hollow roar of aircraft.

"There's an airplane getting closer," says Ammar.

"Please," Omer says, maybe prays, to no one in particular, "don't let it see the van."

T he roof of Rabih's red van is unmarked. From above, it would not be hard to mistake it for an ISIS vehicle, there in the no-man's-land of Pepsi Road. And because the men are isolated from the rest of the civil defense team, which has retreated, and because no army is in sight, and because the last airstrike could not help but unnerve even a veteran like Thanoon ("Yesterday we loaded seventeen dead bodies"), he and Ahmed are unsure whether it's safer to stay inside the shop—where they're protected from bullets and shrapnel—or outside, where they can perhaps warn the army of their presence. Ahmed is convinced that inside they're likely to be stumbled upon, or seen peripherally, and so shot by soldiers who'll assume anyone still in the area is ISIS. He therefore has been lingering in plain view at the edge of the broken shop front. Thanoon disagrees, but for a moment all the men are outside anyway, watching a helicopter. Not so high above them, half a block in the distance, it banks, hovers, then launches a pair of missiles. These fly overhead, white contrails in their wake, and detonate out of sight with another tremendous crash.

"Get inside," Thanoon urges the group, leading the way.

"May God help the guys up there," say Omer.

"May God help the surrounded civilians," says Thanoon.

"Someone might say, 'Where's civil defense?'" says Ammar, sarcastically, at the expense of the retreated Baghdadis.

Omer's phone rings.

"Hey," he answers, "we got to al-Pepsi street, got to Muqaddim Street. . . . After that one crew of the civil defense was hit. . . . Yeah. Gunshots, killing, and airplanes."

Ammar, listening, says to himself: "We have to do it."

"Brother," Omer says into the phone, "there is no clear way for us to get out now."

Beyond the doorway, the gunfire resumes, louder, incoming.

If Omer and Ammar make a run for it, they may die by bullet or mortar fired by ISIS or the Iraqi army, or by airstrike launched by the international coalition, almost certainly America in particular. Or they may survive, may even rescue their uncle and return by the smoke-addled light of dusk to what new homes they've cobbled in their displacement. But which? Or grievous injury in between, some unforeseeable disaster? Each step they've taken to this doorway is their own, and those beyond will be the same. ISIS can't make them run, nor can America. And yet this choice of life and death is not their own, precisely, either.[14]

They decide to make a run for it.

"If Colonel Rabih comes back," says Ammar, "tell him."

"Okay," says Thanoon as though conceding a point in an argument he expects to win later, "go ask the army, but walk close to the wall."

The army is back where they came from, past the street of the sniper, past the body, over the intersection—a safer direction than the uncle's street and front line beyond. Known danger, at least.

"Yeah," agrees Ahmed, "wait for the army's orders."

Omer and Ammar don't answer. After a moment on the threshold they step outside. As they do, the incoming crack of fire echoes loudly in the shop. The cousins retreat, startled.

"This is not a game!" Thanoon shouts at them. "This is death!"

"Come on!" Omer gathers himself again. "Be brave and go."

"Just to see how the situation is out there," says Ammar, almost apologetically.

And they dash onto Pepsi Road.

2.

Correspondence (I)

THE WHITE HOUSE
OFFICE OF THE PRESS SECRETARY
FOR IMMEDIATE RELEASE

August 8, 2014

TEXT OF A LETTER FROM THE PRESIDENT
TO THE SPEAKER OF THE HOUSE OF REPRESENTATIVES
AND THE PRESIDENT PRO TEMPORE OF THE SENATE

Dear Mr. Speaker: (Dear Mr. President:)

As I announced publicly on August 7, 2014, I have authorized the U.S. Armed Forces to conduct targeted airstrikes in Iraq. These military operations will be limited in their scope and duration as necessary to protect American personnel in Iraq by stopping the current advance on Erbil by the terrorist group Islamic State of Iraq and the Levant and to help forces in Iraq as they fight to break the siege of Mount Sinjar and protect the civilians trapped there.

Pursuant to this authorization, on August 8, 2014, U.S. military forces commenced targeted airstrike operations in Iraq. . . .[15]

I am providing this report as part of my efforts to keep the Congress fully informed, consistent with the War Powers Resolution (Public Law 93-148). I appreciate the support of the Congress in this action.

Sincerely,

Barack Obama

3.

Excavation of Bodies
off Pepsi Road

Ahmed and Thanoon wait. It's not the first time they've waited for Rabih under less-than-ideal circumstances. The cousins haven't come back, either.

"When the gunshots have passed," Ahmed says, "this will be different."

"The smell is foul," remarks Thanoon.

"I'm going to sit on the stairs," says Ahmed, retreating to a set of steps in the back of the shop. Behind him, a door lists into the darkness of the wrecked building. The source of the smell. Neither investigates. They speak instead about the last time they were on this belt, some ways down, on a block since secured. An explosion killed half a dozen or so after they'd arrived that day, bodies everywhere. But before that, before all this, they'd done their shopping on Boursa, the next belt over. Ahmed recalls good markets.

Soon, his phone rings. "Hello, Mohammed," he answers, stepping out to check the street. "One of Baghdad's crews was hit. . . . Yeah. I don't know, we're still in Boursa. They moved on. . . . In Boursa! Yeah, tell him that we are in Boursa, tell him to make sure to inform us. The Baghdad team retreated. . . . Yeah. Once Lieutenant Colonel Rabih came over, they retreated. . . . Okay, bye."

He hangs up frowning, but then his expression inverts, lights up—Rabih has reappeared. He's strolling down Pepsi Road to cover in his habitual slouch, talking on his mobile phone. Arriving at the shop front, he holds the phone away from his mouth.

"How did it happen?" he asks Ahmed, at the absence of Baghdadi fire trucks.

"He was shot in the car."

Rabih shakes his head and resumes the phone call. The Abajis' street, in his determination, is not yet secure enough to begin digging for survivors or bodies, and it's time to retreat. Presently, and with excellent timing, the cousins return, breathing hard. All scamper back into the red van and sink low into its seats, as far beneath the windows as possible. Thanoon starts the engine, takes a breath, and shifts into gear.

They make it safely back to the street of shell casings. Omer, clearly discouraged, is impatient to go home for the day. He got within sight of his uncle's house but couldn't get close enough to dig through the rubble. I ask him, "Is it necessary to do these airstrikes?"

"If there wasn't an airstrike," he says, "this wouldn't have happened to my uncle. . . . We want peace. Tell him," he tells my fixer, "all we want is peace."

Omer scans the staging area. Rabih is in consultation with Qusay and various army officers, looks like he will be for a while.

"Take down my phone number," says Omer. "If you want me, you can call me on this mobile number."

He hurries away to find a ride out. In the distance, more explosions. Sometime after Omer is gone, Rabih announces that the new plan is to go to the Abajis' house as soon as the army declares the area properly secured, maybe tomorrow.

Back at the station, Thanoon and Ahmed help prepare the evening meal. Times are lean—no sugar, rice donated—but not so lean as just before liberation, when some of Rabih's men took to hunting and eating cats. These days it's chicken, pickles, bread, and Mosul's famous grape juice under the usual tender banter of men working together in combat. Some lounge in front of the television, some retire to sleep on the roof. It's cooler, and the view of the city at night is dynamic: tracer fire and scattered flames, the sweep of distant headlights, the darkness broken by points of generator-powered light. The night is loud. Though sleeping men don't hear as they do awake, the brain continues to register vibrations of the eardrum. Noises creep into our dreams. The noises of the Mosul night, if they don't sync with explosions the men are actually dreaming of, might manifest themselves in some other dream form. Thunder over your home-town, an ice floe breaking up. The midnight crash of a spouse dropping milk in the kitchen might become an explosion in the dreams of suburban parents. Tracer fire might turn to cat's howl, in Thanoon's dreams. All seen or heard or smelled or previously imagined might appear. Even words written about civil defense teams elsewhere, about the White Hel-mets, for example—the Syrian civil defense group, carrying out work similar to Rabih's—might appear in a dream, if the dreamer happens to have read of the White Helmets on his phone, perhaps just seen the head-lines. Many articles have been written about them. A documentary on the topic won an Academy Award.[16] And yet for each civil defender, reporter, and reader, though the raw material may be shared by all and necessarily recycled and repeated, each dream is original. Nothing can prevent this process. Neither torture nor imprisonment can stop the dreams of a sleep-ing man. Neither hunger nor thirst, nor the rise of a fascist state, nor an inadequate healthcare system, nor any inequality. Even as the earth heats and oceans swell, nothing stops an innocent man dreaming except death, brain injury, or certain narcotics which, in our irrepressible creativity, we have engineered. The men of Mosul's civil defense all have reasons they risk their lives for trapped strangers, but each reason intersects with the desire to prevent early death, and, consequently, the end of dreams, how-ever unlikely or illogical, whatever they happen to depend upon, whether a common story of rescue workers, or tracer fire seen a thousand times or even only once, imagined.

No one sleeps for long. At around ten o'clock that night word goes around: a new mission, also on Pepsi Road. *Word goes around* in springs and flows, breaking down, dammed and exaggerated. Facebook pages report on certain neighborhoods. Texts arrive from unknown numbers. The army makes requests, too, and the militias, and the bereaved, and friends, neighbors—the whole city, except the airborne Americans who actually collapse the buildings. Not their responsibility, perhaps. In any case, in Ras al-Jadah station Colonel Rabih is arbiter of it all and doesn't always explain the politics behind whom they must try to rescue and when, and soon it's time to get back in the van.

Night missions are common and in some ways preferable—not as hot. Under the Mujasar highway approaching Pepsi Road, however, a stink of bodies still spices the cool night. Staging there, Rabih and Qusay hop an army Humvee to consult with a Ninth Division general at the front, leaving their men to tell stories in the roadside dark. One concerns a father who rushed from bombarded ISIS territory over the line to an Iraqi Special Operations Forces position, carrying a dead boy in his arms. The father, in shock, somehow thought the boy alive. Told by soldiers the boy was dead, the man began to wail. What happened? the soldiers asked. He told them an airstrike had killed one of his sons, and so he decided to try to escape with the remaining one. He'd quickly dug a shallow grave, the closest he could come to *halal* burial under the circumstances, and laid the dead son down, and covered him. Then he scooped up the surviving son and fled. But in his panic he'd taken the dead boy and buried the living one.

Other stories circulate in the darkness, jokes, boredom. After an hour or so Rabih returns. The army has changed its mind, and forbids any rescue operations off Pepsi Road that night.[17] The men return to their stations to sleep.[18,19]

In the morning, Rabih's red van crosses Pepsi Road without incident and parks at the near corner of the Abajis' street. A pair of army Humvees holds the far end. The men of civil defense, in red or blue jumpsuits, keep to the street's sides in deference to sounds of continuing gunfire—safely distant, they're told. Metal gates and stone walls run the length of the street, behind which concrete buildings stand, one to three floors each in various degrees of destruction and hues of sand. Some boast stone columns, others razor wire, others gaping mortar holes. All are bullet and shrapnel marked.

In the center of the block, where the damage is most severe, lies the Abajis' house. The homes on either side are shorn open in cross section, so that it is possible to see into a carpeted hallway; a bedroom with unmade bed; a study, its books overturned and scattered across the floor, a Koranic verse framed on the wall above a soldier swiveling in a black office chair, looking out over the devastation. Which is utter, a massive pile of brick and concrete, rebar thorning out. It's difficult to imagine anyone alive beneath, but civil defense has made some surprising rescues. Colonel Qusay paces the pile in aviator sunglasses, urgently directing his men. Shards and slabs of stone grind beneath his stained brown boots.

Center pile, the Baghdadis' lead man, Hussein, forty-three, hefts a gas-powered hacksaw. He's over six feet and broad beneath his blue helmet. A Texas "Fire and Rescue" patch in that state's shape adorns the left biceps of his red jumpsuit. A friend gave it to him during their training by American contractors in what was once known as Baghdad's Green Zone. Hussein was top of his class. With a yank on the pull starter he brings the saw sparking to a piece of rebar. The rubble's twisted skeleton, rebar must be broken up so chunks of roof and wall can be separated and cleared. The pile is like a giant puzzle in which each piece must be removed carefully, to prevent slide or collapse. The cutting is laborious. Hussein leans into it as other men take turns holding his belt from behind, lest he lose footing. When he cuts through to an open space, men chip around it, expanding the hole until it's large enough to enter, which Hussein does.

Then, from down in the pit, he shouts, "It's ISIS," and, for evidence: "They have a weapon!"

He's found a body. A pocket in the crush suggests the possibility of survivors. They would be on life's edge, unlikely to have eaten or drunk in nearly four days. A strong basement is the best chance, but the pile still stands two stories above street level.

"Boys," shouts Colonel Qusay, "nobody else down there . . ."[20]

Lieutenant Jabar paraphrases his commander's order to the men at greater volume, according to habit. "Boys, nobody go down! Only the team." Then he softens. "Once they become tired, I'll put you in."

Hussein shouts evenly from the pit: "We have two bodies here."

From all sides, shouted suggestions. Like many groups of men faced with a problem of spatial reasoning—say, packing suitcases into a trunk—the civil defense group argues about the best way to proceed. One of the most vocal is stubbled, pouchy Adil, who sometimes hovers near Colonel Qusay, and other times disappears entirely from the pile. He wears a white bandanna around his chins and a red T-shirt over his prodigious gut. Printed on the shirt is a cartoon of a half-naked, enormously muscled Caucasian fireman, holding a drooping fire hose and flashing a thumbs-up. ONLY THE BEST ARE IN THE FIRE DEPARTMENT, reads the German caption.[21]

"Sir, if you go from here," Adil says, "and we pull them out, it would be better. There's lots of rubble on them."

Colonel Qusay ignores him, shouting down into the hole: "Check them! If they are ISIS, don't bother with them, leave them. Check them; if all of them are ISIS we'll video them and go back."

"Sir," calls back Hussein, "two of them are ISIS here."

"Record them," says Adil. "Record them." He sounds unusually eager for them to be ISIS rather than civilian.

A bulldozer driver who has been observing this exchange suggests a more careful process. "Sir," he says, "let's take out the rubble and *then* identify them."

"There's one of them lying on his stomach," calls Hussein. "You can't identify him."

"Hussein, come out," orders Colonel Qusay, and then to another man, "Bring the bags!"

As men help Hussein up and out of the hole, Adil asks him, "Hussein, are they wearing military clothes?"

"I don't know, it's dark."

"They're wearing military clothes, right?"

ISIS fighters aren't consistently uniformed, but they often wear military gear.

"It's not clear, ISIS or not ISIS," a nearby fireman interjects from behind a mask.

"Do they have weapons with them?" Adil wants to know.

"No weapons," says Hussein.

"I heard there are weapons."

"The smell is too much," says the masked fireman. "There must be a lot of bodies here."

Top of the pile, a handful of soldiers stand smoking, watching the civil defense men at work. Faisal, from Diyala, late twenties, M16 slung over his shoulder, says, by way of hello, "Every day we're getting thousands of these bodies."

Then, realizing I'm American, he perks up. "I'm sick," he says. "I have stones in my kidney. Do the Americans have any hospitals here?"

"There are two, one in Mosul Jadida and one in the mosque," my fixer tells him.

"Can you bring medicine, when you come back?"

"I think this is our last day here."

Faisal is unimpressed. "When we liberated this area," he says, scraping grime across his stubble,[22] "we came before sunset, and the day after, the civilians told us, 'There is a family under the rubble there, they're yelling for help. . . .' We were shouting, 'Is there anyone alive?' But there wasn't a response. I think," he concludes, "they were ISIS yelling, but when we told them we were army, they didn't say anything."

Majid, a youthful and equally grimy friend of Faisal's from the Ninth Division, has been listening. He announces more personal concerns. "In

four days, we haven't taken a shower. Man, there's no water in this area."
He shakes his head, pointing to the hole. "If we stay any longer, we'll
smell like them."

"You guys never shower anyway," replies Faisal.

"You're saying we're dirty?"

"No man, the Ninth Division is good. Not like the Eighth Division.
We're like Um Allawi's division."

Laughter. Um Allawi is a mythical Baghdadi prostitute.

"The Mosul guys told us there are three [bodies]," says Majid, chang-
ing the subject.

"The doctor's family?"

The house, word is going around, belongs to a doctor.

"Yeah. A doctor came and told us there are three."

Adil, who has been hovering at the edge of this conversation, interjects. "He's a liar!" Adil says. "They're not three. They're twenty, maybe.
Even al-Abadi"—the prime minister—"is calling us about this."

"If you were coming here yesterday," rejoins Faisal, "that would've
been better. Maybe you would have found someone alive."

"We tried to come yesterday," says Adil, "but we couldn't make it."

"The other house," Faisal gestures vaguely down the street, "there
were thirty-five people under the rubble."

This quiets the group. Or perhaps it's the arrival of Colonel Qusay.

"When we first came to inspect," the colonel says, watching a bulldozer struggle with the Abajis' twisted gate, "we called and there was
no response."

He's talking about Rabih's lone reconnaissance up the street. Which,
suddenly, Faisal claims to have witnessed.

"Yeah," he says, "I saw civil defense come for inspection."

"Thanks God," adds Adil, sly. "You're the witness. Because maybe
the journalists and the media would write something else about this."

"I swear to God," says Faisal, "if I came here and someone was alive,
I'm not gonna pull him out? I'm gonna pull him out, somehow."

"Four days ago, Colonel Rabih came," Adil repeats the point. "There was nothing."

"*Inshallah* they are alive," Faisal intones.

"*Inshallah*," the assembled agree, "*inshallah.*"

Adil taps his chest in the ensuing pause. "If we hear someone," he says, "and he's alive, we'll get them out. We Iraqis have guts!"

Conversation wanders as the soldiers watch a bulldozer work. Ostensibly, they're guarding the operation, but they don't look alert. After watching them for a few moments, Colonel Qusay asks Faisal and Majid a question.

"Why didn't you tell us there was a sniper? Yesterday we came and he shot our cars and one of the guys got wounded."

"Where did you come from?" asks Faisal.

Qusay answers, pointing. "That street that has the bump."

"Yeah," says Faisal, "that's known."

Qusay is a higher-ranked and more commanding presence in every way, but the young soldier replies with a boredom verging on insolence. As though being armed—though least of the armed—he's more important than any unarmed civil defense officer.

"When we slowed down," says Qusay, "he started shooting at us."

"Which bump are you talking about?"

"When you go left, then straight."

"There's another way. That one's new, only yesterday they opened it. I've been using the other one for four days."

Qusay's nostrils, flaring. "We didn't know," he says. "You should've told us the way. When you go a few meters left, the bump is there, and that's the street where we got shot."

"No." Faisal is unapologetic. "Go straight and take a right, next to the school."

Adil, perhaps sensing the direction of his commander's mood, gets onside. "So why didn't they tell us the other route?" he demands.

Three seconds of incoming fire scatters the group to the lower reaches of the pile. When they reassemble, the conversation resets. Faisal has barely moved.

"That's ISIS," he says, "but it's far. The day before yesterday, an ISIS guy blew himself up on some soldiers from the Sixteenth Division. Seven martyrs, and the officer badly injured, and three other soldiers wounded."

"And how far is ISIS now?" Adil wants to know.

"Around four hundred meters."

"Where's the central high school?" Qusay asks. "Did they take it or not yet?"

The central high school, just visible beyond the Humvees at the end of the street, is drab, square, badly scarred.

"Yes," Faisal reports, "they took it. They're right behind the central high school."

"What about the fuel station?"

"Yes, it's liberated."

Colonel Qusay harrumphs and moves to business elsewhere on the pile. The bulldozer has managed to rip off the front gate and is pushing it across the street.

"There were lots of airstrikes, artillery, helicopters until we took it," says Faisal, resuming the conversation in the colonel's absence. "We have airstrikes supporting us, good, but they should fight them out by Tal Afar instead of surrounding them here."

Adil disagrees without hesitation: "No," he says, "let them die here."

Tal Afar is a smaller city to the west, still under ISIS control. The Iraqi army and the Coalition will, two months later, take it with little resistance or damage to the civilian population. As opposed to Mosul, where the Iraqis and Americans pursue an encircling tactic of "annihilation,"[23] in Tal Afar they will leave a corridor of escape for militants and civilians.

"If they die here"—Faisal spreads his arms over the pile—"it's a massacre. Look at this."

More incoming fire. The bullets seem to be angled such that the pile is safe, but some men still crouch at the volleys—Adil, for one.

"Let them all die here," Adil repeats, regaining his posture, "because maybe tomorrow they'd come back. They have money. They could get passports and go wherever they wanted."

The shooting intensifies, more men crouch. Conditions are not ideal. Hussein works with the hacksaw, the men with pickaxes, shovels, their hands. Faisal remains unbothered. "This is nothing," he says. "Yesterday we were in a house, and ISIS was in the house next door. We were fighting by throwing grenades. This street is fine—the next isn't safe."

"I think we need more weapons with us," says Adil.

"No, no, it's safe, just don't go to high places, and don't be out in the open." Faisal is thoughtful for a moment. "The best military plan would be to get them out into the Tal Afar area, toward Jazeera, and fight them there. And kill them there in Jazeera. Brother," he takes the point up again with Adil, "this is total devastation—and in the Old City, there are thousands of families. Those families will die there."

"Shit on them," says Adil. "Let them die. At the beginning they could've gotten out."

"No, they couldn't."

"They could, they could, they could. This is a *doctor's* house. He's supposed to be educated and leave here. But they like them, they *like* ISIS, they welcomed them!"

"No, it was difficult for them."

"You want me to show the footage?" Adil reaches for his phone. "The first day when ISIS came? Everyone is saying 'Thank God you saved us from the disbelievers. Thank God you came here.' Come on, man, you know this."

"No," insists Faisal. "No. Not all of them."

Across the pile, someone still hoping for survivors yells: "Get the phone numbers and call them!"[24]

"They don't have coverage," Adil says. "How can we call them?"

"Inshallah, they are alive," intones Faisal.

"Inshallah," says Adil.

Eventually, the pit is big enough for several men. Saleh, a Muslawi from Rabih's unit, climbs down to join Hussein. He's even bigger than Hussein, six and half feet tall, plainly mighty but also gentle, with no equipment but a baseball cap, a white surgical mask, and red gloves. He's known for heroism. The day before, he single-handedly carried an unexploded missile from the basement of an old man's home to the street, comforting the wide-eyed elder along the way. Now Saleh stoops, scrabbles, passes warm stones up into the light. The temperature is 105 degrees or so when he finds the body of a woman.

"Do you want the pickaxe?" a voice calls from above.

"Give it to me," commands Lieutenant Jabar. At the pit's edge he runs the operation like everyone's stern uncle, like the assistant director on Maestro's final shoot. Seen it all before. "Nobody come through here, nobody come through."

Saleh pulls another stone loose. Only the woman's arms and head are exposed. It will be hard and delicate work to free her without damaging her body. For a moment, Saleh leans against the side of the pit, breathing heavily. Someone tosses him a bottle of water. He catches it, pulls down his paper mask, tilts his head back, pours half the water into his mouth, gargles, then spits it all out. It's Ramadan, so he's fasting, won't even drink. He stoops to dig again.

Colonel Qusay[25] calls down to Hussein beside him. "Hussein, how is it? Do you want the fork to move rubble? Abu Akil! One more scoop!"

Across the street a mortar lands, sending aloft a wispy plume of smoke.

"Sir," someone shouts, "come here, a mortar just landed there!"

Lieutenant Jabar adds calmly, "Watch out."

"Everybody keep going," orders Colonel Qusay.

In the bottom of the pit, Saleh exposes the fullness of the woman's body. Brief silence from the men amid screeching saws and bullets.

Noon light as lamplight, a dome of dust. Golden bracelets ring the corpse's bloated wrists.

"Get them the blue bags and a blanket!" orders Qusay. "And no one come around here, rocks will fall on the guys who are working down there. . . ."

Body bags, also known as cadaver bags or human remains pouches, vary in quality. The bags standard to American hospitals retail at a little over twenty dollars. More durable versions—manufactured to prevent contamination, or contain infectious disease—run up to two hundred dollars apiece. Qusay's are cheap, bright blue, and made, probably, of polyethylene, the world's most produced plastic—constituting soda bottles, recycling bins, much of the plumbing in the wall. Polyethylene is also found, increasingly, in the oceans. One of the highest concentrations discovered so far lies in a gyre of the northern Pacific Ocean and is known as the Great Pacific Garbage Patch. Though some sailors have reported great swaths of floating debris, the patch is actually invisible, innumerable microscopic particles. Few of the men of civil defense have ever seen the ocean, or likely ever will. Certainly the woman won't, now, rotting in the pit, and her own particles are unlikely to mingle with polyethylene in the oceans or atmosphere anytime soon. But one day they will.

Mighty Saleh folds a blanket around her body. He tucks her bangled arm away and, with Hussein, hoists her, wrapped so, into one of the blue bags. But then he can't close the zip. It's stuck.

Saleh pulls, fiddles. At pit's lip, men shift, embarrassed, on their feet.

Colonel Qusay calls down, "Close the zip!"

Lieutenant Jabar: "Pull the bag closed!"

Saleh struggles with the mechanism, kneeling, his broad back in the sun, his huge red-gloved hands fumbling.

Twenty-one bodies remain.

S even more have been extracted and lie in six body bags along the broken sidewalk (two children sharing) when the brothers Abdulilah arrive. Both are slightly paunched, in late middle age, their hair sensibly parted and receding. Muad's is snowy, but Moghdad's retains some iron gray and rusty brown from when he was a younger man. At this moment the lines around his eyes and jaw, half a nickel deep, are trembling, but in his pressed plaid shirt he holds a dignified silence. You can see it costs him, there beside his brother Muad, who, by contrast, sobs on his feet. Their father and stepmother, they suspect, lie in the rubble, perhaps other relatives.

Rabih immediately identifies the brothers as bereaved and steers them through a fractured wall to the shade of a neighboring courtyard. We join them there.

"Tell him," Muad shouts at my fixer, spittle in his beard, his breath hot. "Tell him it is all death, death, death! Death! Death! Death!"

Moghdad, quieter but enraged: "America caused this."

"Tell him to write three words. Mosul is death, death, death. There are twenty people, my dad is one of them. My dad and my dad's second wife."

"This was by airstrike, or mortar?"[26]

"Airstrike! An *American* airstrike! The missile lands exactly in the center of the house"—a screech of metal erupts nearby, but Muad shouts over it—"into the basement."

"Was ISIS with them?"

"We don't know, we weren't in the house," says Moghdad. "Sometimes, only one ISIS is there and twenty or twelve or fifteen civilians die."

"Let me be clear," Muad objects, index finger in the air, "not even a quarter of an ISIS was here!"

"America destroyed us," says Moghdad.

Where Moghdad is exhausted by grief, Muad is energized, and in his rage appears ready to lift the pile himself, or perform some other act of strength defying the conventions of society and physics.

"America, America, America!" he screams. "They kill more than they liberate! This is America's fault!"

The men of civil defense have heard such screams before. Lieutenant

Jabar soon takes Muad and Moghdad to identify bodies. The brothers can do only so much. The Abaji house, it turns out, was sheltering the Abdulilahs and several other families besides—Hassawis, al-Numas, Hamdanis.[27] The brothers identify a single corpse of those so far collected: The woman with the gold bracelets is their stepmother. Moghdad massages his temples in absent grief as, with the bag open, Lieutenant Jabar explains the care with which his men account for all valuables— never stealing anything, like these gold bracelets.

"Come on, come on," Muad cries, snot running into his mustache. "Cover the face and close the zipper!"

A young man in jeans and a maroon shirt, pistol on his hip, no uniform to mark him, declares of the bodies: "Nothing is clear, you can't recognize them."

Muad crying, steps away from his stepmother's corpse.

Colonel Rabih, meanwhile, has walked two streets over in pursuit of another body. A woman called him with its rough location, pleading—if Rabih would just please find the body and bring it back to his station, she would collect and bury it. Reluctantly, Rabih had agreed to look. He recruited some Ninth Division guys to help. They found the body, bagged it, brought it to the edge of the Abajis' street. But the woman has not answered Rabih's calls since—and now the civil defense phone with her number on it has died.

Rabih sighs and casts his eyes down Pepsi Road. The body lies against a wall spray-painted with ISIS's symbol for "done"—meaning inspected for phones, books, and other contraband. It will have to be repainted. On the curb in the late-afternoon swelter, several men stare into space, waiting for orders, chatting. Adil is one. Rabih's eye falls upon him.

"Call [the woman]," he tells Adil, handing him the dead phone, "to see if she is still waiting to take the woman's body. If she's still in the station, we'll take the body."

"I don't have charge in the phone," replies Adil, examining it.

"Take out the SIM card," says Rabih, "and put it in another phone. Maybe she's waiting for me in the station."

"I swear the phone is broken."

"Take out the SIM card and put it in another phone!"

"I don't know how to take it out. I need a pin."

"If I don't know if she's waiting for me," says Rabih, slowly, "I can't bring the body, and I have to leave it somewhere."

Adil looks at him blankly.

"Give the phone to someone," says Rabih, "who knows how to take it out!"

Just at Rabih's feet, a member of Mosul's east side civil defense team, in an orange safety vest, watching this exchange, begins to complain loudly to the men seated around him. Maybe for Rabih's benefit.

"Why did they bring us here?" he asks in rhetorical anger. He's in his mid-thirties or younger but aged by fatigue. His skin glows orange in the sunlight reflected off his vest. "We don't have any salaries, and the guys who *get* salaries are at home. They didn't bring *them*. Why do they use me as a civil defense employee, and they don't use them?" He looks up at Rabih. "Why don't you ask *them* to come here? Are they special? And when they ask them, they say 'No, we won't come.' Why? What's our fault? Why did they bring us for these missions?"

He has a point. Civil servants who managed to flee the occupation could register with the central government and, in theory, continue to draw pay, even displaced, not working. Those who remained trapped by ISIS in Mosul couldn't—but since liberation, they'd been ordered back to work. Rabih tells the man in the orange vest, "If it was in my hand, I would send you back now to the east side."

Ahmed, arriving on the scene, his undersized flak vest strapped tight, has news. "Sir," he says, indicating a nearby Humvee, "if this car is going, we're going with him."

Understandably, Ahmed wants to travel in convoy with the army.

"Just wait," says Rabih, "let me solve the problem of this body. What luck. Once we find the body, the phone breaks." He turns back to the guy in the orange vest with a face-saving idea. "You'll go and stay in my station in Ras al-Jadah."

The guy in the orange vest isn't interested. "Why do the employees from the provinces in the Nineveh Plain get their salaries," he demands again, "and they don't use *them*?"

Beside this argument, Adil is trying to pry open the problematic phone with chubby fingers. He gives up and hands the phone back to Rabih, whose eyes close for a long moment.

"Get a needle," Ahmed suggests, "from the ambulance driver."

"Or a syringe!" shouts Rabih, recovering. "Ahmed, please solve this situation, or I will fall over. A syringe!"

"*Where* is this van going?" The guy in the orange vest nods at Rabih's red van.

"To the station."

"But, sir," he pleads, "we want to go back east."

"Then call the general," Rabih says, now sitting on the curb beside him, exhaling like an old man, "and tell him Rabih said to provide a car, and leave it at the bridge to take you guys back east. You deserve to go back home."

It's not clear if Rabih is serious. Generals, of course, don't take orders from him. But then, Rabih doesn't sound quite like he's joking, either. He sounds more like he's *in* on a joke—someone else's joke, a joke so vast, so complicated, that the punch line is a thousand years in the future. Or maybe already come and gone.

"Man, come on, calm down," says Rabih, slapping Orange Vest on the back, "we're doing this every day, it's your first hours and you're complaining."

"Sir, lemme tell you something. We worked harder than this. Sometime ISIS was forcing us to go to their fires, and the Coalition was over us. We used to work with some guys wearing explosive belts, grenades in their hands, weapons on their shoulders. That was worse. Here is like heaven, totally safe! You're with police and the army!"

Orange vest is on a roll now, the men on the curb around him nodding in rapt agreement.

"Sometimes they were forcing us, they were putting their pistols to our head. That's worse than this. Now, these guys are working." He gestures at the Baghdadis. "We thank them, they are brave, but we also saw bad situations here."

Rabih elevates his eyebrows. "So," he begins, "many times, I go with the Humvees to the front lines. For example," he looks around, "this one. I used a Humvee and ISIS tunnels to get here. . . ."

A shadow falls over him, interrupting the story. He looks up.

Standing above him, Adil proffers, with some ceremony, a syringe.

4.

Correspondence (II)

from: Col USAF CENTCOM CCCI (US)

to: Nick McDonell

cc: CDR USN CENTCOM CCCI (US)

date: Fri, Oct 14, 2016 at 2:52 PM

subject: FW: CIVCAS Query/ —— request

security: mail.mil did not encrypt this message

Mr McDonnel,

How can we assist you in your research about civilian casualty avoidance?

Please let me know when we can chat, or start up the conversation by email. —— referred you over to us here at Central Command public affairs.

We at CENTCOM have been openly discussing our civilian casualty avoidance processes and approach for some months now. In the midst of a tragic topic, we think we have an important perspective and an important story to tell.

I hope to hear from you soon.

——

Colonel, USAF

CENTCOM Public Affairs

III.

Allies

5.

Iraqi Special Forces and the al-Jadida Airstrike

S ergeant Ma'ad, twenty-eight, Diyala Brigade, Division Two, Iraqi Special Operations Forces, father of five, craving a smoke. He sits on the ragged corner of a bed in West Mosul, lunching on pickled vegetables, bread, and grape juice. Beside Ma'ad lounges pudgy Corporal Abbas, shirtless in gym shorts, eyes clear, cheeks full and bright. His scars from the war include quarter-sized entry and exit wounds through his left forearm and belly fat. A skinny private lies on the bed, too, against the wall, watching videos on his phone. The room has the intimate air of a slumber party except one's nose is always full of dust and sometimes, when the wind moves, the purple stink of corpses. Now and then other soldiers arrive, flop on the bed for a few minutes, get up, leave. The house is about eight hundred kilometers back from the front line, whose geometry is, at that time, variable. Through a barred window, the ancient Great Mosque of al-Nuri is visible, its famously leaning minaret cocked heavenward beneath the frequent passage of aircraft.

Rolling over on the bed, Abbas demonstrates how he requests American airstrikes.

"If you get ambushed," says Abbas, zooming in on a Samsung tablet, "you can immediately send your coordinates—"

Ma'ad spots a soldier in the doorway and calls out, interrupting. "So you still didn't bring back our *nargileh*? Come on, bring it back! The guys want to smoke!"

"All our work depends on this," continues Abbas, holding up the tablet. Brightly colored dots indicate various units around the city. "This is the main tool of our fight. *We* give the airstrike targets. For example, if you see here, this is a suicide car here. And also it shows us the distance between us and other areas. When you point it, it shows you the distance from you and you can read the numbers. I will give it to my boss here, and then he transfers it to ISOF operation room, and then they call the Coalition. Even if a suicide car comes toward you, you give them the target of the street immediately, and when the airstrike comes he will find the suicide car—"

"These targets are not one hundred percent," Ma'ad interrupts again, before Abbas finishes his thought. "These are probabilities."

"And once we go to new area, we give them new targets. We update the map, we send our position: Do not shell us." Abbas zooms in. "This is the school, we are here beside the school."

An explosion shakes the walls.

"It's far," says Abbas.

Ma'ad points out the window: "No it's very close. See, you can see the dust."

Abbas looks, instead, down into the screen. "See the green point? This is us. This is the street on the left, this is the street on our right. See, we are in Rashan neighborhood, and right behind the school is al-Saha. These are the front lines." He points. "And this is the Old City. See, it's clear, it's obvious, you can see everything. Now take it and zoom, but you have to wait a bit until it becomes clear and—"

Abbas pauses as Ma'ad's radio crackles. A captain downstairs needs a ride. Ma'ad stands and swats the skinny private on the bed, tells him to get up.

"Come on, there are two drivers," the private complains.

"I'm telling you," says Ma'ad, "take him. Go or I'll fuck your sister."

The private, theatrically reluctant, gets up.

"Now he goes because he's happy you're going to fuck his sister," says Abbas.

"What am I doing?" says the skinny private, shuffling off. "I take people, and I bring them back. And I don't know why."

"Just take him, motherfucker," says Ma'ad.

Ma'ad sits back down, without a *nargileh* for a post-lunch smoke, and brushes crumbs from his black Special Forces T-shirt.[28] The T-shirt is a popular war souvenir and like many foreign reporters I will eventually take one back home. I will give it to a woman I know who is undergoing treatment for lung cancer. The idea that courage is the same for everyone—for her, and Ma'ad, and ISIS fighters—is implied, even explicit, in much coverage of the war, when reporters quote soldiers or witnesses saying that *whatever you think about ISIS, they're brave.*[29] The division of courage and virtue is perhaps too readily accepted. None of this comes up in that house, though, and soon a young soldier in a different black T-shirt walks in and drops onto the bed. His shirt doesn't have a Special Forces insignia; instead, it's printed with a red heart and looping cursive text: *Let me stick it in your butt.*

"What does it mean?" Abbas asks, grinning.

Ma'ad rolls his eyes, gets back to talking about ISIS's own airstrikes. They use drones, too, the cheap Chinese kind you can order online, jury-rigged to drop IEDs. From there Ma'ad gets to talking about why ISIS fighters are the way they are. He doesn't mention Sunni disenfranchisement or any of the common conspiracy theories about Iranians, Jews, Saudis, or Americans backing ISIS. Instead, he says, "ISIS is unconscious, like, nothing in their mind. They told a big lie and then they believed the lie. Most of the ISIS we kill are kids."[30]

Most of the Iraqi Special Forces seem like kids, too, but somehow more than that. Young but raised in war, many possess an extreme fatalism, a calm more typically associated with age than youth.

It's tempting to call this demeanor ancient, but probably more accurate to think of it simply as a function of repeated trauma. Saif, for instance, twenty-seven, a kilometer or so down the line from Ma'ad, the kind of sniper who blows you a kiss as he walks through the door. He's living, for a few days, on the second floor of an abandoned ISIS safe house, which is where we're talking, after dinner, after he and his guys have cleared plastic plates and tidied the room and smoked together and laid down blankets. They graciously offer me a prime spot in front of the fan, between the guns and the hookah against the wall.

Saif's from Kut, a city in eastern Iraq and site of political intrigue for thousands of years before T. E. Lawrence visited during World War I.[31] Nine decades later, in Saif's adolescence, the local military outpost housed American soldiers, but Saif didn't much care. He was away to earn for the family, trading on his square-jawed charisma to sell vegetables in Baghdad. He lived in al-Hurriya, bought vegetables wholesale in Dora, carted them all over the capital's poorer quarters, never finished high school, and came to hate selling vegetables, being so poor. Much better to join the Iraqi army and then, best of all, make the cut for the Counter Terrorism Service, CTS, and ISOF. Saif doesn't think he will ever become an officer and, like Ma'ad and Abbas, knows nothing of civilian casualty counts or policies on this particular, slow-to-cool evening during the battle for Mosul.

Nor does Allawi, twenty-six, his best friend, wearing skull rings and a silver necklace, losing the hair on the top of his head but sporting a thick mustache. They met early in training—"that black hour," deadpans Saif—and have been CTS for years now,[32] become sage veterans of urban combat in Ramadi and Fallujah, though in the home screen photo on Allawi's phone (case styled like a Washington state license plate, "Evergreen State"), they lean on each other like kids.

As we're looking at the photo, a third soldier, Mohammed, interrupts, pointing.

"Who do you think *took* the photo?" he asks.

Allawi rolls his eyes. Mohammed is twenty-three, soft compared to the others, and quick to bring up the shrapnel in his legs. He's a non-commissioned officer for media, and his courage is therefore suspect, especially since his uncle, General Khadir, is a big shot back at head-quarters. Unlike Allawi and Saif, who are held close to unit command because, having demonstrated berserk bravery, they can be counted on to keep unit command alive, Mohammed seems to be held close because to lose him is to incur the wrath of superiors, of *Higher*—in some ways, more dangerous than a sniper. Still, the three young men seem to love one another.

The country is separated into different tribes," Allawi explains. "For example, this guy," he points at Saif, "is from the Soudani tribe. I'm from Sabihawi. So, if there is a problem between me and him, not just anyone can go and fix that problem. The big men from the tribe, they go and sit and talk and fix the problem. Like me, in the military, I have my boss, Major Khalid. If I fight with someone from another brigade, it's not me who goes and fixes the problem, it's my boss."

Mohammed laughs. "You tell your *boss*," he says, "if you make a problem?"

"Yes," says Allawi, "I just said so."

Allawi never takes Mohammed's bait. Saif quietly backs him, as usual.

"Yeah, he gave an example," says Saif.

"Chabawy," Allawi goes on, naming Mohammed's tribe, "cannot fix a problem between Sabihawi and Soudani."

Leaning in from the next room, lanky Haider, a gunner, is impatient for a game of dominoes.

"Are you done?!"

"Come on," yells Allawi, mock put-upon, "I'm still in the interview!" He turns back to me, composed. "The tribe you belong to—it's like the army, you belong to your brigade. And we have a box we put money in.

Every month we collect money. The money is for any problem facing the tribe. For example, a wedding, and someone doesn't have any money. That box is the most important thing in the tribes."

Mohammed, smirking, keeps at him: "You sure you give money to the box?"

"Every month. Even before I came to Mosul, I put money in the box."

"You're lying, you didn't give any money."

"I swear to God, I gave it to Abu Issa, and Issa took it to the box." Allawi, in an aside, fills me in on Issa: "The head of our tribe. My cousin."

"Issa?!" Mohammed almost squeals. "You gave it to Abu *Issa* and you're sure Abu Issa is going to put it in the box? He won't put it in the box!"

"We have sheikhs," Allawi ignores Mohammed. "We give money to the sheikhs."

Mohammed sits up from the blanket where he has been lounging. He clearly wants to talk about his own tribe. His black shirt, printed with a picture of a handgun, reads: THIS IS MY GLOCK. THERE ARE MANY LIKE IT BUT THIS ONE IS MINE.

Mohammed begins to explain his lineage, then hesitates. "We belong to . . . Aswad al Kindi. It's in . . ."

Allawi chuckles. "He doesn't know where they're from."

My fixer prompts Mohammed. "The main town? The big city?"

"Amara . . . !" Mohammed remembers, triumphant, grinning.

Allawi shakes his head. "You guys are a small tribe."

Later, elsewhere in Mosul, I will be made, jokingly, an honorary Sabihawi.[33] This is better in the moment than American Abroad, which is my most obvious tribal association and not a popular one in Mosul. The next day an Iraqi general will yell at me: "All that is happening now, I blame on the Americans! Before 2003, even a bird couldn't come into Iraq! They opened all the borders! The American army, they still have bases in Germany!"[34]

That night, though, after dinner, Allawi and his friends leave such points alone. "Americans are not on the ground with us," Allawi says, "but in the sky. They support us with their planes. We have some stuff we call 'Coalition jobs.' Like, for suicide cars, we call airstrikes. When Haider is on the .50 cal and a car comes at us, Haider shoots it. But if the car is parked, we call the airstrike. . . . They don't go without our targets. That's my job, to see something and report it. But his job"— Allawi nods at Mohammed—"is to film it with his camera."

Saif and Haider laugh at this, and Mohammed scowls, then laughs loudest.

A llawi shows me the wreckage of an airstrike when we go to buy groceries the following evening. It's Ramadan and we're hungry, walking the main drag of recently liberated al-Jadida, a neighborhood not far from Colonel Rabih's station. We're buying lamb for *iftar*. In a shadowed stall the butcher wrenches joints between his strong hand and a curved knife. A cloud of flies disperses, recombines. Allawi points out where the bodies fell. "Remember the eight bodies that were on the ground," he'll reflect to Mohammed, on return to the house. "Those eight bodies were right where we bought the meat . . . right in front of the butcher."

The bodies on the street have been cleared, but no one knows how many remain under the masses of rubble abutting the market, a whole city block brought down. According to CENTCOM, in Tampa, Florida, at 8:24 one morning some weeks earlier an American aircraft launched a GBU-38 missile at a pair of snipers situated one block from the butcher. The snipers were harrying Ma'ad, Abbas, Allawi, Saif, Mohammed, and their fellow Counter Terrorism Service members as they advanced on the Old City and Tigris, killing every militant they found. From CENTCOM's post-strike assessment:

> CTS commanders and the [Target Engagement Authority]
> determined that it was a military necessity to neutralize the

ISIS snipers in order for CTS to achieve its maneuver objective of seizing the sector from ISIS.

There was, famously, no plan for what would happen to Mosul once CTS reached the river, captured the al-Nuri mosque, and raised the flag. No Iraqi or American politician ever articulated, publicly at least, a substantive strategy beyond defeat of the enemy—even though the enemy, it was widely acknowledged, emerged in part from failures of political foresight during the preceding decades of (near) unilaterally waged war.[35] This GBU-38, short for Guided Bomb Unit 38, would in particular have significant, unplanned-for consequences. The final Coalition count is two dead ISIS snipers, 105 dead civilians, and an additional thirty-six civilian deaths alleged but undetermined at the time of the report. The airstrike was the sixth of eighty-one executed in Mosul that day.

The market, though, one block over, is almost unscathed. We collect our lamb and turn to vegetables. A single three-story building between butcher shops and rows of vegetable carts is crumbled from the top, like a ruined cake, but the street is busy that evening, a vein of life. Long-lost friends greet each other with almost hysterical laughter, an astonishment at mutual survival. Teenagers bark wares—*Juice! Fresh Juice!* Baklava, fat watermelons, onions, blackening tomatoes, cucumbers for salting, primary-colored cellphone cases, Hello Kitty backpacks far from home again. The din is terrific: bargaining, the backfire of motorcycles, the rumble of Humvees, the yap of kicked dogs, the clicking of Kalashnikovs against the metal buckles of men in a hurry. One of the sweets sellers bobs his head to a beat as he transacts business, and when I ask he removes a shining earbud and hands it over, so I can hear the house music drowning it all out for him.

And at some point between sweets, meat, and vegetables I notice a girl, perhaps seven years old, blond, with eyes of blue and green, staring at me. She holds the hand of a smaller, even blonder boy. I point out the children to my fixer, surprised, and he looks at me with disappointment. He tells me: *We have children who look like that, it's normal.* And then they're gone into the crowd and I am abashed again. White Americans are at least as exceptional for the depth of our biases as our good intentions, and the two are married.

It's an often disastrous psychic setup. But there are some worse ones at play in Mosul in those days, which really are days of tragedy. ISIS publications insist human existence as we know it is approaching an end, some apocalyptic inflection point. Beyond the battle in every direction, many secularists are doomsaying, too, though on account of science rather than myth. It's during the campaign for Mosul that a portion of the Larsen C ice shelf, roughly the size of Delaware, breaks off Antarctica into the ocean.[36] Discussion of the wider world, however, rarely occurs on the battle lines. Few Muslawis seem to care about Americans, for example—they just want security like the Americans have. Likewise, in New York, few care about the plight of the Muslawis. They just don't want such trouble for themselves. By default we tend to desire before empathy. In myth, the consequences are often fatal. Icarus drowns, Narcissus wastes away, the House of Atreus falls.[37] Myths in Mosul at the time are less didactic, closer to horror stories or jokes. Many circulate among Allawi and his comrades. ISIS fighters, one runs, have a single fear: being killed by a woman. Within their cosmology, apparently, if you're killed by a woman, you lose your place in heaven. ISIS's great fear, therefore, is female snipers, several of whom have been trained and deployed by Kurdish Peshmerga.[38] I twice hear a story of a lone female sniper driving back a whole ISIS line. No battalion of women, though, is sent to liberate al-Jadida.[39]

Instead, the GBU-38. The U.S. military investigation into the incident, known as a 15-6,[40] is headed by an Air Force brigadier general. The press release promises a link to a full report detailing the incident, which, it notes, was "approved in accordance with all the applicable rules of engagement and the Law of Armed Conflict." The link never appears, but the executive summary asserts that on piercing the roof of the building in which the snipers were positioned, the GBU-38 caused a "sympathetic detonation" of previously emplaced IEDs, which destroyed the entire city block. "Subsequent engineering and weapons analysis," it reads, "indicates that the GBU-38 should have resulted in no more than 16–20% damage to the structure, localized to the front of the second floor of the structure. . . . The target engagement authority was unaware of and could not have predicted the presence of civilians in the structure prior to the engagement . . . could not have predicted the compounded effects of the secondary explosives emplaced by ISIS fighters."

The United States almost always does predict the violence it causes, though—generally, if not specifically. Later in the summer, the U.S. secretary of defense will say, at West Point: "Civilian casualties are a fact of life in this sort of situation." Then, in almost the same breath, he'll say: "The American people and the American military will never get used to civilian casualties." [41,42]

B ack in the abandoned house, Allawi is in an expansive mood after we unpack the groceries. "Feel as though you are the guests of the Sabihawis," he says, with grand irony, before beginning the story of how he came to be fighting in Mosul. Back when Saif was carting vegetables, Allawi was mopping floors. As a twelve-year-old, he dropped out of school when a cousin got him a maintenance job on the Iraqi side of a Coalition base, for a foreign contractor called KBR. In Allawi's telling, he's good at the job and so is promoted quickly to the American side, and eventually to a military college, where he's put to work in a bakery.

Mohammed enters from the fly-baffled kitchen with a modest tray of melon wedges.

"Tell my story," Mohammed pleads. "Come on."

"You make . . . bread?" I ask, catching up to the translation.

"I can't make bread. I was an accountant."

"But you were twelve years old . . . ?"

"Like, the officers' kitchen." Allawi is patient, communicating through our fixer. "They need twelve hundred *samoon*, they were putting them in boxes. I was writing: 'twelve hundred *samoon* to officers' kitchen.' Or: 'four thousand *samoon* to finance.' They would come in and pick it up, and I was keeping account."

Samoon is diamond-shaped Iraqi bread. Allawi grins conspiratorially.

"And if there were two hundred *samoon* extra, I sold them. To the soldiers."

"And the money?" I ask.

"To my pocket, for me. Between me and you." He laughs. Then he shouts to Haider, in the next room. "I'm explaining how corrupt I was when I was working for the Americans."

Saif, who has been out of the room, returns and sits.

"You're *still* talking?" he asks.

"We talked about you," Allawi tells him.

The melon is almost gone, but we also have a box of baklava, for which Saif reaches. He's always eating. Allawi watches. When Saif was out of the room to mix us the chalky protein shakes he likes, Allawi told a story of his bravery. How, in the midst of a firefight, Saif had leapt from their Humvee and run, grenade in hand, directly at an ISIS fighter across open terrain and killed him, saving Major Khalid and Allawi.

"You told that story?" asks Saif, indifferently.

Mohammed, watching this exchange, wipes melon juice from his chin. He is clearly saddened by his exclusion, this time, his face momentarily delicate. Allawi notices.

"Let's not forget Mohammed," he says. "Once we were advancing on Gogjali. He was recording us, and he got shot in the leg." He nods seriously. "Let's mention it. This is for history. And we have evidence!"

Allawi scrolls through his phone for the picture. Then he lowers his voice, but not so low that Mohammed and the rest of the room fail to hear him say: "He stayed home for a long time and fucked up his job.

The Americans treated him and he felt *relaxed* because of their American hands, all over him. . . ."

The fixer and I and the other soldiers erupt in laughter over Mohammed's protests, but Saif does not, absorbed in the baklava.

"And we have Saif," says Allawi, teasingly, as though to reintroduce him from scratch, "who eats all the sweets."

Saif, his mouth full of crust and honey, looks up from the pastries. Then he asks Allawi, with only the barest hint of interest, as though the interpreter and I aren't in the room: "He's gonna mention this?"

Maybe it's this attitude—his story is unimportant, his life is expendable[43]—which suggests the word *ancient* for Saif. But it seems more tactic than truth, from him, as though actually desperate to live, he treats death with indifference, to keep it at bay.

Six weeks later, ISIS kills two of Allawi, Saif, and Mohammed's commanding officers—Lieutenant Idris and Major Khalid. Allawi is lucky he's not driving them at the time. The officers die in a suicide car bomb attack, referred to as a *mofakhakha*. This is one of two words that stop everything, wherever you are, whatever the circumstance. If someone hears it shouted through the din, he shouts it in turn, and everyone runs for cover, shouting *Mofakhakha!* The other word is *qanas*, which means "sniper," though reactions are not as hurried for snipers. Allawi has heard the words shouted in warning hundreds of times, lost dozens of comrades. And yet, over the course of our ranging interviews, there's only one topic that upsets him. It's late, after dinner on the day we go to the market, and I ask him how many people he thinks died in the Jadida strike, targeting that pair of *qanas*.

"They say one hundred and seventy or one hundred eighty civilians got killed," Allawi tells me, voice rising, almost cracking, "but we weren't the cause of that to happen. We're not the army, we're not the federal police, we're the Special Forces, and it wasn't our fault . . . ! All this happened, not because of the U.S., but because of ISIS using the houses!"[44]

The question of *fault* aside, the United States claims to have executed the strike for the Special Forces' safety. In the al-Jadida investigation report, CENTCOM's justification runs as follows:

> If the ISIS snipers were left to continue to engage CTS forces, CTS would incur unacceptable levels of casualties in the seizure of the sector.

That is: Without the airstrike, too many men like Allawi—and Saif, Mohammed, Ma'ad, and Abbas—would have died.

The logic of this proposition depends not only on their mission as defined by its creators, but on the definition of "unacceptable." That summer, the U.S. and Iraqi militaries not only accept the Mosul operation, they trumpet it as a great success in the offensive against the Islamic State, a major victory in the larger war against terrorism. On the basis of its success, in fact, the U.S. Office of the Secretary of Defense asks for $1.8 billion in funding for the following year's training, advising, and assistance in Iraq and Syria—despite noting, in its budgetary justification, that CTS "suffered 40 percent battle losses in Mosul."[45] Nearly every other soldier. Before year's end, the U.S. Congress grants the funding in full.

"Honestly," Allawi tells me, "I don't know what to say about political stuff. We don't have TVs, we don't follow the situation of other countries, we're here fighting the war all the time. . . . We hear, sometimes, what's going on, but you know," he shrugs, "ours is not politics. Ours is military. I hope this situation finishes. I don't care about other countries, revolutions, protest. I only hope this situation finishes."

6.

Crazy Horse

In the years I am describing it was often said in the United States, among people who talk about such things, that there was a bad war, and a good war.[46] Iraq was the bad war, such talk went, and if only we had focused on Afghanistan—the good war—then neither would be so problematic. The level of access I was granted to American forces and their allies in these wars did not map cleanly onto this idea, and was not consistent. I'm convinced the reasons for this are circumstantial, having more to do with luck and credentials than any substantive issue relating to civilian casualties. In my experience, American conduct in the two countries was similar. The same counterinsurgency doctrine held sway. The same drones flew overhead. The same fast food franchises serviced our forward operating bases (FOBs) and combat outposts (COPs), which in both countries were named, occasionally, for Native Americans the United States had fought in earlier wars—Geronimo, Crazy Horse. For a soldier, diplomat, or journalist embedded in the American machine, life in the two countries was in many ways indistinguishable. And with specific regard to civilian lives, the same promises were made.[47]

7.

The Afghan National Army and the Security of Outpost Shamalan, Helmand

F ar from Iraq but at another edge of America's alliances, out beyond Lashkar Gah and the colorful trucks tilting her potted streets, out past white egrets stalking the banks of the Helmand River and through acres of poppy, lies Afghan National Army Outpost Shamalan.[48] The ranking man is Sergeant Mujahed, his high cheekbones stubbled, his hair thick with grease. He's a long way from his own green and mountainous province, Takhar,[49] and looks older than his twenty-four years. As in Iraq, the official American mission in Afghanistan is to "train, advise, and assist" Mujahed to prevent terrorism, and so it is from outposts like Mujahed's that airstrike requests are meant to originate, in his country, in the fifteenth year since America arrived.

OP Shamalan comprises a low, leaning guard tower, four uneven perimeter walls, and three flat bunkers, all of mud. On this winter afternoon, Mujahed watches an American squad walk through Shamalan's simple gate with a gift: an Afghan flag. He sends a man up an unsteady ladder to fasten it in place with plastic zip ties more commonly used as handcuffs. Down below there is grinning, thumbs-upping, and back-slapping, but no shared language among the men of the allied armies as, with a new flag shifting in the breeze, they sit together in the OP's dirt courtyard around an American mortar tube pointed at the bright, pale sky.

Before anything else, Sergeant Mujahed tells me he loves Americans. As opposed to the higher-ups in his own army, he says, gesturing at the mortar tube, the Americans sometimes bring him ammunition—which he needs, because the guys a few hundred meters across the road attack every day. Their compound is superficially identical to his, save the white Taliban flags flying overhead. The Americans call it *the chicken farm*, but Mujahed tells me it's not a chicken farm, and he doesn't know why the Americans call it that.

They also call the potatoes his men eat—for lack of other staples— *French fries*. On arriving at OP Shamalan that day, several well-fed Americans mention the fries like a rapport-building joke, something to talk about, as if they have nothing else in common.

Salaam alaikum. Cookin' any French fries? How are the French fries?

Yes yes, French fries! Good! Good! say the Afghan soldiers. *America good.*

Good as any I've had in the States, says one of the Americans.[50]

Mujahed, instantly, orders his men to fry potatoes.

As we sit beside the mortar pit he offers me a cigarette, crosses his sandaled ankles, and points through the perimeter wall at his enemies. He's never had a job outside the army.

"There's not more than ten or twenty people over there," he tells me. "They attack at different times. Sometimes twelve, sometime eleven, sometimes four, sometimes six . . ."

It's midafternoon. Beyond the two outposts, a road bends north into a scattering of farm compounds. Scooters occasionally putt by, raising clouds of fine dust. More villagers pass on foot. They are at some risk, in those moments between opposed forces. Two days prior, Mujahed was pinned down near the OP by heavy machine-gun fire, just barely crawled to safety. Regarding the locals, he is earnest and defensive.

"As an Afghan soldier," he tells me, "I swear that I don't want to hurt any civilians around here. Yesterday civilians with kids came by, and I swore to God that I didn't want to hurt them. 'The Taliban is trying to use you,' I told them, 'to use your women and children.'"

In seven years with the Afghan army, Mujahed has fought across Gereshk, Marjah, and Nawa, and is familiar with civilian casualties. Most recently, a father and son on a motorbike died of an IED blast just down the road. "Those people that are getting hurt," he tells me, "it's the Taliban that hurt them! But unfortunately, the media is showing that *we* hurt those people. People don't see the facts. We don't hurt anybody. . . . They are always telling us: 'Make sure you don't hurt the civilian houses! Make sure you don't kill anybody, because they are our own people!' Especially the guys with the heavy weapons."[51]

Sergeant Mujahed's men are half listening, half goofing with the Americans—one of whom, in wraparound sunglasses priced roughly at Mujahed's monthly salary, is kneeling to examine the mortar setup. Mujahed juts his chin at the weapon again.

"Right now, for example," he says, "my mortars are angled for five hundred meters, because I know at five hundred meters there are no civilians. If I get contact from five hundred meters, it's Taliban. But I know, *nine* hundred meters from the position, there are civilians over there. If the Taliban try to shoot me from *nine* hundred meters, I won't shoot a mortar, because I know, probably, some civilian will get hurt."

What comes next is not audible in the recording—and I doubt the timing could be as dramatically perfect as I recall—but it is just about at this moment that the American in sunglasses looks up from the mortar system and explains which critical pieces it lacks, how their absence makes aiming the shells impossible.

One of Mujahed's men[52] gathers bad news across the languages, frowns in response, and rummages in a nearby ammo box. He comes up with a cardboard disc on which trigonometric ranging information is printed in English. Nodding as though he has solved a puzzle, he hands it to the American. The American spins the disc slowly in his hands, shaking his head. Mujahed carries on talking, noting at one point, in his long answers to my questions, that he has not been paid in over two months.

It's possible America was once allied with the men on the chicken farm—more likely their fathers and uncles. Across Afghanistan, the United States once armed insurgents to fight Soviets, only to face those arms years later.[53] Likewise, for years before invading Iraq, American officials allied themselves with Saddam Hussein. And so the United States helps Mujahed, now, but it's not hard to imagine that, one day, it might target him. Now and then, America betrays its allies—or, put another way, switches sides.

America's allies switch sides, too. As Mujahed tells me that afternoon: "I've worked [in Helmand] for five years. There were people who would take tea with us, and now they have become Taliban commanders." The most dramatic examples of this phenomenon, green-on-blue attacks, are named after the Coalition color code for Afghan and American forces, respectively. In such attacks, local forces turn their weapons on Americans with whom they are partnered. Mujahed shooting a U.S. soldier, for example, would be a green-on-blue. Such incidents are regular features of the war. After each one, Coalition and press ask the same question: Why?

The green-on-blue I am most familiar with involved a man named Abdul Raziq, early twenties, hometown Musa Qala. On a clear Helmand night, on a base called Puzeh, not far from Shamalan, Abdul Raziq shot and killed three U.S. Marine special operatives,[54] then escaped across high summer fields. A Taliban spokesman, in response to queries, posted a video of Raziq explaining his actions. In it, he jumps at small-arms fire in the background, sports a fresh Pakistani hat, and pulls at his achingly young beard.[55] As in every green-on-blue case, his explanation is consistent with insurgent messaging but marred by obvious suppressions.[56] Commentators on the phenomenon point to *cultural misunderstandings*—the differing treatment of dogs, for example, or women. Greed, blackmail, and ambition are also popular reasons why. All surely swim together, in each case. Less discussed is one of the most common complaints, which Abdul Raziq repeatedly cites in the video and which is shouted from insurgency bunkers to palace steps: The United States and her allies are killing innocent people.[57]

The shadows of the soldiers lengthen. The light turns dusky, then blue. Mujahed invites his American guests into the best-fortified room of the compound, his quarters. Blankets, a paraffin lamp, ammunition, the damp. He calls for tea, and soon the French fries arrive. The American officers, having asked for and received assurances that their men are also getting fries, eat by the polite fistful. Mujahed relates some of the local goings-on. The Taliban have been making busted locals eat their contraband SIM cards but, generally, everything is fine.[58] He asks for more guns, more ammunition. All this through an interpreter, "Randy," who speaks in a rapid baritone, repeating the construction "you know." His translation is slangy and partisan. "Bitterest enemies of our people" becomes, for example, "douchebags."

The Americans pay close attention, especially a Lieutenant Nate. He is two years older than Mujahed but looks younger—tall, white-toothed, unlined, powerfully jawed. He's cramped on the dirt floor but moves with athletic grace, was in fact captain of the football team at West Point, America's elite military academy. Though he's only a lieutenant, the combination of linebacker pedigree and good looks has made *Higher* particularly aware of him. Later, I'll ask him, "Do you think that what you're doing over here is directly related to the security of the United States?"

"Gosh," he'll say, "you ask tough questions."

"You're a smart guy, you're a West Point graduate."

"Yeah," he'll say, after a moment, "I think it does. Anytime you put a ground force out into a different country, it provides some security. We're everywhere, and it's more of a presence, I guess."[59]

He'll talk about duty, too, the call to serve, being part of something bigger than himself. But that's all back at the American base. In the meantime, in Mujahed's room, we cock our ears to gunfire, soft in the distance. Mujahed is unconcerned. Some of his men actually want the fighting closer and, to that end, one sticks his head in the room and makes an excited request, which Mujahed conveys to Randy, who translates for the Americans.[60] Mujahed's men want permission to conduct *recon by fire*. This involves standing on top of the wall and shooting at the chicken farm, to see if anyone shoots back. The hope is that the Taliban do so, because if they do while the Americans are present, the Americans, being threatened, are likely to respond, and on responding will kill very effectively, with their overwhelming technical superiority, training, and maybe even air support.

The Americans look at one another: Should we let them?

Battle at the chicken farm is beyond the day's mission, and any engagement increases the likelihood of civilian casualties. But Mujahed is at the front edge of the war, and these Americans are his allies, and for the moment they're outposted together, and every round in the distance, every day of their training, tilts to the violence that is the status quo.[61]

Mujahed watches the Americans intently, waiting for an answer.

"In case America ever goes into war with a superpower," Mujahed insisted to me, earlier that afternoon, "Afghanistan will always back America."

The Americans shrug.

Sure, go ahead.

Mujahed nods at his subordinate, who rushes off. Soon we hear rounds outgoing across the village road.[62] Promising continued friendship, the Americans finish the French fries, leave for their base before dark.

8.

Correspondence (III)

from: Nick McDonell

to: Col USAF CENTCOM CCCI (US)

cc: A CDR USN CENTCOM CCCI (US)

date: Sun, Oct 16, 2016 at 7:43 AM

subject: Re: FW: CIVCAS Query/—— request

mailed-by: gmail.com

Dear Colonel —— and Commander ——,

Thank you both for reaching out. I also think CENTCOM has an important story and perspective re: CIVCAS, and I'm looking forward to learning more.

As mentioned in the email forwarded below, I'm on contract for a book with Penguin/Random House to write a modern history of civilian casualties in U.S. and other conflicts.

My goal is a top to bottom understanding of how the U.S. estimates, causes, avoids, and tracks CIVCAS. To that end, I have three requests that I'm hoping we can discuss.

1) To embed with OFS and/or RS personnel tasked with CIVCAS tracking in Afghanistan. . . .

2) To embed with a Joint Terminal Attack Controller active in Afghanistan. A JTAC attached to OSF/RS forces in Helmand (currently 1st Cavalry and/or 10th Mountain, I believe) would be

ideal, as I have made several trips to the province in previous years.

3) To interview personnel tasked/involved with setting Non Combatant Cutoff Values for airstrikes—in Kabul, Doha, Tampa, or wherever they are located.

What do you think?

I know I have much to learn on the topic—please correct any mistaken assumptions I may have made. To tell the CIVCAS story properly, I think it is crucial not only to interview but to see the U.S. Military in action. As you write, it is a tragic topic, but in my research so far it's clear that the U.S. has the most robust CIVCAS avoidance policy and process in the world (and in history). How we got there, and what it looks like up close, is a story worth telling. The goal is not a scoop, or particular number—it is a thorough, accurate understanding of how the U.S. works on this extremely difficult issue.

I appreciate your attention. I've just arrived in Kabul and am available to discuss anytime.

Very Respectfully,

Nick McDonell

IV.

Operations

9.

The Targeting and Killing of a Helmandi Combatant

In the tactical operations center the general and I are watching out for innocent people like you, very closely, on-screen. We're in southern Afghanistan still, a short helicopter ride from OP Shamalan, but most proper nouns inside the room are classified, and in exchange for entry I have agreed to leave my phones and recorders outside, so what I will describe comes from my notes and memory, can be verified only by those who were present. It is not necessarily their mission to tell the truth, but eventually I interview and record all of them separately outside that room, too, and without exception they believe themselves to be doing the right thing.

The operations captain, John, keeps dice on his desk and shakes them in his fist while he coordinates airstrikes. There is, on my arrival, much talk of how *we don't joke, we don't cheer when we hit 'em*, but soon everyone loosens up—like *I'm cool with Hiroshima* and *You can't say that shit in front of the reporter!* [63] And the word for a man who has escaped an airstrike and is running for his life on-screen is *squirter*. How could they not banter? Some of them are still kids, in that steel and plywood room. Not the chaplain, Sidney, though.

"And tell me one more time what you did in your life before you were in the military?"

71

"Yeah, I was actually in college."

"Where did you go to college?"

"Originally I started going at Wallace Community College in Cullman, Alabama. I was a paramedic and bouncer in a strip club before I joined the Army."

"You'd probably do both your jobs in one night, then, huh?"

"Well, actually I bounced at night and worked the ambulance during the day."

"What was the name of the strip club?"

"It was called Dream Girls. It was on Rideout Road in Huntsville, Alabama. I don't even think it's there anymore."

Sidney, a Southern Baptist from a family of coal miners, tells me that the ends never justify the means and that everyone in the tactical operations center, deep down, agrees. He is tall, cheerful, bald, youthful in his late thirties, and watching the screens, too, providing confidentially privileged spiritual guidance as requested, or as he deems necessary. Some of the screens are crisper than others, but on each we are looking at a typical Helmandi compound, and you can almost, but not quite, make out the faces of the men who are about to be killed. The compounds are mud brick and roughly built, cut open to daylight by a few precious windows.

It is jarring to square these shapes with walks I have made between such compounds, through bronze leaves fallen to dust, moving north or south through the pixels. Despite this realization, and despite the blimps and insectile drones I have seen, and against shrewd advice, I have not taped over this laptop's camera, preferring to put my faith in irrelevance over increased security. We hold these surveillance devices close. To be in that room is to feel the immense power differential which flows from their control. The view is imperfect but godlike.

Captain John, with the dice, has dark circles under his eyes.

"How long is this deployment gonna be for you?"

"That's kind of up in the air right now. Most likely until next July."

"How long will that be?"

"That'll be nine months."

"Nine months. That's nine months—will that be every day in that room, looking at those screens?"

"Yes."

"Do you dream of those screens sometimes?"

"Yes."

First, they *soaked* the area, which meant keeping cameras on it and watching the screens—which everyone was half doing all the time, and fully doing some of the time, like when the general was in the room.[64] I will note here that in addition to giving up my phones and recorders to enter this room, to watch the soaking of mud-and-timber compounds, I signed an agreement, as I have signed similarly before every American embed, running as follows: "Intending to be legally bound, I hereby accept the obligations contained in this agreement in consideration of my being granted access to classified information. . . . I hereby agree that I will never divulge classified information to anyone unless . . ." And it goes on. Two public affairs officers witnessed my signature of this agreement with regard to classified information acquired during the five days in question—but agreed also that it should have no bearing on my reporting before or after that period. We amended the document to emphasize this fact, and I am glad we did, because in chapter 13, having signed no agreement to the contrary, I will report classified information acquired under other circumstances regarding the death of hundreds of Afghans.

The watching of screens, meanwhile, is not classified. Neither is the Collateral Damage Estimate Methodology, which governs the strike that morning and is laid out in *Chairmen of the Joint Chiefs of Staff Instruction 3160.01*, among other places. It requires that the team's strikes, or *target packets*, meet a series of criteria, or *pillars*—positive identification, for example. It is the business of the room to *build pillars* in order to *execute target packets*, and the lawyer in the room, Bobby, agrees that the process is somewhat like building a capital punishment case. Bobby'd been a litigator in Texas, has the physique of a weightlifter, and drinks cartons of milk with his dinner—which he usually eats out of styrofoam takeout boxes beside Captain John, watching the screens, instead of in the dining facility.[65]

"In the American legal system," I say to him later, "we talk about 'beyond a reasonable doubt.' If you were to describe the standard that you need to reach here, how would you describe it?"

"Somewhere about probable cause."

On-screen a man is digging behind a stone wall on the edge of a field. It's farmland in every direction. Five other men are nearby, pacing, sitting, reclining in the dirt, watching him dig. The room snaps to[66] as General D.A. enters. We'd been in his office for a formal interview when the digger was spotted shooting at an Afghan National Army outpost on the other side of the field. The general crosses his arms beside Captain John and asks, *What's the situation?*

Captain John tells him: types of jets and drones they have in the air, grid numbers, the nearest object on the no-strike list—*historical ruins*, at a safe remove from the expected blast.[67] More besides. The no-strike list names buildings that require high approval[68] to destroy: mosques, orphanages, nurseries. Only occasionally do we hit such buildings, like the Médecins Sans Frontières hospital in Kunduz, and kill the people inside.[69]

The digging man sits down, stands up. On-screen, behind him, is a hole in the ground with a few logs over the top, a crude bunker. This bunker is an *established fighting position*, and though the team does not know the names of the men they are watching, they have built a target packet for the bunker that has received approval from command in Kabul, so, if the general agrees, they can launch. They are obviously eager to do so.[70]

General D.A., short for Douglas Arthur, is an affable, white-haired forty-eight-year-old Army football fan. He played baseball himself and has the lean physique of a shortstop, though he'd be small for the majors and in fact did not play ball at West Point, which he attended like his father before him. He smokes cigars and wears authority easily, warmly. He's served multiple combat tours in Iraq and Afghanistan, and eventually we'll have the following exchange:

"Are they the right wars to be fighting?"

"It's not my choice, right? I mean . . ."

"I know, but now that you're a general officer, you don't get to . . . You have to . . . right?"

"All I do is . . . And nobody's asking me, but at some point all I do is offer the best military advice. I mean, really, that's all I'm doing. If you were to ask me would I rather be shooting pheasants with my dog right now, going to my daughter's softball games, or sitting here talking about this? I'd choose the former."

"Of course."

"But that's not my choice."

It's December. A few strands of tinsel hang around the tactical operations center. A plastic Santa Claus clings to a secure phone receiver on which a young lieutenant relays coordinates. Like any office, but almost all male: candy bars, coffee, inside jokes, catchphrases, fantasy football. Most of the men in the room have a wife or girlfriend at home, most have children. Half a world away these children wait for their fathers, become distracted on Skype calls, play video games. Half a world away in vast university libraries, graduate students sleep in the crooks of their elbows, type, finish their books. Their books collect dust, are checked out, returned, uploaded into the single searchable text that is the Internet. Borrow a volume, if so inclined, read it to a child tonight— *Justice*, for example: "A volunteer army," writes the political philosopher Michael Sandel, "fills its ranks through the use of the labor market—as do restaurants, banks, retail stores, and other businesses. . . . The soldiers are 'volunteers' only in the sense that paid employees in any profession are volunteers."[71]

Sandel teaches at Harvard, which General D.A.'s father-in-law ('52) and brother-in-law ('92) both attended. General D.A. himself has completed a fellowship at the Massachusetts Institute of Technology.

We are all looking at the screens.

I cannot tell the age of the six men. Whether they are young or old. They are too tall to be children, but not to be teenagers. I don't know many Helmandis but the ones I do tend to be short, by American standards. The shortest I know is also among the bravest, a mustachioed police officer named Asadullah. He was once wrongly accused of killing Marine special operatives and imprisoned for some weeks with men he had previously helped lock up. The subtext of our talks about his imprisonment was that he had been abused in that cell. He was eager to get back on duty.

I spent some months speaking with him and his father, Shamsullah, taking down the story, and when we finished they insisted I accept a gift, a carpet to bring to my own father, which I did. Asadullah in a green police jumpsuit, his wide eyes manic; Shamsullah, deeply wrinkled beneath a beige turban, knockoff Armani glasses on the tip of his nose, pigeon-gray eyebrows, desperately adoring of his son. On worn carpets we ate dates, chain-smoked, made optimistic phone calls never answered or returned. Asadullah spoke often of vengeance. I discouraged the idea, as did Shamsullah. I wouldn't have recognized either of them on-screen in the tactical operations center.

But even if I could have, even if those screens were perfect, in each moment was the question of whether killing Talibs was right or wrong. Some of the key personnel weren't sure. Back in Kabul the month before, Mark,[72] forty-seven, an erudite and combat-tested lieutenant colonel just removed from his position as head of the Civilian Casualty Mitigation Team, told me about a phrase a colleague of his liked: "ten-dollar Taliban." Mark came from a line of Bengal Lancers and sat for his interview with unusual grace, as though on a barge floating the Nile, or at a university high table, after dinner. "They need ten dollars today," Mark explained. "They need ten dollars tomorrow. So they'll join the team for the sake of earning that ten dollars in order to put food on the table. And what joining the team may mean: that they drive a leader from one part of the province to another, or they provide accommodation for him, or they provide food for him. Or actually they provide the cordon for the laying in of the IED. You know, is that guy Taliban, or is he civilian? And if we are gonna win this, isn't he, you know, the swing voter that we need to be focusing on instead of killing him? Because that guy is supporting— he's got eight or ten dependents. And we've just killed the guy."

On-screen, the digging man fires a rifle over the wall at the Afghan National Army outpost.[73]

The tactical operations center goes quiet save low radio chatter. There are quick glances from all corners at the general. A junior officer half breaks the tension.

Squirters, he predicts, *are gonna run southeast like Usain Bolt.*[74]

What's the slant? asks the general.

The *slant* refers to the number of men, women, and children present in the target area. Written, the numbers are divided by slanting lines, in this case: 6/0/0.[75]

The screen I am watching freezes into static. Text appears: *Media server error. Retrying in 15 seconds.*

I t's a common complaint among the men that too many people watch these strikes, causing the feeds to freeze and skip.[76] Later, in our official interview, I ask Captain John about this.

"So how many people could've been watching that, then?"

"Anybody," he says.

"So . . ." I try again, "how many people are on the ———— system? Do you know, Kay?" I ask, turning to the woman across the table. She's an Air Force public affairs captain who is chaperoning me throughout this embed. She is thoughtful, diligent, considering a career in the foreign service when she gets out of the Air Force.

"I don't know, actually, but . . ."

"A lot," finishes Captain John.

"Like, one hundred thousand people?"

"The majority of people in the military have a ———— account"—
Kay chuckles—"so . . ."

As of this writing, the United States has 1.2 million active military
personnel.

"I get bored sometimes," John says, "and pull up videos from Iraq,
or pull up live feeds from Iraq. . . . I just go see what's going on in Syria,
zoom in, and watch a feed."[77]

At this point, jets are streaking to a target under the guidance of a
joint terminal attack controller, or JTAC, a blond lieutenant named
Rob. JTAC training is rigorous—requires air traffic control under simu-
lated fire, in the wilderness, sleepless—and Rob has a certain swagger.[78,79] His banter is high quality, generous but not lame. He wears a
mustache and is in constant direct contact with the pilots, whom, if kept
aloft unengaged, he describes as *burning holes in the sky*.[80] But mostly,
on the job, Rob speaks in call signs and coordinates. For all his swagger,
it is easy to imagine that machines will replace him, one day soon. The
way we kill from the sky is in a process of lock-in,[81] especially as we use
more drones and fewer jets. Standards we set now—protocols to abort a
strike, say—will define future lives as surely as the gauge of railroad
tracks defined the American West, as Twitter's character limit has defined the language of America's forty-fifth president. But the process is
not up for debate, and mostly the men don't think it should be.[82]

"Do you think that regular folks, in Gardner, Kansas, own a piece of
it?" I ask Captain John.

"I think they empower us to own it for them," he tells me.

Gardner is his hometown, population 21,000.[83] Captain John speaks
in a flat Kansan drawl past a wad of chewing tobacco.

"Do you talk to people about this when you go back to Gardner?"

"Not too much. People I grew up with, my best friends from home, one's a car salesman, one's a high school basketball coach and teacher. They really don't relate on the same level of what we do, so not really."

"Do you think that they should? Do you think that they should have a better grasp of what's going on with the kind of work you do?"

"I don't know. I don't know if it's really necessary for them to."

"Because they have empowered you to do it, and they voted the way they voted and that's . . . ?"

"I think so. The more levels involved, the way our government's set up, we're empowered to do what we do. We have the checks and balances and the chain of command in place the way we do in order to make sure we're making the right decisions. We're trusted to make those decisions. Putting it up to, maybe, people who don't have the same training or the same sense, it's not necessarily—they need to just trust us with that decision, which I think, on the whole, they do."

Whether or not Americans trust the military and intelligence communities, we celebrate them, attend the funerals. Even, especially, in media. I attended one for a long-serving Moscow station chief, in a white church in a seaside town, crisp leaves pinned against clapboard by a salt wind. The politics were excellent, all of ours were, on those dark pews, flexible, intellectual, kind. There was a cousin who had shaved his head and taken saffron Buddhist robes, there were champions of Wall Street become philanthropists, there were on-air correspondents. All taught their children to work diligently, learn languages, respect religion, get a job at the premier institution in the field. All were generous, righteous, did not even have to stoop to ad sales, mostly. Did they intuit they were the crest of the American power? And are they, who admired elegant eulogies for CIA operatives, now so surprised at how mightily they must fight for *truth*, in late middle age?

On-screen, the final minutes of their lives are passing. Bobby the lawyer points out that despite the media error, several feeds remain operative, as I can see, allowing for *unbroken positive identification* of the digger-shooter and the five men around him. They are clearly within a blast radius predicted by the *fires* team—the targeteers, who sit a couple seats over from the JTAC. The top targeteer is Chief Warrant Officer Ron, thirty-two, of Biloxi, Mississippi.[84] He worked as a dishwasher, before he enlisted.

"You're the guy who picks out where the thing's gonna fall?"

"Yes."

Chief Ron is on his fourth deployment. He is watchful and possessed of a low-volume certainty that puts other men at ease. He has four kids, and ten years in.[85] He is looking forward to getting out.

"Oh, yeah. Already told my wife. I was like, 'You know what? When I hit twenty, I'm out.' She goes, 'Why? Why don't you wanna stay in if you want to?' I was like, 'No. Kids'll be fourteen, be able to stay home and be with them.'"

"Aside from raising your kids—that's plenty, but do you think you'll do something else, too?"

"You know what? Maybe I'll just find some mindless job where I don't have to think. I just show up, do something."

On this deployment Chief Ron works from nine a.m. until about eleven-thirty p.m. every day. It is he and his men who generate the collateral damage estimates, predicting how many people will die and what will be destroyed in any proposed strike.[86] This is a technical process, which requires special training. Chief Ron received his certification in collateral damage estimation in 2014 at Fort Sill, Oklahoma.[87]

"Was it hard?"

"Oh, yeah. It was hard."

"Why is it hard?"

"It was hard at the time because everything was manual. Everything was on paper, so they'd hand you the print-off, and you'd have to manually calculate the heading for the mitigation techniques. . . ."

A *mitigation technique* is any practice that makes an airstrike less deadly. A fuse, for example. If a bomb explodes when it hits the roof of a house, it's likely to kill everyone inside. If, instead, it rests in the earth on a fuse before detonating, there is a greater chance for inhabitants to run outside and survive, and the earth dampens the explosion. Such mitigation techniques are variables in any collateral damage estimate.[88] The process, these days, is on-screen. The relevant program looks like Google Maps, but with a specific set of tools for planning and predicting the consequences of a strike. Chief Ron picks *aim points*—spots where the missiles are supposed to land—with the click of a mouse. Likewise, he measures distance from aim points to the nearest object on the no-strike list—in this morning's case, some unspecified *historical ruins*. He compares blast radii for different weapons—a five-hundred-pound bomb versus a two-hundred-pound bomb. Some of his options are binary, others appear in the form of long pull-down menus—for example, *collateral structure functionality*,[89] which looks like this:

Population Density Tables

Valid for: (AOR/Country)

CDE Level 5 Population Density Reference Table

Collateral Structure Functionality	Estimated Population Density		
	Day	Night	Episodic Events
Residential Structures			
Single Family Urban or Small Town, Upper and Middle Class			
Single Family Urban or Small Town, Lower Class and Slum			
Single Family Village or Rural Scattered, Lower Class			
Multi-Family Unit (Apartment, Condominium, Dormitory)			
Institutions/Public Service			
Religious			
Museum			
Library			
School			
College/University			
Hospital			
Public Service Outlet			
Store			
Restaurant			
Hotel/Motel			
Office Building/Industrial Facility			
Light Manufacturing			
Heavy Manufacturing			
Chemical, Refining, Cement			
Heat Processing (i.e. foundry)			
Craftworks			
Transportation Facility			
Station (Air, Rail, Bus, Subway, Gas)			
Transportation Repair (Garage, Hangar)			
Warehouse			
Recreation/Entertainment			
Indoor (Theater, Gymnasium)			
Outdoor Intensive (Stadium, Racetrack)			
Outdoor Extensive (Park, Zoo)			
Auction			
Indoor			
Outdoor/Intensive (Theater, Gymnasium, Casino)			

Notes:
1. The table is based on population density per 1000 square feet.
2. Combatant commands are responsible for tables for their assigned AOR. Combatant commands may use multiple tables to account for the disparity in population density throughout different regions of various countries.
3. Day and night refer to socialized cultural norms for daytime/nighttime functional activities. Special consideration must be given to unique cultural practices and periodic events (i.e. religious holidays) that may influence the population density during daytime/nighttime hours as well as episodic events.

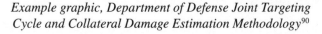

ACLU DRONES JOINT STAFF 000037

37   UNCLASSIFIED//FOUO

Example graphic, Department of Defense Joint Targeting Cycle and Collateral Damage Estimation Methodology[90]

The zoo ("outdoor extensive") is most striking, to me. I visited the Kabul zoo, once, with mustachioed Asadullah's father, Shamsullah. Together we observed a half-blind lion, who, rumor had it, had lost her eye and mate to a Pashtun out to prove his courage. Other foreigners I knew who'd visited the zoo remarked, as I did, on the poor state in which the animals were kept, particularly the bear,[91] patchy and trembling in its cage.[92]

I never visited any zoos in Iraq, but read they had similar problems. It was a trap to assume anything about Iraq based on Afghanistan but unavoidable for many, and Chief Ron, like most soldiers I met in that tactical operations center, had served in both countries. The collateral damage estimation process for both countries was identical on paper. Only the variables changed. The estimated population density[93] of zoos, for example, or the availability of certain missiles, or who could approve a strike, or why we said we had gone to war, or whether we were killing Iraqis or Afghans. Those last two are not included in the pull-down menus, but Chief Ron is wise and I think his plans for retirement have as much to do with the variables he can't control as the ones he can. Shamsullah, for his part, loved the zoo, grinned as we stood at the bear's cage.

General D.A. gives the okay. I can't recall exactly how he puts it, whether it's *Go*, or an *All right, engage*, or a *Proceed*, or what, but in the seconds afterward a gear shifts into place, or warm-ups are suddenly over, and the routine sharpens. Captain John repeats the general's order to the room. The young comms lieutenant alerts higher American units in the area, and *the Afghans*. Chief Ron's out of the room, but his junior targeteer, a thickset sergeant named Albert, previously employed in an applesauce factory—picking rotten ones off the line—confirms the collateral damage estimate, which is zero, structural or human.[94] Rob the JTAC translates the order to the pilots in Air Force jargon. The pilots radio back that they copy, bank their supersonic machines. And for a moment, everyone waits.

There's a story I heard a few times in which, just before striking, a pilot refuses to fire missiles because of civilians—a kid running suddenly into view, for example, or a bigger crowd than expected. I was always on the lookout for such a pilot, but no American I spoke with ever admitted knowing one—just that the thing happened, from time to time. The point of the story was never the heroism of the individual pilot, or that the airstrike might have been poorly conceived. It was rather that our Air Force was the best in the world. A corollary: Even our missiles could be turned aside, midair, into the dirt. Certain stories reaffirmed the mission for the people who fought it, consoled them with exceptional moments of competence within the frame of what even the most *hoo-ra* grunt usually knew, on some level, to be bad news.

I did eventually meet a pilot who claimed to have lived the story. He was a young Iraqi, his skin shiny with oil and creased with acne scars. In a faux French café in Baghdad we were smoking a shisha. He told me he had been flying low over Anbar one day when he saw some kids around a target and, disobeying orders, held fire. He did not want to specify or go on the record and described an air force of great dysfunction and danger to its people, though he was proud of being a pilot, showed me pictures on his phone of his squadron in formation against a horizon of enormous, gentle cumulus clouds. He did not, he told me, believe that speaking publicly would change the situation, but he was certain it would jeopardize his career.

There's a version of this story for drone operators, now, too, which Captain John relates in the tactical operations center. Not all of the screens in that room run surveillance feeds—some display text, and a big one in particular resembles a chat room. It's called *merc-chat*, in reference to the slang to *merc*, meaning to kill, most likely from the word *mercenary*.[95] Drone-feed analysts and operators, earthbound from Nevada to Qatar, communicate with the men in the tactical operations center via this chat screen. In Captain John's story, one of them objected to a missile launch on merc-chat. When asked what the problem was, he wrote back, in black letters upon that white screen, *I don't like to see people die.*

The sentence resembles nothing on merc-chat in register or content. According to Captain John there was no danger of civilian casualties for that particular strike, and the analyst was crazy. The records are classified—I never see them—but the story rings true. The tone of the analyst's objection echoes a familiar strain of indignant video-game bro culture, and as Captain John mentions to me, the job is "like playing Call of Duty all day." He also mentions that everybody says this, and he's right. The video-game comparison has recurred since the beginning of the recent wars in accounts of both journalists and soldiers.[96] The dehumanization it implies is as obvious as the superfluity, for some, of speaking with a bank teller to withdraw money, or a grocer to buy vegetables, or a librarian to read a book, or a driver to ride in a taxi. Less frequently mentioned than this rapidly expanding robot culture is the inversely proportional relationship between access to automated luxuries and the likelihood of getting merced by a drone-flying young man who cannot control his rage or alienation long enough to stop typing even when everyone—the generals and the spies and everyone—can see what he writes, the moment he hits return.

The missile flying toward the target is just under ten feet, nine inches long. It has a diameter of approximately eleven inches and weighs 510 pounds, of which slightly more than half are steel casing designed to shatter into shrapnel. The rest is navigation and guidance, for which the missile employs two systems, laser and GPS. In the former, aircraft or ground units first *paint* the target with a laser beam. Imagine a super-high-powered pointer of the sort used during presentations or lectures. When the beam hits the target, it bounces off. You can't see it, but like all light this beam has a particular electromagnetic wavelength—defined on a spectrum running infrared in one direction and ultraviolet in the other—which can be represented mathematically. The missile is equipped to detect the beam's particular wavelength, to adjust fins and flaps, and to fly to it. The other system—GPS—depends on the military's network of satellites. Like a smartphone providing directions, it triangulates location by bouncing radio waves between earth and space, then adjusts the fins accordingly. The missile's price hovers around $20,000 and is paid by the U.S. Department of Defense to Lockheed Martin or Raytheon, depending on the contract and year.

Such industrial defense companies do more than provide the missiles. They also provide contractors who perform integral tasks—like intelligence analysis. In the tactical operations center, a contractor from BAE Systems—one of the largest of these companies, controlling assets of some $30 billion—is among the people who synthesize the intelligence that guides the missile in a more general sense. Chief Ron, the targeteer from Biloxi, reminds me what is at stake in this particular job: "It all depends on the intel," he says. "I don't walk in there and be like, 'I wanna hit these buildings.' We let intel build itself, and then once we gather all the intel, then we identify the positions that need to be possibly engaged."[97]

"Is intel the most important part of this process?"

"Yes."

"By how much?"

"All of it," he says. "All of it."

It starts long before lasers and radio waves. What we know, or think we know, or say we know, what we've discovered with spies and cameras, or in the rubble of office buildings in lower Manhattan or Dar es Salaam. Imaginary weapons of mass destruction, or tanks rolling into Kuwait, or the bombing of Pearl Harbor. Intelligence is history and informs every step of a war. No intelligence, however, exists in a vacuum, or independently of our values. By seeing some facts as *intelligence* and others as *the status quo* we make decisions before our decisions, before any vote or executive order or tear gas canister tossed in a crowd.

This is common sense, and soldiers I was embedded with knew it on some level already, as they opened the door, in darkness, in Mosul, years ago. They shone white lights in the face of an old man and asked for information, first gently then less so, as he shooed children inside, away from the door.[98] How old was he? A sergeant took him by the elbow, brought him into the street to scan his retinas. Suddenly his age was intelligence, of new value, though the intelligence with which the Americans justified their presence that night was long since debunked. His beard was white, his cheeks pitted, he was not a fighting-age male, like the digger-shooter is said to be. But would we have known, from a camera, from above, in the dark, if he was younger—young enough that his lower lip didn't tremble as the sergeant raised the *haj box*[99] to his rheumy eyes? Perhaps we would have had additional intelligence. We could have analyzed his stride, what he was wearing. We could have intercepted a phone call. We could have been soaking his house for days.

The intel that justifies the strike on the digger-shooter and his compatriots, I read in my notes, consists of "no farming, visual-ops, firing, ISR, humint." That is, the men on-screen are suspiciously *not farming* on that farmland; they have been conducting *visual operations*, i.e., looking at friendlies; they have *fired on* friendlies or been in proximity to someone doing so; and there is additionally relevant *imagery, surveillance, reconnaissance,* and *human intelligence.*[100]

The BAE contractor who synthesizes such information in the tactical operations center, in concert with a small team of military intelligence officers and NCOs, is named Callie.

Callie is thirty years old, from Crane, Missouri, population 1,462. She says she lives by three rules:

1. "Shit happens."
2. "Life's not fair."
3. "Nobody owes you anything."

Her father was a truck driver, her mother became a pharmacist after the divorce. Callie holds a master's degree in sustainable development and has worked as a television actress. She was one of the first female combat-line platoon leaders in Afghanistan, clearing IEDs ahead of infantry and Special Forces in Kandahar between 2010 and 2012. All that, before she began work for BAE and landed two seats to the right of Captain John. She is married to Captain John's predecessor. The job allowed her to be deployed with him, but he rotated out before her contract was up.

"You know I have a passion for sustainable development," Callie tells me, "and building developing nations, but to be honest that doesn't pay the bills. So while I try to figure out what my path is, this is a job."

"So do you think what's going on in that tactical operations center," I ask her, "is contributing to the sustainable development of this country?"

"I do in the aspect of . . . something has to happen."

What, exactly, she isn't sure—but she has a theory. Afghanistan needs a strong, moral leader,[101] she says, and after that: "You have to ensure that an assassination doesn't happen." Callie elaborates, unbidden: "You know, in Africa, there's been a lot of great leadership that would've made something better of their country, and they were assassinated before they received the opportunity."

"Who are you thinking of, for example?"

She pauses, stutters: "I . . . um . . ."

"You mean like Patrice Lumumba?"

I am helping, here, but I am also laying a trap, have done so before I can even think. The way you snap at someone you love over dinner and realize by dessert that you've only betrayed yourself. This unconscious aggression is the heart of partisanship. There are no cameras here, no judge, no witnesses for cross-examination—so how best to understand Callie, to do justice to the word *synthesize* rather than redeploy it in anger, to encompass ignorance of the local language, the truck stop, the master's degree, the satellite feeds, the partial power over life and death, her long sigh?

"No," Callie says, finally, "'cause I don't have enough knowledge to wanna make a statement, but, you know, corporations get in the way a lot, right? And that's part of my struggle, my own struggle in sustainable development is, I want to have my own sustainability, my own family, but yet do I feel like, you know, I'm working for a corporation who is takin' advantage of other people?"

She is pale as a plate and freckled, brown-haired.[102]

"Well it's funny you bring up the African leadership," I say, "because that is one of the places in the twentieth century where the United States is most famous for assassinating leaders, who some people, like Patrice Lumumba in the Congo, it's sort of widely understood—known—that the CIA assassinated this guy, and it wasn't great for the country."[103]

"I mean," she says, conciliatory, "just like the British were here doing that in the 1800s, you know, colonialism is what it is."

"Do you think we still do that kind of stuff?"

"Personal opinion? I don't know at what extent, but I'm sure it still happens."

"So does it freak you out?"

"I mean the world is complicated. It's gray, there is no black and white, anywhere."

"Yeah. You got your three laws. I appreciate someone who lays down axioms in the middle of an interview. That's great. And did you say you had kids, too?"

"No. No."

In asking about kids I am gently attacking her. I do not mean to, but I am, somehow. To discuss childbearing in this context, to interpose it suddenly in a moment of political tension is nothing, but it is everything. It is every interaction on a base full of men, another mote of disrespect, small but airborne. She is the only woman in the TOC that day, aside from my chaperone, Kay. I try to link it all back to something else, to reverse.

"You said something about raising a family, and um, the future of sustainable development. . . ."

Callie is unfazed. "Even single," she tells me, "you want to have a livelihood, but at what cost is my livelihood affecting somebody else's? But that's just a third world–first world all-around moral dilemma. . . . I think we all ignore some pieces more than others when it comes to first and third. . . ."

She continues her non sequiturs, floating them like moondust kicked up at great risk to her body, her eyes, back when she was on patrol, not at a desk as she is now, responsible for managing intercepted information and contextualizing it in the local culture, about which she explains:

"You know, you and I are talking, and in our culture, we tend to trust what each other are saying. In Pashtun culture, you know, they know that the person they're talking to is probably going to stab them in the back with something, so I'm gonna try to beat you to the punch. . . ."

We are sitting at a long table in a conference room with no windows, down the hall from the tactical operations center. We are approximately 7,500 miles from Crane, Missouri. We are in a small white building bordered by the rubber walking paths which like capillaries carry us around Camp Shorab, formerly Camp Bastion, formerly logistics hub for the U.S.-led international coalition in southern Afghanistan. On my previous trips it had been crowded, tens of thousands of men, hundreds of aircraft. This time it's almost deserted, fences bent down to the wind, the Afghan National Army occupying only a fraction of the desert offices their foreign allies built, a few hundred Americans garrisoned to advise them, fly drones, watch, and strike.

"I'm trying to figure out," I tell Callie, "in my own head, in my own heart, whether it is appropriate sometimes to kill innocent people to get what we want."

"In this world you have good people and bad people, and sometimes the bad people are evil, and I'm not sayin' we have to go to their level but on a personal level, I can understand having to take steps to mitigate the evil so that that does not enter the world on a larger stage."

"When you say 'mitigate the evil,' you mean what I was saying about killing civilians?"

"No, well, no, I'm talking about enemy."

"I'm talkin' particularly about civilians. I'm saying, is there a moment when it's okay, when it's right, to be willing to kill a civilian, to do what you need to do?"

"I just think that's how the world works. I don't think anybody would say that's *right*. I just don't know if there's a mitigation on how *not* to do that when you're fighting an enemy who will protect himself with women and children," she says. "I mean, that's the evil, right? An evil person is going to protect himself with women and children. . . ."

These words, good and evil, lie in every childhood. I cannot forget the feel of dirt under my fingernails from a potato field where I pulled and lobbed clod bombs at my younger brother. A sweat in the autumn air, the whiskery bales of hay, the cold skin of a pumpkin against a cheek, playing games of war, or cops and robbers, hide and seek. Universal games, and there are pumpkins in these fields, too, cold and therefore near impossible to see on-screen during the night shift when the thermal imagery is hypnotic, the men in the fields white hot, or black hot. But there is no lens to reveal our halos or small cruelties, our intent or guilt or innocence as we step into whatever field lies out the back door, without the luxury of choosing our family, neighbors, countrymen.[104]

On-screen, the explosions resemble red flowers.

Good effects on target, says someone.

A plume of black and gray smoke obscures the view. Two of the six men emerge, running from its edge. The surveillance drones follow as they sprint away through the fields, over a wall, along irrigation canals, into a stand of trees, where we lose sight of them.

General D.A. nods—*Good work, everyone*—and leaves quickly.

Several men in the room predict the *squirters* will be back for the dead. Or someone will. After a few minutes the wind carries away the smoke, revealing a crater where the digger-shooter had been. The bunker, several men point out to me, is untouched, so precise was the missile.[105] And within half an hour some men do return and collect scattered remains from the crater, by hand. I cannot tell if it was the digger-shooter who escaped, or one of his compatriots, but everyone in the room is satisfied with the outcome. No one admits any doubts—to me, at least. Not about this strike, about the apparently unarmed men who died in the same field as the digger-shooter, nor about the wider policies, which I discuss with General D.A. at length in our interviews.

"If you believe," I ask him at one point, "that it is appropriate and necessary to tolerate foreign civilian casualties to achieve national security objectives for the United States of America, are you comfortable going to those people, the families of the Iraqis or the Afghans, and saying, 'Look, I'm sorry that your daughter had to die, but this had to happen for X, Y, and Z'?"

"Comfortable? No. Would I do it if I was told to? Yeah."

He collects himself, continues.

"I'll give you a personal example, and this is a disturbing story. I'm up in Urozgan, an operations center in Shah Wali Kot. . . . I get a call, late at night of course, that one of my platoons moving on Route Bear had taken fire, they had maneuvered to suppress the enemy that was firing at them. And in the process, they'd fired at a guy who had an RPG. What they didn't realize was—they did everything right, right?—what they didn't realize was . . . all the way over this ground that was about seven to eight hundred meters away—they couldn't see that it dipped down. When they arrived on the scene where the guy with the RPG was, they found that their forty-millimeter rounds had landed in a Kuchi[106] camp, and in the process killed an eight-year-old little girl. A bunch of sheep, and an eight-year-old little girl."

In his spare office, General D.A. speaks in tones of disappointment and disbelief at the troubled world, but also pride and certainty in his own actions.

"And the guy with the RPG," he goes on, "was a dude that had a bed roll, that when he saw the Strykers coming, he just took off running. And with the cameras, it looked just like a dude with an RPG. So the next day, I fly down to make the solatia payment. I take the cash out to this Kuchi father for his eight-year-old girl. And what he's most concerned about is the fact that he hadn't been paid for his sheep yet. I gave him money for his daughter, that didn't really matter to him. What he really wanted to know was, how much money was he gonna get for the sheep we'd killed?"

General D.A. puts his hands in the air, like, *What can I say?*

"Now if it had been his son," he goes on, "that might have been a different discussion, but it was his daughter. And it was the weirdest conversation I've ever had. I remember going out there and being like, 'Man, how am I gonna face this father?' Because I was a father at the time of a ten-year-old little girl. 'How would I face this father who just lost an eight-year-old girl?' And it was crushing. And I went out there."

General D.A. leans toward me.

"Now, I'll tell you," he says, "who it was really harder on than that man, was the crew of the Stryker that had fired the volley that had killed the eight-year-old little girl."[107,108]

S ome men don't love their children. Perhaps the soldiers who killed that little girl do suffer her death more than her own father. Who can know the infinite variety of men? But some types repeat. Years before, on the same base, in a similar office, one of the general's predecessors, a man who survived shrapnel to the throat in Iraq, spoke to me in the same tones of easy authority, using a long poppy stalk as a pointer against the wall map. The war had already confounded America for eight years by then, but he was likewise certain of everything. Every general I've met has been like that.

No one starts out a general, though, and relatively few officers get the star. Far below, the more diverse mass of soldiers keep their own counsel on the dead, make their own decisions about eight-year-olds. Once, on a different embed in Helmand, I was riding in the back of an MRAP when a pair of small boys rushed its sides and hatch, yellow jerricans in their arms. These were common housing for IEDs and the Marines around me, believing the truck in imminent danger, yelled up at the gunner. *I see 'em*, he shouted into his mic, and swore, yelled something else along the lines of *I really don't want to shoot these kids.* He kept a pile of rocks up there for such occasions, not infrequent, and began winging them at the children. It was hard to imagine these kids would blow up the truck, but then suddenly, it wasn't. One of them made it all the way onto the running board. The young captain, cramped beside me, yelled to *Shake him off!*[109]—which the driver accomplished by accelerating, then slamming the brakes. The kid bonked his head and fell off into the dirt behind us.

That afternoon the Marines were searching for a drone fallen to earth, though their patrol had been due back to base an hour before. *Oh, fuck that,* the driver had said when the order to search had come across the radio. Eventually we stopped close to an Afghan police base and looked out over the fields, to the mud compounds in the distance. Dark was falling and no one wanted to keep driving around, wrecking crops, exposed in a district where small boys frightened heavily armed men in armored trucks. *Okay,* I remember the captain saying, *what's everyone got in their wallets?* And out of their camouflage the men pulled wallets. Vinyl and Velcro, a few of battered leather. They counted out their money and handed it over. The captain collected around two hundred dollars to hire the local Afghan police to recover the drone, in whatever manner they saw fit, so we could return to base. He saw one future—staying out there—and decided to buy another.

This seemed to me a wiser course of action, and replicable. Even for big problems. No amount of money will make a truly committed man switch sides in a war, but money *without* war can be convincing. And there is no shortage of money. Only, it is concentrated in the hands of the super-wealthy, of magnates and politicians and pop stars, one of whom was playing in the truck that day, on an iPod rigged to the comms system. In the seat beside me, a teenager in a Puerto Rican flag bandanna sang along in a full-throated tenor as we returned to base, smooth enough his truck mates didn't mind. *If I die out here*, he told me, *this is the song I want to die to.* I had actually met the pop star he sang along to once, backstage at the taping of a television show, and the story helped me with the soldiers. She was formidable, also married at the time to a comic who wrote about politics and identified as an anarchist. *Baby, you're a firework / Come on, show 'em what you're worth,*[110] went the song that the young soldier said he wanted to die to, if he had to die, and in that sweating steel box he was Sinatra, he was Sam Cooke, he was Pavarotti. Days later on that embed, a few minutes behind us on the road leading into the base, an IED would disable a truck, killing several men, but the day of the singing we were back inside the wire just after dark, able to imagine not only what might have been, but what might be.

Through it all, intel to targeting to the gathering of limbs, Corporal Ryan enters data. Up in the first row he's positioned in such a way that he must crane his neck to look at the screens, but mostly he doesn't look as he combines and proofs and retypes everyone else's reports into new reports for *Higher*, all the relevant numbers and captions. He is the skinniest, youngest, and lowest ranking guy in the room, a helpless magnet for its banter. *Corporal Ryan is the kind of guy who would have a Star Wars tattoo,* someone speculates when the new Star Wars movie comes up, and as though fated to humiliation Corporal Ryan blushes, confesses that he does, and is forced to roll up his sleeve and reveal an intricately drawn light saber. He is from Falls, Pennsylvania, population 34,300.[111,112]

"I kinda got it," he tells me, "because, honestly, I thought that light saber was pretty badass."

Corporal Ryan says he doesn't want to kill any innocent people, hopes he's never in a position where he has to weigh civilian lives against some greater good, hopes that no one is *ever* in that position. He's uneasy throughout the interview, worried about getting into trouble or looking like a fool, which he is not. At the end of our interview he tells me that he does feel responsible, in part, for every airstrike.

"There's really no other way to put it, you do. Like, you helped contribute. And again it's . . . I'm trying to think of a way to put this . . . accessory, essentially the way I think about it. Yeah, you contributed. It's almost like . . . I don't know how to put this. I don't wanna say murder, 'cause it's not really a proper way to put it. But then again, that comes down to perspective, really. Yeah, I do feel responsible for the count, I guess."[113]

"Okay. And how about after the Army?"

"After the Army . . . ? I'd always weigh my options, but if I had my way I'd probably try and be a police officer."

I hope to see him, then. Sometimes when I'm in the United States I run into servicemen I've met on embeds. An ex-CIA officer once told me—after relating the practice of *canoeing*, in which Special Forces operators compete to shoot targets' skulls open into a V shape, like the bottom of a canoe[114]—that 5 percent of any army is psychopathic. And that may be. But almost every soldier I've met was decent, and several were heroic, within the confines of their bloody work. And soldiers are good company. Drinking too much in a dive with a former Marine who wants to run for office. At a school reunion with a Navy SEAL. Over sushi in D.C. with a cavalry officer, years after a grenade blew up a patrol we'd walked in Mosul. That last guy and I were both about twenty-five when the grenade went off. I ducked so low I fell to my knees, but he was up and running and scanning, yelling at me to follow. His men had started shooting, and the alley resounded with shots. Someone spotted the attacker, we all gave chase, and eventually they shotgunned the lock off a gate, battered down a door, and I ran in behind to watch the apprehension of a teenage insurgent.

Back at the combat outpost a staff sergeant sitting on a cot across from mine asked if it was my first time in combat. I told him that no, it wasn't, I'd been in Darfur and been shot at there, which was a lie. I had actually been stuck in a sandy river with some African Union troops, and we heard gunfire in the middle distance. I didn't mean to lie; it just came so easily, before any thought, driven by fear and pride. The sergeant looked skeptical—knew my deception, I suspect—but told me I did good. I'm not sure whether this was generous or not. There is no guide for whom to confront and when, which lies we must kill on sight and which we must let pass darkly beneath us. There is only the fragmentary interaction with our environment, whose most brightly shining shards are the stories we tend for a while, polish, and often enough discard.

The light saber is one of several tattoos that run up Corporal Ryan's forearms and across his chest. All are comic book related. The "HA HA HA" up his shoulder, he tells me, is the signature exclamation of the Joker, the anarchic enemy of Gotham City. He got it in the All-American Tattoo Parlor in Clarksville, Tennessee, when he and his fiancée split up.[115] We talk around comic books and movies for a while before, eventually, we get to this: "All right. Well, let me ask you: Now you've been in a real war for a while, two deployments—is the make-believe of war, of these stories we tell ourselves, anything at all like real war?"

"Make-believe stories?"

"Like the stories we tell ourselves. Like, *Star Wars*—it's a war story, right?"

"Yeah."

"I mean, is it anything like real war? We're not swinging light sabers in here, but you know what I mean? Like, the larger story."

"I'll just say," the corporal says, "from my perspective, and this is the way I view it, is, I really wasn't here for the war. Like, if you talk to anybody, the war's over."

I do solemnly swear," runs the Uniformed Services Oath of Office, "that I will support and defend the Constitution of the United States against all enemies, foreign and domestic; that I will bear true faith and allegiance to the same; that I take this obligation freely, without any mental reservation or purpose of evasion; and that I will well and faithfully discharge duties of the office on which I am about to enter. So help me God."

Captain John took this oath a few years ago, General D.A. decades before. Enlisted men like Corporal Ryan take a slightly different oath, which mentions obeying superior officers, and the Uniform Code of Military Justice.[116] All are obligated, however, to disobey unlawful orders. And this is the great challenge. Not to avoid any of the misdemeanors or felonies, the adulteries which bring down presidential candidates or the drug prohibitions that discharge you dishonorably back to your small town for smoking hash over a chessboard with a Kurdish terp. Nor to run across the Fallujah street in a firefight, nor to walk the path laden with IEDs. These are common enough and trained for, and indeed the desire for battle is thick on many forward operating bases. The great challenge faced by soldiers is not to obey orders, but to disobey them. And if the law is unjust, to change the law, and if it can't be changed, to break it. The last sermon Sidney the chaplain delivered, in the days before the digger-shooter and the other men in the field died, concerned such a dilemma.

"I don't know how familiar you are with scripture," Sidney tells me, "but basically the angel comes and tells Mary she's pregnant and that she's gonna birth the Messiah. And she goes and tells her betrothed husband, 'Hey, I'm a virgin but I'm pregnant.' And according to Jewish law then she should've been stoned to death. And so what I focused on was basically calling it 'Joseph's Dilemma,' and just, the choice between law and love. . . ."

"It's not one or the other, law or love," I say, "or is it?"

"Well, if you're going to err on any side, I would always err on love."

That evening we are in the empty conference room where he leads Bible study, next to his bedroom. Alone of all the men, Sidney keeps private quarters. Even the general shares a building with other officers, but not the chaplain. The logic behind this arrangement is that soldiers are more inclined to seek him out if no one is likely to see them coming or going, in search of understanding or solace for the killing to which they are party.[117]

Other sources of solace are available. History, philosophy, the reassuring study of the sky. Biology, breathing and sweating in that tactical operations center, is most relevant, perhaps, though little discussed. American campaigns float within the genetic drift, not beyond it. That the United States raises armies for the same reason the peacock raises feathers and the snake exposes fangs increases rather than diminishes the value of its highest ideals.[118] These are worth dying for. And if you are still young, the military will train you to fly, to kill with a knife, to jump from airplanes. It will give you brothers and sisters. It will pay for college, teach you mathematics and physics and how to hold your breath under water. It will pin medals on you. It will give you dominion over other men, heal your body when it is wounded and strengthen it in the meantime. It will provide a pension. It will celebrate and mourn you. It will take you around the world. It will give you secrets, make you most lethal, even turn you, perhaps, into one of the polyglot warrior poets who sometimes emerge from the machine. Then it will welcome you into the tactical operations center.

And it may seem impossible, inconceivable in your one-stoplight town, if that's where you are, among decorated uncles and fathers and mothers, whose martyred parents fade upon the mantel in Garmsir or Falls or Crane or Gardner or Tikrit, but there are other options. These options exist, are no less honorable. Many are more so, and may finally rest easier upon your head. For while on the first day of the embed, though I do not ask, Captain John says, *No way,* he will not tell me how many men he has killed—*my number*—on the last day he stops me in the hall and says that he does want to tell me his number. It is 136.

10.

Correspondence (IV)

from: Nick McDonell

to: Col USAF CENTCOM

cc: A CDR USN CENTCOM

date: Tue, Nov 1, 2016 at 5:28 AM

subject: Re: FW: CIVCAS Query/ —— Request

Hi Colonel, Commander,

Writing to following up on this and keep you posted on our previous correspondence. My embed request remains under review with RS and I appreciate how responsive a Lt. —— has been so far. Thanks for putting us in touch.

Regarding my second request—to speak with anyone involved in setting NCCVs, if there is some problem with the request or it should directed to another office, please let me know. Am available to talk anytime. I would also be happy to visit CENTCOM to have the conversation in person if that is a better option.

Best,

Nick

V.

Numbers

Solatium, n. 1. A sum of money, or other compensation, given to a person to make up for loss or inconvenience.

—*Oxford English Dictionary*

Solatia payments: Iraq: Up to $2,500 for death; up to $1,500 for serious injury; and $200 or more for minor injury. Afghanistan: Up to 100,000 Afghani ($2,336+/–) for death; up to 20,000 Afghani ($467+/–) for serious injury; and up to 10,000 Afghani ($236+/–) for nonserious injury or property damage.

—U.S. Government Accountability Office, *Military Operations: The Department of Defense's Use of Solatia and Condolence Payments in Iraq and Afghanistan*, Washington, D.C., May 2007

11.

Revelation in Pleasantville
of Anticipated Civilian Casualties

T wenty."

In a Starbucks in Pleasantville, New York, a former targeting officer explains the rules for Baghdad. Above him, wall-mounted speakers play Beyoncé.

"There was a cutoff of twenty civilian casualties, twenty anticipated civilian casualties in any airstrike."

The officer, Marc, is an American born in 1970. When I first meet him, he is conducting research for the federally funded Center for Naval Analyses. He's since gone on to the United Nations to investigate Syrian war crimes. He began his career on the operational side, though, as a contractor with the Defense Intelligence Agency. By the invasion of Iraq in 2003, he'd become chief of high-value targeting for the Department of Defense, against the war but highly qualified to wage it. Drawing on a vast, almost affectionate knowledge of munitions, he oversaw weaponeering, targeting, and sequencing—what to drop, what to aim for, and in what order. He was therefore responsible, in part, for deciding who died as collateral damage.

"Any more than twenty, you needed national-level authorization, which meant sec def or president."

"So who came up with that twenty number?"

"You know, that's a great question," he says. "I have no idea. No clue."

12.

The U.S. Civilian Casualty
Mitigation Team

For the first time in the recent wars, in 2017, more civilian casualties are alleged against America than Russia.[119] This fact seizes a few headlines, but knowledge of the numbers remains rare. In the United States, foreign civilian casualties are seen to be unfortunate, but even less relevant than usual given novel pressures on the American experiment created by the forty-fifth president.[120] On Fifth Avenue in Manhattan during the Women's March after his inauguration, posters address an array of issues, but none that I see mention the policy to tolerate the killing of innocents, or the ongoing wars abroad.[121,122] A few days later, a senior American diplomat, a friend, forwards me a newspaper report on the reopening of secret prisons with a note that runs: "So depressing . . . Mitigation of civilian casualties will seem so quaint, in not too long."[123] I don't write him back immediately, thinking instead about *quaint*, what is old-fashioned versus what is new. Decent citizens may be torn between arguments—the greater good versus human rights—and new ideas—the responsibility to protect versus sovereignty—but the soul of the problem remains unchanged. The ascent of a demagogue throws it in relief. What ideals are more valuable than a life, lives?

In Berlin, the gray stelae of the Memorial to the Murdered Jews of Europe stand in morning light. During the tragedy to which those stones are dedicated, George Orwell argued, "Pacifism is objectively pro-fascist. This is elementary common sense."[124] Later, he characterized the statement as a "propaganda trick." "The important thing," he wrote, revising his position, "is to discover which individuals are honest and which are not, and the usual blanket accusation merely makes this more difficult." And yet the beaches of Normandy remain shockingly wide, every step down to the water recalls the unzipping of air. Such a long walk, under such fire, and here is a popular idea, in that gray air, under a new and more bellicose administration: without certain exercises of American violence, the world would be colder, darker, more brutal. The United States both contributed to and opposed the rise of the Third Reich, the failures of Communism, the distortions of jihad. These phenomena are different, and it's best to take each case on its own merits; and yet. Frequently the United States caused the problem before addressing it—as in helping Yazidis trapped on Sinjar's mountaintop to escape, saving[125] them from fellow Iraqis driven to extremism by illegal and immoral invasion—and yet. As ignorant men have visited violence upon the innocent, the United States of America has sometimes stood beacon to victims, even, very occasionally, intervened successfully on their behalf, fighting for those who were in the moment defenseless.

I wrote that diplomat back soon enough. Like our most thoughtful leaders, he takes seriously the question of killing. Such leaders are not ignorant of arguments regarding *ends* and *means*, and neither are all the citizens they're meant to represent. Knowledge is more virtue than power. The great challenge is to establish facts in the face of lies, which are ubiquitous. The day after the last U.S. presidential inauguration, for example, the new White House press secretary disputed attendance figures at that rainy ceremony, contradicting all data. He was emboldened to do so on account of earlier, grander deceptions. Among the most grievous is how many civilians the United States has killed in the on-going wars, over a decade and a half—the numbers, daily and in total.

An array of organizations chase those numbers, or claim to. The United Nations, the International Red Cross, and various NGOs, jour-nalists, state media services, peer-reviewed academic journals, the armies themselves, the breadth of America's opponents and allies—all have figures. And everywhere, in every case,[126] the United States admits to causing fewer civilian casualties than any of those parties estimate. The U.S. number is always lowest. And the number the U.S. will tolerate is, almost always, classified.

O ne man who determines the U.S. count in Afghanistan is Sergeant First Class Rogelio. In America's military headquarters in Kabul, he's part of the Civilian Casualty Mitigation Team, or CCMT.[127] He is a smiling, thick-necked twenty-nine-year-old with a firm handshake. When he isn't deployed with the National Guard, he's a police officer in Duncanville, Texas.

"I go by 'Roger.'"

His reaction on assignment to the CCMT, he tells me, was: "First of all, what is that?"

We laugh about this.

"Second of all," he says, "you know, this is not what I came here to do. But after spending some time here, my views changed. I do think now that the CCMT is important. Not only because of the moral aspect of it. You know, every single civilian casualty does have a strategic im-pact on what we do here. Because, not only is it horrible, it lends a cred-ibility to the insurgents . . . ammunition for recruiting, ammunition for arguments against GIRoA [Government of the Islamic Republic of Afghanistan]. . . . I will say that, unfortunately, as a reality of war, it's gonna happen. Unfortunately."

Working from that assumption, Sergeant Roger and the CCMT per-form three functions:

1. Training, advising, and assisting
2. Consequence management
3. Reporting

The investigation of particular deaths—of the corpses that add up to the total number—falls under "consequence management."

"So," Sergeant Roger explains, "whenever we receive an allegation, we convene what is called a CCARB, Civilian Casualty Credibility Assessment Review Board. And so basically what we do is we take the allegation and we compare the date, times, locations, and other relevant information contained in the allegation. And we compare that to all the tactical reporting we have."

"Video."

"If we have it, right."

"Tactical reporting from units on the ground."

"Right. And so—"

"Anything else I should put in there? Intel?"

"Intel. We also look at GIRoA reporting, for instance from the provincial governor or district governor."

Such reporting varies dramatically and is treacherous in both Iraq and Afghanistan. Some officials never venture into the districts they are meant to govern. Others do, but play both sides of the conflict. Others dig in with the foreigners, a pistol ever present on their desk. For all sides, assessing the honesty of partners is difficult.[128] Within the Coalition, officers are often made to seem liars or fools by their superiors and representatives. This is also true for U.S. citizens at large. When I was younger, I told many Iraqis and Afghans that America doesn't go to war *just* to plunder oil, and I believed it, and then America elected a president who said the country should have kept Iraq's oil when it invaded, and might take it in the future.[129]

He was speaking a deeper truth. The history of pillage abroad is not ended, it is only tempered and re-formed.[130] Certain totems convey this reality as well as any number. I once watched a child-faced lieutenant colonel, Bill, his blond hair sucking up the sunlight, present a pair of Mameluke swords to a jowly Helmand district governor named Abdul.

The Mameluke sword is curved and fearsome, worn by officers at dress occasions and unsheathed dramatically at the beginning of old television recruitment advertisements. It became associated with the Marine Corps in December 1805, during the First Barbary War. That war, between the United States and what were then known as the Barbary states—including present-day Morocco, Algeria, Tunisia, and Libya—saw Marines fire cannonballs across North Africa in defense of American shipping interests. This is what the Marines are singing about when they mention the shores of Tripoli in their hymn, and the song carried to Abdul's district, Nawa. The story about the sword is that a viceroy of the Ottoman Empire presented the original to a lieutenant who'd led a handful of Marines and a few hundred mercenaries to victory in what's known as the Battle of Derna. It was the first American battle fought abroad, and considered a decisive victory in which many locals were slain.[131] District Governor Abdul accepted the swords gratefully and in my recollection did not ask about their history.

He was a gracious man.[132] In his sandbagged, perennially besieged office he answered ignorant questions from foreigners who had no interest in his language. He learned to salute in the American style. Then Bill's Marines left, new ones arrived, and Abdul continued to govern.[133] A few years later all the Marines left[134] and Abdul was ambushed on the Kabul–Kandahar highway, shot in the head for supporting a government backed by U.S. officers who insisted they would support him, even as their intelligence agency did business with the narcos and insurgents broadly responsible for his death.[135] I wonder, sometimes, where the swords are. But Abdul is not the kind of civilian casualty Sergeant Roger and his team count.

"Okay, so, you get the CCARB and then . . . you decide whether it is credible or not?"

"Right. Exactly right."

"And how many people on that CCARB board?"

"So, minimum of five. . . . We have the chairman, which is usually a lieutenant colonel or above, and then we have—"

"I have his name somewhere here. . . . Jones?"

"Right."

This is the man who has replaced Mark the Bengal Lancer.

"He's double-hatted as a targeteer?"

"Right. He's the chief of targeting."

That is: The chief of targeting for the airstrikes which cause civilian casualties is now *also* chairman of the team to assess civilian casualty allegations.[136]

I don't think I've ever met anyone in the American military," I tell Sergeant Roger at one point, "who's like, 'Yeah, fuck it.'"

"Right," he says, "Right."

"You mostly don't meet people like that."

"You probably haven't talked to many."

We laugh again. I have met such people, and the small lie stays with me.[137] Maybe such lies are unavoidable in the flow of interviews, a necessary part of the process of empathy and conversation. And there's flow to every process, even counting the dead. After Sergeant Roger's team assesses the credibility of an allegation, it either denies and closes the case, or pins it for review pending new information. In rare circumstances, members of the team will investigate further, even more rarely visit the site itself.[138] The majority of allegations are deemed not credible.

The few which are tend to be significant and the subject of questions from media. Self-reporting of civilian casualties also occurs, which the CCARB, naturally, finds credible. But you don't hear about those deaths because, if no outsider asks about a civilian casualty, the U.S. military doesn't announce it. The process concludes in command's Public Affairs Office, which is responsible for disseminating the findings to whoever asks—or not, if ordered to keep them secret.

13.

Sar Baghni and the Deadliest Civilian Casualty Incident to Date

S ome secrets about civilian casualties do not emerge for years. The biggest I've come across—numbers-wise—attended an airstrike on August 2, 2007, which was conducted on the village of Sar Baghni, in Baghran district, Helmand. A U.S. spokeswoman at the time said:

> Over the past weeks, several media have reported erroneous information on numbers of casualties from ISAF [International Security Assistance Force] operations following Taliban extremist propaganda. But rushing to deny casualties is not the way ISAF communicates. We refer to confirmed facts, not hear-say and that obviously takes time. Unlike the Taliban extremists, we value the truth and our credibility.

In tandem, her office issued the following statement:

> In response to allegations that the strike may have caused civilian casualties, ISAF sent a task force to conduct an assessment. . . . There is no evidence of civilian casualties caused by the above mentioned operation.[139]

Ten years later, Coalition officials decline to discuss the incident—often claiming, gently, that it was before their time, and so not their responsibility, though they wish they could help. Absent their comment, I propose we proceed in fives:

Tazaa Gul, Anaar Gul, Zhar Gul, Shah Noor, Gul Zaman.

These names appear on a list I hire several men to compile by interviewing residents of Baghran. Like everyone I contact about the incident, they say, first: it happened a long time ago. This is one of many challenges, though it is also a mercy kind as sunrise that we are less troubled by deaths as days pass by. Another challenge is forensic.[140] As one of the UN officers who followed the case at the time points out, the missiles would have done such damage to the crowd—the bodies so mixed up, just *pink mist*[141]—that an accurate count on the day itself would have been difficult, even for a world-class forensic team. Such a team isn't present anywhere in Afghanistan, and the strike occurred in remotest, Taliban-controlled Helmand. But if certainty of a number is impossible, a range compatible with common sense is not.

Faiz Mohammad, Ajab Khan, Shir Khan, Khan Mohammad, Gul Mohammad.

An equal challenge it seems to me is identifying *with* the victims. In low moments, I wonder how to do so. Who would I be, if I couldn't read? Who would you? According to USAID, the literacy rate in Helmand where these people died is less than 10 percent for men, less than 1 percent for women.

Abdul Khaliq, Salaam, Tazaa Gul, Mohammad Lal, Abdul Kabeer.

A key and literate Helmandi in this case is Senator Sher Mohammed Akunzhada. Before he became senator he was the province's governor, but lost the job over allegations of drug running after British commandos discovered nine tons of opium in his compound. He claimed to be storing the drugs for destruction. He admitted, however, to sending men to fight for the Taliban.[142] Classified U.S. documents describe him as "most nefarious," and intimately familiar with the strike. I set out to visit him one autumn morning, as a light wind stirs Kabul's maple trees.

On the way, my fixer and I discuss the wisdom of leaving our blue sedan in the care of Akunzhada's men. We are careful, at the time, have been bellying down on the pavement to check the chassis for sticky bombs. We decide the vehicle will be safer under Akunzhada's protection than on the street. It is obvious, in retrospect, we don't need to talk about it—there's probably no danger. But often we talk of nothing, of anything, of everything, of music videos, of sunglasses, of whether pornographic actors are welcome in heaven, or not, of other running jokes, of the weather, of what to have for lunch. The fixer says he isn't trying to convert me, and he only half is, only tries tenderly, off work and a little stoned, for my own good.

Malan Wali Jaan, Niaz Mohammad, Shoo Khan, Toor Jaan, Mohsen.

The guards at Akunzhada's gate are irregularly uniformed and armed with light machine guns. In the courtyard, a few bow the legs of plastic chairs, leaning back, staring. Children dash across the garden. It is a family compound, and resembles compounds belonging to other powerful criminals. Many have at one time or another enjoyed American support. In Khartoum years before I'd lunched with a logistician of the Darfur genocide beneath framed certificates awarded him at Fort Benning, Georgia, where he had trained as a helicopter pilot.[143] Children roamed that compound, too, and as we spoke the logistician delicately fed his grandson a green and viscous stew.

On another trip to that blacklisted country I chanced upon—to the evident dismay of their aides—a quartet of American lawmakers[144] in the basement of Khartoum's most expensive hotel.[145] Not a congressional delegation, or *codel* as they are called—but a *no*del, as one of the aides joked, uneasily, physically barring my entrance to the conference room. I wanted to ask my representatives how they were working with the treacherous regime. Surely they knew, as the logistician surely knew, as Akunzhada in his compound of children surely knows, that cruel men are capable of kindness, that cruelty and goodness are not segregated. (Shakespeare's Fool in *Twelfth Night*: "Anything that's mended is but patched. Virtue that transgresses is but patched with sin, and sin that amends is but patched with virtue."[146]) Perhaps they used this common knowledge to justify partnerships with men who little value life. With a Saudi air force that bombs indiscriminately, shattering holy sites in Sana'a as brutally as ISIS in Palmyra or the Taliban in Bamiyan. With Iraqi army units that execute teenage prisoners. Or with a series of corrupt Helmandi governors. Akunzhada is rumored to have ordered murders himself.

Ahmad Shah, Jalat Khan, Noor Mohammad, Sheen Gul, Torman.

Inside his dark and gaudy living room, we drink tea. Two other men await an audience, one snarl-toothed and both silent beside the unctuous aide-de-camp with whom we have arranged the meeting. All jump up when Akunzhada himself arrives, trailed by large-bellied associates. He's not much over five feet, turbaned in black and gray, and has the largest belly of all. He smokes loudly and says he doesn't have much time. With little preface I ask if he is aware of an airstrike in Baghran in the summer of 2007.

"It was the biggest ever," Akunzhada answers, without hesitation. "Other strikes only had twenty, thirty, or fifty casualties, but none this big, to have two hundred and fifty."[147]

He goes on to cast doubt on other sources, insist on his righteousness, crow of his family's service to Helmand, attack the Brits and Pakistanis. But within all that, some details of the strike chime with what I've heard elsewhere. The number, for example: around 250. And since Akunzhada remains an influential man in northern Helmand, with contacts in that difficult place, I ask for introduction to those contacts, and will hire two of them to help collect names. As a tribal leader, former governor, and senator, Akunzhada is well placed to help gather information, though any information he helps provide is necessarily suspect.[148] Not only because he is an alleged drug runner and mafioso, but because he has been accused, quietly but specifically, of providing intelligence for the strike in question, and then stealing funds intended for the widows and orphans it created—the brothers, wives, and children of men like:

Mohammad Wali, Mohammad Lal, Gul Zaman, Salih, Gul Zaman.
As you can see, some names repeat.[149] You'll also notice, reading this list, very few women. This owes, at least partly, to the conservatism of Sar Baghni, where men commonly confine women indoors. It is a small and very remote place.

"Baghni," an eyewitness to the incident recalls, "is surrounded by different beautiful tall trees, long mountains, fountains, bazaar, shops, and nice graceful fields with a shrine and a big madrassa."[150]

The shrine[151] is the village's distinguishing feature, and draws crowds weekly. It is dedicated to Abraham of the Old Testament, who demonstrated faith in God by willingness to kill his son Isaac. The villagers know, our witness explains, "not to kill snakes or cut down trees near the shrine, because snakes won't bite and the trees are sacred."

Abdul Qasem, Mujahedullah, Noor Mohammad, Badar Khan, Peerzo Mohammad.

August 2, 2007, is a Thursday. As usual in Sar Baghni, people arrive in the morning to visit Abraham's shrine and go shopping at the nearby *mela*, or weekly market.

Everyone has a market and they're all centers of life, arterial. In Garissa, wiping dust from a Somali blacksmith's scissors, or in Longyearbyen, hefting a frozen reindeer leg as snow obscures the aurora, or along Brooklyn's East River, opening ribboned mason jars that could walk the runways of Milan. Or watching livestock in Livingston, or between *gers* on the edge of Ulaanbataar. All the same in their to-and-fro, in the excitement preceding consumption. Livestock markets especially resemble one another, scholar ranchers everywhere enjoy the comforting smell of manure. And I'll even qualify the equivalence here, sitting on the fence. The *mela* in Sar Baghni is not precisely any other foreign market, Lecce's blessed *burrata*, Silver Lake's Sunday coffee, Kabul's pine-nut cart outside the mosque. But markets share a smell. They share types. In the shadow of Central Asia's Khangai Mountains, lost in dusk, I once watched an adolescent boy beat a horse, knew him in bullies back home,

that boy too quick with the switch. One of the boys at the *mela* is probably like that, come to hang out and take a look. Because not only is the
mela the premier social event of the week, on this particular day there
is to be a hanging. A local Taliban commander, Mullah Bulbul, is planning to execute three men who have been fighting for the government.

"Bulbul asked," our eyewitness reports, "all the Imams of the area to
call on their people, to come on Thursday, and watch the execution of
three traitors."

Local elders object to Mullah Bulbul's plan to hang men from the
shrine's trees, but Bulbul ignores them. Our witness, at the edge of the
crowd, notices that "many more people came to watch the hanging" than
typical for the weekly market. Others confirm his assessment. This is
the crowd on which the bombs will fall.

Abdul Wahed, Allah Daad, Badar, Agha Gul, Haidar.

We are at forty names.

"Nothing left," recalls the eyewitness. "No trees, no fountains, no cars,
no people, everybody and everything was mixed up with blood and dust."

W ere they civilians, or Taliban fighters? Any large gathering in
northern Helmand in 2007 likely included Taliban sympathizers
at least. In this case, we know one Taliban leader—Bulbul—was present. (The hanging never takes place, but he survives and shoots his prisoners.) It's reasonable to assume some fighters were in the crowd, too.[152]
A note in the United Nations Assistance Mission in Afghanistan Report
for the year confirms "the strike resulted in numerous casualties," but
"so far it has proven extremely difficult to verify how many of these civilians were in fact [*sic*]." The report continues:

> Most of the available evidence supports that the strike targeted
> a large gathering of Taliban. . . . This suggests that [a] substan-
> tial majority of the up to 200 people reported killed were in
> fact combatants and as such a legitimate target of attack.

How then do we know that *anyone* present, any of these names, was a civilian?

The answer can be found by asking, as it could in any town. My list is just a list of neighbors, known to one another, and to the survivors, met in interviews or called up, asked questions. Where was he from? Who was his father? What did he do? Did you see him every day at the bakery? At the checkpoint? With a gun? People know, and in aggregate they can know rightly. The UN assessment *suggests* based on what information was available. But *available* is a tricky word. Vast quantities of evidence were and remain available, given time and resources. What wasn't available, really, was attention: to the wounded photographed at a Lashkar Gah hospital in the following days, to the statements of the men who brought them in, to the multiple independent witnesses and district residents living in a province constantly overflown by cameras and raided by American Special Forces.[153] Without forensic evidence, their word was never heard over a U.S. message about what is, by definition, a massacre.

The UN note concludes:

> However, HRU [Human Rights Unit] has received information that at least some of those killed and injured in the strike were also non-combatants. For example 5 boys under 16 years old were amongst a group of 19 males who claimed to have been civilians injured in the attack and who received treatment at Kandahar hospital. Up to 40 injured individuals were also reported to have received treatment in Lashkargah (Helmand). However this incident remains extremely difficult to verify.[154,155]

No casualties from this incident are included in any official tally.

Though the United Nations avers each death is of consequence, its officers at the time see this incident to be of secondary importance in the quest for wider reduction of civilian harm. They are trying to effect change quickly, diplomatically. They believe it impolitic to poke the United States in the eye over this strike, and that making a mistake— getting the number wrong—would set their broader diplomatic mission back significantly. It is considered too dangerous and expensive to conduct enough research to get it right.[156]

All this is understandable. For my part, I do not know exactly how many civilians were killed that day, either. My own list is 234 names long, but I've heard and read and recorded conflicting figures, ranging from a low of 90 to a high of 312.[157] Of all the organizations and researchers, only the Coalition claims official certainty, a particular number. Their number is 0.

Unofficially, different numbers. Classified documents—produced by a U.S. military intelligence cell, the Stability Operations Information Center—detail the strike and, regarding civilian casualties, cite witnesses, including a longtime Coalition ally, a local elder named Haji Salim Din:[158] "About 500 people killed and 250 injured in the strike . . . Three tractors (flatbed trucks) full of body parts were removed from the area." The document neither endorses those figures nor provides an alternative estimate, but concurrent secret documents advise a payment of "approx. 800,000 USD" in compensation for the families of the dead and wounded. At the time, American compensation guidelines call for no more than $2,336 to be paid per innocent death. Eight hundred thousand dollars, therefore, would cover up to 342 dead Afghan civilians. According to a State Department employee then working in Helmand, the actual amount paid was $836,722, which would cover 358 dead Afghans.[159] The classified report, authored by a Marine major, concludes:

> From all local accounts, casualties suffered in this one airstrike were enormous and left a lasting scar.[160]

The insignia on his report includes a motto—*Victoria per Scientiam*, or in English, *Victory Through Knowledge*. This motto is commonly associated with Marine Special Operations. It is unlikely the motto is intended ironically, but language may be reinterpreted up until the moment of death and so among the men and women who obscured the casualties some difference of opinion remains possible, though will certainly not be mentioned in their own obituaries alongside their names, ages, survivors, and the honor with which they served their country. No final line, in an obituary or here, is equal to their lies about the innocent dead. It is probable that the bombing of Sar Baghni is the deadliest civilian casualty incident of the war in Afghanistan. To date, none of these casualties have been acknowledged publicly by the United States.

14.

Official Spokesmen

The chief spokesman for the Afghan Ministry of Defense never smiles, that I see, but at one point during our interview he begins to laugh. I'm asking about the Sar Baghni case and others, trying to get permission to meet the Afghans officially responsible for counting and confirming casualties—his ministry's Sergeant Rogers, as it were. The ministry's public position on civilian casualties, like America's, is aggressive investigation and transparency.

"To really understand a process," I'm arguing, "you have to talk with the people who *do* the process. It's like, to understand the way people make bread, is it better just to ask the man who owns the bakery, or is it better to go stand by the oven with the man who makes the bread?"[161]

The spokesman shifts in his padded chair. His waiting room is staffed by two captains at a single desk and crowded with supplicants, but his office is large and airy, with a view over the city.

"Well," he tells me, "even if I set up your meeting with the team, they won't show you the system, they will just answer your questions the way I am doing. It will be like showing you the bread only. And"—he smiles—"if I am trying to hide anything, I can have *any other person* introduce himself as a member of the investigation team."

This is the point at which he leans back and begins to laugh.[162]

G iven such duplicity by Americans and Afghans alike, I suspect the best hope for an accurate count of civilian dead in U.S. wars lies with the United Nations, despite omissions like Sar Baghni. The UN's process varies mission to mission, but the organization is at least nominally dedicated to peace, rather than national self-interest. In Afghanistan, over the course of the war, a handful of ambitious diplomats designed a standardized civilian casualty monitoring system dependent on three-source verification. Their mission continues to pursue investigations, and Coalition officials continue to insist their numbers are too high.

The UN Assistance Mission for Iraq claims an equally involved process, and likewise receives criticism from the Coalition and Iraqi governments.[163] I was therefore surprised when UN officials in that country ignored months of emails and calls regarding how they count. One spring afternoon in Baghdad, as the heat settled over the city center and its brilliant noise,[164] I decided to visit their quiet office to inquire about the process in person.

O n my search for the relevant senior official—a long-serving Australian-Italian lawyer[165]—I get to talking with an Iraqi working in a bare office, Ali. Black hair, full of face, checked shirt, a neat bureaucrat. He's a human rights officer. This is 2016, and civilian casualty numbers in his country were on the rise before the flowering of ISIS and the fall of Mosul, Fallujah, and Tikrit, two years earlier.

2012: *3,238*

2013: *7,818*

2014: *12,282*

2015: *22,370*

2016: *19,266*

2017: *8,079*

After I sit down, Ali confirms his involvement in the publication of such numbers and warily agrees to chat.

"Can you tell me about the sources," I ask him, "and how you find them, and so on?"

"Just by relations, like friend or somebody in the ministries around Iraq, we just call them and check with them. Ministry of Defense, maybe Ministry of Interior."

"So for the Sadr City bombing," I say, about a recent incident, "who did you call? You don't have to tell me their name, just—"

"Sadr City, a lot of my friends, one of them living there, one lives close, also I call my Ministry of Interior focal point, he is working in MOI [Ministry of Interior], he gave me also the numbers of the victims over there."

"Did you get several different numbers for the Sadr City bombing?"

"Of course it is different numbers."

"And how do you decide which number is the best number?"

"Actually we also have a media search. So we just compare between the numbers. If it's too low, and the media says it's too high, also the officials says it's too high, we can compare it with them."

"And then, but, how do you decide which one?"

"If there is a huge difference between the numbers, we can go with the highest one." Ali stutters, as though unsure of what to say next. "I mean, not the highest." He shakes his head. "For example, my friend said two killed, and two wounded. It's not logic, in that huge incident. And the MOI said it's maybe twenty, forty. Look, it's big difference between the two numbers. We have to go with this one."

He indicates the higher number on the pad we have been using for scratch.

"Why do you have to go with this one?"

"Because that one is not logic."

At this point the landline on Ali's desk rings, and he answers. He listens for a few moments, whispers rapidly, then hangs up.

"Can you stop it?" he asks, pointing to my recorder.[166]

After that, Ali tells me he can't talk anymore, that his boss had called and said I should make an appointment, that I should go into another room, which I do. An assistant appears and advises that the senior official is busy, but will be back in touch about my interview request. I follow up a few times but never hear back.

I can imagine reasons why Ali asked me to stop recording. Perhaps he is worried about losing his job. Most Iraqis who work with foreigners see the United Nations as a jackpot—good money and a chance to get out. Why should he risk anything, let alone his clean desk in that converted school of Saddam's, prestige, safe and air-conditioned, for a number—or for me, one of the invaders, no matter what I say?[167] Ali has family, has likely suffered some loss by violence, like nearly every Baghdadi I know. Iraq is, of course, dangerous.

How dangerous changes constantly. Eight million people in Baghdad get on with their lives daily, but danger is why Ali and his colleagues don't visit the scenes of civilian casualties. The same is true in Afghanistan. Mostly, UN and NGO workers and the media receive reports of such deaths by phone. And because official points of contact for such inquiries in the Iraqi and Afghan governments are in their respective ministries of health, it's most often hospital bosses, doctors, nurses, and morgue workers on the other end of a researcher's line.[168] It turns out that the number of civilian casualties reported depends very much on what such people manage to remember, or to forget.

15.

Record Keeping
in the Emergency Room of the
Baghdad Teaching Hospital

I s this going to be a positive or negative piece?"

Jinan, media director for the Baghdad Medical City complex, lavish frown, middle-aged, regal at a particleboard desk.

"Because when foreign journalists come by, they only focus on the bad things. But they do not write that there are exceptional circumstances, that even in war we are providing."

I tell Jinan I'm sympathetic. She cuts me off. The windows of her office are darkly tinted, her headscarf is taut, immobile.

"The city of medicine," she says, "is six hospitals, eight specialized centers. . . . It became operational in 1970. Baghdad Teaching Hospital has one hundred and ten beds. . . . The Baghdad Medical Center has six hundred doctors and three hundred specialists, funded *completely* by the Ministry [of Health]. The outpatient facility receives three thousand patients a day."

I ask if she might provide any information sent to the ministry for the accounting of civilian casualties—the kind of information the United Nations claims to base its figures on.

"We do have statistics, but we cannot divulge them."

She declines to elaborate, but prints an authorization letter for my visit to the Baghdad Teaching Hospital,[169] and shows me the door.

In the following days, most casualties arriving at the Baghdad Teaching Hospital come either from another bombing in Sadr City, or a battle in the nearby town of al-Subhayat. To observe what counting might occur, I follow chief resident Rafid, thirty-six. Casualties arrive every day, he tells me, mass casualties about once a week.

Dr. Rafid is a general surgeon who walks like a rooster. Before the casualties arrive he spends a quiet morning signing pay stubs, looking at his phone, and recounting stories of sectarian mayhem. A nurse who, on discovering her patient was Sunni, ripped the cannula out of his arm. A Sunni patient who, on realizing his doctors were Shia, jumped out of bed and ran from the hospital in his dressing gown. Dr. Rafid laughs in the telling and is proud of his personal alliance with the Imam Ali Brigade, a local militia known for its Shia nationalist politics, and for severing heads.

"I ask them to protect my doctors and my patients," he says. "They cooperate with us. And as a gift, we provide services to their men."[170]

These are some of the men who burst through the ER's double doors after Rafid's phone rings and we rush downstairs. The white and blue room is crowded, loud, but a hush envelopes the largest knot of militiamen. Gathered around a stretcher, they're watching a young doctor in smudged glasses peer into the back of a man's open skull. According to several of the militiamen, the injured man, Khamees, had been standing beside a Humvee when it was struck by an RPG.[171]

Dr. Rafid looks over the younger doctor's shoulder.

"This man is passed," Dr. Rafid tells him, quietly.

But the young doctor intubates Khamees anyway, then hands the air pump off to an enormous bearded militiaman in a tan jumpsuit.

Dr. Rafid, shaking his head, moves on. Iraqi doctors often pretend resuscitation, even if a patient has no chance, lest relatives with militia connections, dissatisfied with a doctor's efforts, demand blood money.[172]

Dr. Rafid pauses by a young man writhing on a gurney soaked in blood.

"I want to piss!" the writhing man screams.

"So piss!" someone screams back.

The writhing man is delirious, and it's not clear where he's been wounded. Rafid tends him alongside a gray-haired physician and a nurse in a lab coat. Without looking, she flips a plastic bottle of iodine over her shoulder. It lands with a bang on a medicine cart, startling an old man with tears in his eyes.

"I called him at the morning and he was fine," the old man, Karim, says, pointing to his son, splayed on a nearby bed. "He is a great furniture painter but there is no work, so he enlisted in the army."

A tube drains the son's torso.[173] "This country," Karim begins crying again, "we're always paying a blood tax. . . . We have the hopes of cats: eat, shit, sleep."[174]

Two beds over, the bearded militiaman in the tan jumpsuit is still pumping air into Khamees. The dead man's chest rises and falls. Frustrated, the militiaman calls for help, and several of his comrades[175] pull the young doctor to the bedside. He examines the patient again.

Dr. Rafid mutters to himself and walks over.

"This man," he shouts, raising a hand in aggressive benediction, "has been martyred! Take him away!"

For a moment the whole ER is quiet save the beeping of machines. Then the bearded militiaman opens his mouth wide and wails. It's a sound with shape, broad and flat, and it fills the room. Rafid moves on to a man whose shoulder has been opened by a machine gun round. A little later, during a lull, the young doctor in smudged glasses catches up with Dr. Rafid at the nurses' station.

"If anything goes wrong," the young doctor bites the words off under his breath, "if there is a problem, you will sell me!"

"I'm known to be selling no one," Dr. Rafid barks back.

Shouting interrupts them. The bearded militiaman is yelling at the gray-haired physician in green scrubs. The older man holds his ground.

"What is this?" he demands. His voice is cold with disdain. "A tribal fight?"

The bearded militiaman looks like he will strike the doctor, but several of his comrades intervene, tugging him out of the ER as he begins to cry. So far I have seen no one keeping records of casualties, civilian or otherwise.[176]

Time seems to flow differently in that emergency room. Moments drag, hours fly by. Seventeen minutes after Dr. Rafid proclaims Khamees martyred, one of his fellow doctors shouts for help. A woman's vital signs are falling, her monitors ringing in alarm. She lies in a corner bed, a civilian. She is middle-aged, a black abaya pulled up to reveal rolls of pale torso. Blue hospital sheets cover her waist, pelvis, legs. She's been there for an hour, perhaps, arrived in the middle of the chaos with the militiamen. There is a problem with her heart.[177] As she goes into cardiac arrest, Dr. Rafid and others rush to help. In her final moments, they try furiously to resuscitate her—a single creature, a dozen arms—but fail. Her relatives scream and soon are shepherded away by nurses. The doctors return to the fighters.

Neither Khamees nor this middle-aged woman are technically civilian casualties. He's a combatant, and she wasn't killed by a bullet or run over by an MRAP or blasted into a canal to drown in an inch of irrigation runoff. He's not a civilian and she's not a casualty. But if, as seems likely, she would have survived given earlier treatment, their deaths both count as *excess mortality*. That is, deaths that wouldn't have happened without the war—either caused directly by combat, or indirectly, by the consequent degradation of public health infrastructure.

In 2007, four years into the fighting, the English medical journal *The Lancet* publishes an estimate of such deaths, based on more than twelve thousand interviews, to a confidence interval of 95 percent.[178] The authors are respected epidemiologists and doctors. Their work—which costs $50,000, paid for by the Johns Hopkins Bloomberg School of Public Health and Baghdad's Al-Mustansiriya University—remains the only major peer-reviewed statistical investigation into casualties of the war in Iraq.[179] The most famous of its findings is that at least 650,000 Iraqis had died as a result of the first three years of the war. The U.S. president at the time, George W. Bush, calls the study "pretty well discredited" but cites no evidence. His number is 30,000 civilian deaths.[180]

Politics and medicine[181] both depend on accurate records, but what record keeping I do eventually see at the Baghdad Teaching Hospital is rudimentary and ephemeral, single sheets of paper and the odd carbon copy, folded with desperate care by relatives blank faced by shock and sorrow. Though the *Lancet* study demonstrates the possibility of statistically significant tracking, no system is in place to follow cases from bombings or battle through the hospital up to the Ministry of Health and the United Nations. The numbers in the press and UN reports, often sourced to this hospital or others like it, are based on phone calls by Ali and officers like him, or the odd reports filled in after the fact by Jinan and bureaucrats like her, to be passed on according to their own whims and incentives. Without exception, however, the doctors insist they are not the right people to count. Without anonymity, backing, or an escape plan, they say, counting is too dangerous. Militia and security officials control the hospital and ministries, and thus the numbers. As one cardiologist says to me: "After everything, if I see my neighbor in trouble, I will not help him. My country is my father, my mother, my wife and two children. It is enough." Rafid puts it another way: "All things are connected, all go to hell."

Still, much depends on these different numbers.[182] Jinan has her secrets, the United Nations issues reports, the press periodically notes a threshold: *100,000, 200,000, 400,000.* Trends emerge and thankfully can be influenced. Currently, for example, in Afghanistan, a majority of civilian casualties are caused by Taliban, rather than Coalition, forces.[183] This is a change since the beginning of the war, multivariable but brought about partly by the public and NGO pressure, which produced the Civilian Casualty Mitigation Team, Roger's job, and a more rigorous count. Occasionally, bowing to such pressure, the U.S. military acknowledges mistakes and publicly emphasizes civilian casualty monitoring. No matter the reform, however, its officers always initially reject conflicting counts. They are particularly hostile to those compiled by their enemies—the Taliban, for example, who regularly release numbers through a spokesman, Zabiullah Mujahid.

16.

Definition of the
Non-Combatant Casualty Cutoff Value

We are 100 percent trying not to harm the civilians in our attacks, so we are against civilian casualties either caused by us or by the enemy," Zabiullah writes me,[184] "and for the development and implementation of this policy, we have an authorized commission in our administration called the Civilian Casualties Avoidance Commission."

"Do you count," our exchange continues, "civilian casualties?"

"Yes, the commission that I told you about is tracking all the attacks, and counts the civilian casualties caused by us or by the enemy."[185]

Though the United States never acknowledges Taliban numbers, when the war is over I suspect this will change—as it has after all the wars, as presidents finally visit Hiroshima, as senators visit the lakes in Hanoi from which they were dragged and beaten as downed pilots. Zabiullah, meanwhile, remains on the target list and maintains his nom de guerre. Really he is two men, at least. You can tell from the different voices on the calls.[186] He can be impatient—once chides me for coming late to a story—but is always willing to talk, and sometimes to email. The original Zabiullah claims to hold a master's degree in religious studies and is reportedly Pakistani, from Chaman, and in his mid-forties.

Though I have colleagues and friends who meet regularly with Taliban officials, I never do. It occurs to me, whenever I weigh the risk, that at least one Afghan journalist I know has similar concerns about meeting American spokesmen. Those spokesmen wouldn't kidnap and ransom a journalist, but there have been enough wrongful detentions to ground the fear.[187] Zabiullah speaks to this issue in another exchange, when I ask, one day, bent over a cellphone, temple to temple with a fixer, straining to hear, if the Taliban considers journalists civilians.

"Yes, journalists are civilians," Zabiullah says. "We never attack journalists if they are local or international. If they are attacked, then that's an attack on the civilians."

The Taliban, though, have attacked journalists.[188] This remains the case even if *Taliban* is a generalization—encompassing as it does official and unofficial groups, drone-flying assassins in Quetta and pumpkin farmers who just want armed foreigners out of their fields. The press corps, mostly, doesn't trust any of them, conscious as it is of colleagues dead and captured.

But that's not how the U.S. military sees the media's position. The U.S. senior legal adviser in Kabul is strident on the topic.[189] He's a broad, bald colonel named Nicholas who tells me "a lot of ridiculous stuff is written in the press." Colonel Nicholas is usually more precise than that, more lawyerly, cites examples. Usually, in his view, "the journalist hasn't departed from journalistic ethics, because they're not making something up—but they are reporting something that is inherently lacking in credibility."

"Can you give me an example," I ask, "of a CIVCAS in the press, that you read about and you thought, 'These people don't understand what's going on here'?"

"Anything that says 'Taliban spokesman said.' The idea that there's any equivalency between RS [the NATO Resolute Support mission] or the USFOR-A [U.S. Forces in Afghanistan] spokesman and the Taliban spokesman is ludicrous."[190]

Like Colonel Nicholas, many Americans bristle at the notion of such equivalency. Enemies exist in pairs, though, even if one side is obviously evil—neo-Nazis, for example, versus leftists. The Taliban have figures, flawed or invented though they may be, their highest to the United States' lowest. You don't have to close your eyes and ears to such information, even false information, to remember the bombing of markets, or UN guesthouses, or the American University of Afghanistan in Kabul, or the TOLO News crew bus, or Zabiullah's black mistake when he tells me that "wherever the Americans want to pressure, they don't care about human beings, kids, women, cities, homes of people." That the Taliban have limited regard for facts is clear enough in the multiplicity of Zabiullahs—all of whom take credit, proudly, for indiscriminate bombings and shootings.

"How do you allow them," I ask Zabiullah, "based on religious teachings?"

"We have proof for this," he says, "from the life of our Holy Prophet—peace be upon Him—and His companions. In holy wars, a companion of our Prophet—peace be upon Him—would enter a crowd of enemies all alone and would fight till the end of his life. In such wars death was something certain. Now, in this age, we don't use swords, we enter the crowd of enemies with our guns or bombs. There are many other examples for this. And in the war of Palestinians against Jews, many scholars from Arab and non-Arab countries permit this kind of attacks."

"But what about the innocent people who get killed in these attacks?"

"There are a number of conditions for a suicide attacker to fulfill. . . . He should not harm any civilians. But no one can have full control over an explosive. We may have five percent civilian casualties."

There is no reason in this justification, only superstition. But the percentage he provides—that *upper limit* on anticipated civilian casualties—is modern and straightforward. A maximum of 5 percent works out to one innocent per twenty combatants killed. Such a numbered limit is meaningless in attacks on civilian targets, which the Taliban conduct regularly, as when they shoot adolescent girls in the face for attending school. But the *idea* of a limit, a number, isn't meaningless. The United States has one, too. It's what that former targeting officer, Marc, was talking about in Pleasantville: "twenty."

I t's called the *non-combatant casualty cutoff value*, abbreviated variously as the NCV and NCCV. It's set ultimately by the president, and classified. It does not include the apparently unarmed men who died beside the digger-shooter—they're considered combatants. At Operation Resolute Support headquarters in Kabul, senior legal adviser Colonel Nicholas explains it all to me in general terms.

"The NCV represents a number of civilians that could be killed, that might be acceptable under the rules, not international law, but under whatever restrictions the U.S. government has put on us. I think the way to think of that is, what if you, I don't know . . ." Colonel Nicholas runs a hand over his milky scalp. "Let's just say, Osama bin Laden."

We face each other across the desk in his cramped office. Such meetings could be sterile and boring, but the trip in from outside was always dense with life. I'd ride with my fixer or take a taxi to Shash Darak Road. None of the officers I met knew the name of that road, because they never got off base.[191] They never learned the pleasure of hot bread at the bakery by the blast walls, past the aggressive, legless beggar and the careful local contractors, past the guffawing Georgian sentries. They never knew the pompadours of the teenagers who hung out by that bakery, or the deeper pleasures of the drive to Top Dara, a fourth-century Buddhist stupa that the locals referred to as the Burj-e-Kaffereen, or Tower of the Unbelievers, or of eating *mantoo* and trying to learn Dari from children upon your knee. And then of despairing with their parents at the rejection of a visa application. The officers, instead, remained at HQ, beneath the banners of their sports teams or alma maters—in Colonel Nicholas's case, Xavier University.

He continues talking about the number of civilians America is allowed to kill.

"I could think of a scenario where you would say, 'Okay, Osama bin Laden is the leader of al-Qaeda, and because he is such an important military objective, under international humanitarian law, we're gonna do a proportionality analysis and say, is it proportional that we might kill some civilians in order to kill him, 'cause we know that his family is gonna be with him, or whatever else?' The U.S. government could say, 'You know what? Osama bin Laden is so important that under our own rules, assuming that it's still proportional under international humanitarian law, it would be acceptable to kill five civilians.'"

In his example, then, the NCV = five.[192] That would be the acceptable trade-off: five infants, say, or five toddlers on your knee, killed to achieve the mission objective. During that particular interview with Colonel Nicholas, the NCV for conventional forces in Afghanistan is zero, and in Iraq and Syria, ten.[193] No one will speak publicly about the numbers for the CIA or Special Forces. Conversations off the record suggest they are higher.

Most civilian casualties, however, aren't predicted and tolerated under the NCV. Such casualties are just one type of several. In her insightful book *Accountability for Killing: Moral Responsibility for Collateral Damage in America's Post-9/11 Wars*, the political scientist Neta Crawford defines three categories of civilian casualties:

Type 1: Genuine Accident Collateral Damage

"Sometimes military planners do not anticipate that civilians will be at risk in a particular operation, but civilians are nevertheless harmed."

Type 2: Systemic Collateral Damage

"The rules of engagement and weapons choices are, respectively, cognitive and structural biases that lead to predictable outcomes—normal accidents."

Type 3: Foreseen Proportionality / Double-Effect Killing

"In some cases, the civilian deaths were foreseeable, foreseen, and judged to be worth the military advantage that would result from an operation."[194]

The NCV explicitly dictates Type 3 casualties, but its existence speaks to the other two. The rate at which all types accumulate is a function of political calculation, system design, and priorities, not fixed. According to Anand Gopal and Azmat Khan, on the basis of their analyses of more than a hundred U.S. airstrikes in and around Mosul in 2016 and 2017 for *The New York Times*:

> Our findings reveal a systematic failure to investigate claims properly, to keep records that make it possible even to identify its own [Coalition] airstrikes accurately, and a process that treats Iraqis as guilty until proven innocent, with no discernible path to clear their names, let alone get justice. Additionally, we uncovered intelligence breakdowns that challenge the popular framing of collateral damage as tragic but inevitable. Another kind of collateral damage is the result of a systemic design flaw—for example, the rules or procedures specifying what constitutes actionable intelligence. Deaths that result from actions that are foreseeable and potentially avoidable cannot be considered accidents.[195]

They concluded that the U.S. numbers were low by a factor of 31.

That factor depends on local governments, too. In Afghanistan, the NCV dropped to zero because dead civilians became a deal breaker with the government. In Iraq since 2014, it rose from zero as ISIS grew and Iraqi government officials pled with the United States to tolerate more innocent dead, in the belief that such policy would bring swift victory.[196] I was friendly with a diplomat who had been charged with asking the United States to relax the rules.[197] When I asked him about this, he directed my attention to the Islamic State's razing of ancient mosques, enslavement and rape of adolescent girls, murder of the old and infirm, and messianic delusion. These were evil and had to be defeated, and there was a cost.

The Iraqi people have a high tolerance for pain, that diplomat told me.

We didn't discuss the relevant math that day, but it's simple once you have the numbers. Based on Gopal and Khan's findings for *The New York Times*, a reasonable estimate for civilian deaths caused directly by U.S. airstrikes in Iraq between 2014 and 2017 is 13,862—an average of 4,621 per year. For the sake of a conservative, back-of-the-envelope experiment, let's cut this number in half before we multiply it by the number of years America has been at war in Iraq. This gives us: 34,657 civilians killed—about the population of Beverly Hills, California, or Tupelo, Mississippi. In Afghanistan, there has been no investigation as robust, but starting in 2013, the UN mission in that country disaggregated civilian casualties caused by aerial operations from the rest. Between 2013 and 2017 the average was 375 per year. Over seventeen years of war, this adds up to 6,375 civilians killed—about the population of Pleasantville, New York.

The actual number of civilian casualties America has caused directly is known only to its military, and though caches of data are scattered throughout that establishment, to my knowledge no comprehensive record exists. I'd be surprised if it did. But the NCV remains clearly recorded and easy enough to find. In 2016, as the Coalition acknowledged 4,589 airstrikes in Iraq and Syria, it was 10. This allowed, in theory, U.S. forces to kill incidentally up to 45,890 innocent Syrians and Iraqis to destroy the Islamic State. At the height of the battle for Mosul, the high estimate for total ISIS fighters, worldwide, was 40,000. Between then and September 11, 2001, foreign terrorists killed a total of

411 American civilians. Thus, on paper, the United States was willing to tolerate the incidental killing of 112 innocent Iraqis or Syrians per 1 innocent American killed by terrorists. The numbers differ among Afghans, Yemenis, Libyans, Somalis, Pakistanis, and other people on whom the United States conducts airstrikes, but the theory and research and numbers reveal something simple about how America values foreign lives against its own. It values them less.

17.

Correspondence (V)

from: CDR USN CENTCOM

to: Col USAF CENTCOM, Nick McDonell

date: Wed, Nov 2, 2016 at 9:04 AM

subject: Re: FW: CIVCAS Query/ —— Request

security: mail.mil did not encrypt this message

Nick,

Apologize for the delay, but we are not in a position to discuss NCCV nor have anyone who can even on background.

 V/r,

 ————

 CDR

 US CENTCOM

 Communication Integration

 Sent from my BlackBerry 10 smartphone.

from: Nick McDonell

to: CDR USN CENTCOM CCCI (US)

cc: Col USAF CENTCOM CCCI (US)

date: Fri, Nov 4, 2016 at 3:47 AM

subject: Re: [Non-DoD Source] Re: FW: CIVCAS Query/ —— request

Hi ——,
I see. Can you tell me why that is?

VI.

Solatia

18.

Dirt Worship

It's a matter of choice for me, as opposed to the people I interview, and there are moments during the research, between the unmistakable passage of rounds at ear level and the crash of mortars, when I am ready to renounce principles in exchange for a squad of operators, professionally murdering their way to my rescue, heedless of civilians killed, because when I get back I can dose myself with beauty, walk through dune grass in a salt breeze, and these foreign lives won't seem so pressing. I recall thinking in those moments oh get me out of here and I'll never come back to anything like it again. But in those same moments I have worshipped the dirt, thought, what fine dirt, if this is the last moment I get, to be lying in, how delicate the grain, how vivid the color, under the sky. I never, in those moments, think about the ideas underlying this book. Many have been made succinctly, before. Here by the philosopher Thomas Nagel, in 1972:

> In the final analysis, I believe that the dilemma cannot always be resolved. While not every conflict between absolutism and utilitarianism creates an insoluble dilemma, and while it is certainly right to adhere to absolutist restrictions unless the utilitarian considerations favoring violation are overpoweringly weighty and extremely certain—nevertheless, when

that special condition is met, it may become impossible to adhere to an absolutist position. What I shall offer, therefore, is a somewhat qualified defense of absolutism. I believe it underlies a valid and fundamental type of moral judgment— which cannot be reduced to or overridden by other principles. And while there may be other principles just as fundamental, it is particularly important not to lose confidence in our absolutist intuitions, for they are often the only barrier before the abyss of utilitarian apologetics for large-scale murder.[198]

Such clarity always seems to me both cuffs and key. For if the analysis and study and writing have taken us this far, distilled thought so, the question arises: *What is to be done?*

19.

Provision of Tents and Staples
to the Bereaved

Mohammed Taha, twenty-two, mechanic and father, mustache and soul patch, early riser. In Mohammed's hometown, Albu Hardan, the cost to build his single-family house is roughly 25,000,000 Iraqi dinars, or 21,250 American dollars. This is one-twelfth the median house price in Tampa, Florida, the closest city to MacDill Air Force Base and U.S. Central Command, whose M-Q9 Reaper drones, purchased at a cost of $12,548,710.60 per Reaper, fly over Mohammed's head.[199] Albu Hardan lies on the Syrian border, in the Rumana district of Anbar province, where very few possess bank accounts. The blocky buildings are tan, beige, brown. The desert runs south into the empty quarter of the Arabian Peninsula, but along the banks of the Euphrates, the earth is fertile. Albu Hardan's polygonal fields are visible on the web, but you can't quite see the wheat and rusty barley, the rows of potatoes, crisp white onions. A kilo of onions costs about 75 cents. Mohammed has a small plot but works full-time as a car mechanic at a nearby garage. One can buy the sort of cars Mohammed works on, Kia Rios, for instance, for $6,000.

Mohammed is a young man of habit, goes to work before eight every morning, returns home to his wife, Aisha, and their daughter between four and five. Often in the evenings he sits outside his house chatting with an uncle, Inizi, who lives across the road.[200] They're close. In 2011, they designed Mohammed's place together, mixed concrete, laid bricks, built it by hand. It was a family project, and they had plenty of help—most everyone in Albu Hardan is from the eponymous tribe, and related.

Mohammed, Inizi, and their immediate relatives are unusual, though, because they're Sufis. Sufism is a minority sect of Islam, one of the least austere, most mystical. "Whirling dervishes" are Sufis—Inizi refers to himself as *darwish*. Chanting, meditation, and drum beating figure into his daily worship. At evening prayers in Albu Hardan, long-haired men, old and young, swing their heads in time with the rhythm, whirl. *Tekya* is the word for a Sufi mosque, and Inizi is chief of his local *tekya*. A long-limbed man with a sloping, dignified belly and ash-gray beard, he leads spinning and worship beneath calligraphic flags and the starry desert sky every Monday and Thursday night. Mohammed loves going to the *tekya*. A flat drum of the kind beaten in prayer, a *daf*, costs anywhere from a few dollars to a few hundred, depending on size, craftsmanship, and inlay of stone, pearl, plastic, or bone.

As Inizi leads a service on Monday, June 9, 2014, ISIS conquers Mosul, a few hours' drive north. A spare road connects that city to Albu Hardan, and in the following days ISIS fighters begin to drive down. Inizi, on instructions from his sheikh in Baghdad, lowers Sufi flags at the *tekya* so it looks like a typical mosque. Across the district, policemen ditch their uniforms. A policeman's salary in Anbar, frequently unpaid, is about $600 a month. Unprotected, the mayor and local council members flee for Baghdad, and ISIS moves into their abandoned houses.

The first missile strikes ten days later, destroying an empty pickup truck parked outside the police station. A Hellfire missile costs about $100,000. Inizi, Mohammed, and several neighbors had seen ISIS fighters raising their black flag above the station's guard tower, parking a truck beneath—then, strangely, setting up their base elsewhere. Inizi believes it is a test by the fighters—and sure enough, no other black flags rise after the truck is destroyed.

The airstrikes continue, though. The next, two weeks later, hits a farm. Two cows perish. Average cow prices here run $300 to $500. Three days later, the mayor's office, which ISIS has occupied, is destroyed. A friend of Inizi and Mohammed's, Sameer, is frantic because his father lives next door with both wives and all the kids. They only just survive, escaping through the dust and shrapnel. The next strike, another week later, hits close to a bridge where ISIS has set up a checkpoint. It misses, and no one dies—no ISIS, no civilians, no cows, no soldiers, no Sufis. At that point, in fact, no one from Albu Hardan has died in the strikes—at least, not since the previous strikes, in 2006. Inizi has a feeling the luck will not last. He and Mohammed stick to their routines. As Inizi recalls: "People were so scared, because from one side, the aircrafts are bombing, and you don't know where the new bomb will fall, and from the other side—the *daesh* guys are on the ground."

The next missile lands on a road in the middle of town, about fifty meters from a shop. It's late afternoon and a crowd of kids coming home from school is just on the way in. They often stop by this shop, which sells tea and candy, cola and biscuits, sundries. A cola costs fifty cents. The shop is owned by another friend of Inizi's, Humeed, who lives in the attached large house. Humeed was on the district council and fled before ISIS arrived. Senior militants are rumored to be occupying his place. Inizi is nearby, and among the first villagers who sees what happens. A handful of ISIS fighters, grease on their hands and beards, bolt from the house unharmed after the missile lands. The schoolkids, though rattled, are uninjured, too. Inizi thanks God. There is a sense of relief among Albu Hardanians as they mill around the crater, discussing what's happened.

About fifteen minutes later the second missile hits, completing what is known as a *double tap*.

Inizi: They don't tell the truth. There were a lot of bodies.

Translator, speaking Arabic: How many? Just give me a number. *Just give me a number.*

My fixer wants out of the tent. A UN tent for refugees costs about $380.

The fixer wants to be done for the day, actually. We've already been kicked out of this camp by the Iraqi police, talked our way back in. Or rather, my fixer has talked us back in, and we're woven together by then, friends. And there's the $200 I pay him daily, and his own curiosity, which is formidable. But *just give me a number* doesn't help. *Just give me a number because I have to get a number for this foreigner.* I don't clock the attitude until I read the transcripts. Transcription costs $1.50 per minute.

I can't blame him. I've rushed, too, sometimes, tired and nervous and monolingual, wanting a number so I can get out of a plastic tent—maybe ten feet long by eight feet wide by seven feet high. This one is the color of old milk and smells of cigarettes—two dollars a pack, locally—and feet. Mine, plus those of the seven to twelve men and adolescent boys crowded around me at any moment over the course of our interviews. They lean on one another like the pickup football team they are. Inizi has put the bedding outside to make more room, leaving a single cushion, for me alone, atop the tarp that covers the dirt.

The refugees of Albu Hardan argue about the correct sequence of events with which I have constructed the narrative above. It all takes a few days, but eventually, working it out in front of me, they reach consensus about how many civilians died in the big airstrike: twenty-one.

1. Salam Muhammad Turki, born in 1985 or 1986
2. Bashira Khother Muhammad, born in 1965

3. Bashira's son, Ahmed, who started school in 2004

4. Ahmad Abd Jabbar Muhammad, age unknown

5. Sadaa Ali Muhammad, age unknown

6. Sadaa's daughter, born between 1990 and 1992

Translator, speaking Arabic: What's the name of her daughter?

Interviewee, Arabic speaker 3: I don't know.

Interviewee, Arabic speaker 6: Give any name.

Translator, speaking Arabic: No, no; don't give random names.

7. Adnaan Hassan's son, about nine years old

8. Hawash, age unknown

9. Hawash's wife, about sixty-eight years old

10. and his children: a boy, born in 1988

11. and girl, born 1995

12. and his son's daughter, born in 2010

13. Salam Sharabi

14. and his daughter, Leed, born in 1995

15. and his son, Noory, who was about twenty-one

16. and Noory's son, born in 2010

17. Raed Hammood, maybe born 2000

18. ?

19. ?

20. ?

21. ?

No one can remember the last four names. Inizi is certain, however, about the next airstrike to hit Albu Hardan—it's the one that kills Mohammed, the mechanic, his nephew. The night is hot. Isha prayer has just finished, so it's between nine and ten o'clock. Mohammed's wife, Aisha, and their daughter are visiting an uncle, approximately five kilometers away. Inizi is sitting outside, approximately thirty meters away, across the road from the house he helped build. Mohammed is inside. Inizi is blown off his chair. He estimates he's incapacitated for thirty minutes before he manages to get up and begin ripping at the rubble of the house, looking for Mohammed.

"We could not find the body."

When Inizi tells me this, Aisha, who has been sitting beside him, begins to cry.

Mohammed Taha

We produce three types of tears: basal, reflexive, and psychic. They are distinguished by chemical composition and cause. Basal tears are most common—a continuous tide released from the lacrimal gland, which is located laterally and just above the eyelid. Reflexive tears surge in response to foreign objects and irritants, psychic tears in response to stress. The latter contain elevated levels of Leu-Enkephalin, a pain-regulating hormone whose overflowing presence on the cheek correlates with universal experience: Crying eases pain. Aisha cries for Mohammed, for grief. But we cry for joy, too, for laughter, for love. I have even seen people cry on kissing, though a kiss is only the pressing of lips against lips, or lips on anything else, not necessarily profound or physiologically significant, depends on whose lips. But often enough, like an old car idling on the side of a forested road, the darkest evening of the year, a kiss is a pocket of warmth in the cold. Aisha and Mohammed, newly wed against the desert night. And add to a kiss the infinite variations—the wedding band against the back of a skull, the index finger tracing the cheekbone's ridge—and it is not only warm, but complex. The mouth's corner, the philtrum with its wonderful name, the surprising clicking of teeth. This ageless moment when the hands hold another's head and pull it close until all you can see is abstracted, shapes combined and shifting. And on not seeing, hearing, but unable in certain moments to distinguish the sound of one's breath from another. And on not hearing, feeling—the cracked lips of winter, the grease of balm, the scratch of whiskers, the contained force of a tongue. And on releasing, and retreating to one's own side, inheriting a calm, at least for a moment. A confidence, however fragile, that a kiss felt is a bond, and that one will not be left alone on the side of the road, or in the dubious care of tribes one did not choose, or ripping at the rubble.

A merica rarely pays for its mistakes. In those instances soldiers do make solatia payments to survivors of the innocent dead, the money is commonly drawn from the Commanders Emergency Response Program, or CERP, a fund created in Iraq in 2003 for "urgent humanitarian relief and construction requirements."[201] CERP is equally well understood, in theater, as a supply of cash with which ground commanders may buy off locals.[202] The process is ad hoc, and an American charity—the Center for Civilians in Conflict, CIVIC—has been advocating legislation to institutionalize solatia, in the belief "there are practical, strategic, and ethical grounds for creating a permanent and viable framework to address the harm caused to civilians as a result of US combat operations."[203] Some officials take CIVIC seriously, others not, but either way, in the long view, the willingness of any establishment figures to engage is evidence of an expanding moral imagination.[204] America kills fewer civilians in Iraq and Afghanistan than it did in Vietnam and wars preceding. The chance for moral expansion, however, depends on examination of the status quo. And so: How much, if anything, does the U.S. Coalition owe Aisha?

Perhaps it is disingenuous to ask. Inizi now supports Aisha and her daughter. They live in a refugee camp, funded jointly by the United Nations and Iraq's scattered Sufi establishment. He and Aisha would like, but do not expect, compensation for Mohammed's death from the Iraqi government, or the United States. CENTCOM Public Affairs denies any involvement in the strike that killed Mohammed.

> Please see the answers to your questions below. . . .
>
> Q2. Have there been any coalition airstrikes on Rumana?
>
> A2. No, there have been no strikes conducted in the vicinity of Rumana.[205]

It is possible the Iraqi air force repeatedly struck Rumana without U.S. support or knowledge, but as *The New York Times* reported at the time, the Iraqi air force had "a dozen attack jets . . . less than half are known to be in service, and none are equipped for precision bombing." Moreover, CENTCOM claims to monitor Iraqi airspace carefully as it trains, advises, and assists the Iraqi military. Off the record, American officials tell me: *Of course we know what's going on in Iraqi airspace.* On the record, an Iraqi spokesman tells me: "No one cares about that, who dies from the jets, who dies from the fighters. We send all those people to the morgue."[206]

In any case, it is unlikely that Aisha will receive compensation. She will not knock, perilously, on the door of the American embassy, which cost about $750 million to construct. She is not permitted anywhere near that compound, across the river in the Green Zone, around which the sons of Iraqi oligarchs, made wealthy by the U.S. invasion, raced me on their jetskis, across the oil-slick Tigris, into the darkening night.[207]

20.

Notes on Security

Sometimes looking at a case is like looking over the edge of a cliff. A long fall, a cold whistle in the ears. And all around, other mountains. To stop from falling, it seems to me appropriate, even necessary for security's sake, now and then, to put work aside. You might be equally interested in all that. About how the Iraqi National Symphony Orchestra's rendition of Stravinsky's *Firebird* Suite is frequently gilded by cellphone ringtones, but moving anyway, maybe more so. About how the crowd dresses up, and after makes the fifteen-minute walk, some in heels, over bomb-cracked pavement, in the cool spring night, to Cafe Ridha Alwan. The espresso machines shine silver, the air above the clean tables is homely with cigarette smoke. Regulars include such notables as the conductor, Maestro himself, Karim Wasfi, and Hussein Adil, a young artist who once made news for a conceptual piece in which he went shopping in an enormous bomb disposal suit.[208] "I wanted to show the public what we have come to," he told Agence France Presse, "and plant this question in their heads: What if we all looked like this?" And then, at the nearby Baghdad Writers Union, that night or another perhaps, how several of us discuss the merits of Adil's project (*Too earnest? Not earnest enough!*) at a plastic table under open sky, with other Iraqi artists commissioned to produce work for the Venice Biennale. The Ruya Foundation, which did the commissioning, was cofounded by

Tamara Chalabi, daughter of the late deputy prime minister Ahmed Chalabi, who was often accused of abetting the American neocon establishment's mistakes during the invasion. Fortunately, the separation of culture and politics remains impossible. Likewise politics and the sporting life, which enthralls the city. In those days, a short drive from the Ruya Foundation, former Iraqi national football team captain Sharar Haydar manages the locally famous Karkh athletic club in pipe-cleaner jeans and designer sunglasses, all black. At a basketball game between his club and the unfortunately named Basra Bombers the bleachers are packed. The Americans built the place, but the only Americans still around are a pair of dominant swing forwards recruited to the Iraqi club league after careers in Europe. The money is not bad, and they like playing in the big sports center designed by Le Corbusier. Haydar especially appreciates the architecture, the heroic style and scale. Haydar is a hero himself, known to Iraqi football fans for an extraordinary agility on the pitch long before his torture on the orders of Saddam's eldest son, flight into exile, and finally return because, civilian casualties or not, Iraq is *his* nation, Iraqi sports *his* calling.

S o he tells me. Despite the dangers, he and many others return out of a similar pride. Sheikh Satar Jabbar, for example, grand priest of the Mandaeans, "has his family and children in Australia," a junior priest confides to me in awe, "but returns because he longs for Iraq." We are standing on the banks of the Tigris, downriver from the sports center. The Mandaeans are one of the many ethnoreligious minorities who continue to enrich Baghdad and perform rites at its center. They must worship along flowing fresh water, and their religion dates to sometime in the first three centuries AD. Their prophets are Adam, and John the Baptist.

"Flowing water is considered the secret of life," the junior priest, Anmar, tells me. "We cannot do ceremonies unless we are by the river. Our food and drink is exclusively from flowing water." Anmar estimates

Le Corbusier's gymnasium in Baghdad

there are 250,000 to 300,000 Mandaeans worldwide, of whom 5,000 to 10,000 remain in Iraq. Others cite far lower numbers, but whatever the population, Anmar's temple complex is fine-looking, centered on a delicately hand-built *mashkna*, or mud hut, reaching down to the water. "There are only two in the world, one here and the other in Iran," Anmar says. "There was a desire to build another in Sweden, where many Mandaean emigrants and refugees settled, but the weather was too cold for so much time in the water."

In prayer, Anmar squats on the muddy staircase and washes, drinks, and spits, chanting as the water soaks his robes. Turning to face the *mashkna* he looks skyward and lifts his hands. It is storming that day, and his prayers are lost in the wind and rain, but after prayer Anmar is refreshed and invites me, and any who mean the Mandaeans no harm, to join him at his temple, anytime, for a meal of grilled fish that we can eat together by hand.

And so even looking over the edge of the cliff, there is always music, art, sport, religion. Other, more hedonistic entertainments are available, too, as when Kerada's chief pimp[209] feeds me by hand in the basement of the Palestine hotel. I have been introduced by one of my colleagues that evening as part of a French embassy delegation, but we don't talk politics. Instead, the chief pimp orders cascading rounds of whiskey against our objections but not our will, and applauds seriously when we join the gangsters, militiamen, and call girls on the dance floor. Every one of them, I'm sure, has a civilian casualty story, but I don't ask any-one about that again until the next afternoon, when I ask the pharmacist selling me headache medicine, Salmon. He is bald and gentle, possesses a wry intensity. He works in Kerada, a wealthy neighborhood compara-tively untouched by the violence of recent years—though he still mourns the death of his best friend at the hands of a local militia. He recalls for me a day the militia stole his whole stock of codeine cough syrup at gunpoint. Despite his friend's murder he agrees militiamen drinking cough syrup to get high is amusing. They need a break, too. Salmon says he's a heavy metal drummer formerly of a band called Dog-Faced Corpse, but the scene in Baghdad has disappeared, because Iraq is not safe, because the future is black.

"Take it from me," he says, "get the fuck out of here."

Which is tempting, and what the chief pimp is planning to do him-self, it turns out. A few days later he calls my colleague to inquire as to the possibility of acquiring a visa. He is with the French embassy, *n'est-ce pas?*

No trouble seems to come of the lie, but then, the country has been invaded on false pretenses; lies are told constantly. The dancers onstage in the basement of the Palestine had all been wearing bright blue contact lenses when a friend slipped off backstage that night, to interview them, and in the minutes she was gone I feared for her. Soon the table was up drunkenly searching for her, though of course she was fine, qualified to look after herself as well as anyone making a life by looking at bad news every day. She is one of the few reporters to write a story that actually gets a family of civilian casualties paid—for their car, anyway, which the United States destroyed at a checkpoint in Hatra.[210] Modest victories. Reporting is impossible and worthless without them, and affection for fellow travelers, journalists and otherwise, is the strongest safety line, the only true security, when falling over the edge of the cliff.

In truth I am usually confused, enormously ignorant in Iraq and Afghanistan, and the ignorance too often turns my attention to abstractions. One evening as the sun sets and a cat stalks through razor wire on the blast walls, I sit on a balcony in Baghdad listing what I will not write about. I edit the list still. Just war theory; civilian casualties as stand-in for the inevitable death of family; the perils of utopianism; the idea that you can understand the cost of a civilian casualty only by understanding the value of what you love best; the neurochemical components of judgment and their consequences for justice; the merits and difficulties of subsuming yourself in *the other*; apologies; sex as bulwark against entropy; the respect necessary when speaking of the dead; the perfect scale of the boulders beneath the Aegean Sea around Kythnos; pacifism; alienation of reader versus generosity toward reader; all of our respective love lives; antecedents; the honor of facts, names, and specificity. And maybe it's good to think about all that, but it's simpler for sure to stick to people themselves, their particular stories, casualties and killers and those between. Simplest of all are casualties who survive.

A casualty, after all, is not necessarily a fatality, and we may follow some of them back up the cliff face.

21.

Compensation for Injuries
Caused by U.S. Forces

In Iraq and Afghanistan, a living casualty will sometimes ask Americans for solatia. Zabiullah Zarifi, for example, thirty-seven, *Zabi* to his friends, paralyzed from the waist down, wheezing on the dirt floor. He is high cheeked, his skin wan. In his mud and timber house he recounts, ruefully, how he got a job with the Americans on Bagram Air Base as the war in Afghanistan began in 2001.

"They used to collect gravel from the mountains," he tells me. "I would collect gravel with them. One of the Americans said, 'Let's play a game. If you win, I'll give you a job in the base.' The game was like, keep staring at each other's eyes, the one who blinks will lose. I made faces at him, so he laughed and blinked, I won the game. And they gave me a job."

Zabi lives in Parwan, north of Kabul, in the rising foothills of the Hindu Kush. On the clear fall afternoon we're meeting he has spread before him a stack of papers—printed pictures, mostly. Over a dozen years on Bagram he went from manual laborer to sentry. In the pictures he stands with American soldiers—smiling, arms draped over shoulders, serious. In only one is he alone—shirtless, posing before an American flag.

Zabiullah Zarifi at Bagram Air Base

Zabi is still handsome, but now ravaged with scar tissue.

One of his eight children serves tea barefoot as Zabi sifts the papers. Several are marked with clip art and American military insignias, one is signed by an Air Force master sergeant: "*Certificate of Appreciation* is hereby presented to Zabiullah 'Wolfman' in special recognition of your steadfast support to build a better future for Afghanistan."

Other documents in the stack are medical: "CRAIG JOINT THEATER HOSPITAL / BAGRAM AIRFIELD," reads one, "admit diagnosis: GSW to chest, tension pneumothorax."

GSW stands for "gunshot wound," and the incident occurred in spring, on the fifth of May, 2015.

"GSW to abdomen s/p partial colectomy, shock bowel, splenectomy, diaphragmatic injury, L7th lateral rib fracture, T1 vertebral fracture with incomplete spinal cord injury . . ."

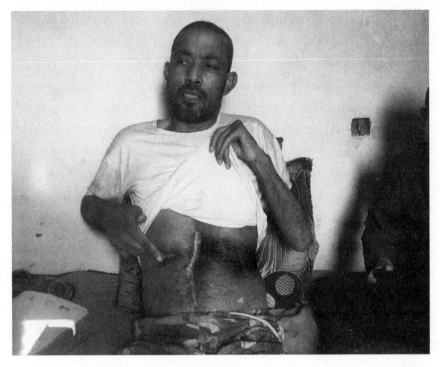

Zabiullah Zarifi at home

Zabi was driving home at dusk.

"I know how the Americans work," he says, careful with the papers. "If they suspect you, they first point the laser light at you, then they shoot in the air, then they shoot the tire. But in my case they directly shot me. I think they were afraid."

Confirmed by multiple eyewitnesses and Afghan officials: An American patrol shot up the car, riddling Zabi. After they pulled out his bleeding body and realized their mistake, they called a helicopter and evacuated him to Bagram. Surgeons stabilized him, but Zabi fell into a coma.

A wind down the mountains slips over russet fields and through the cracks in Zabi's plank front door. My fixer's face falls as he translates.

A few days into the coma, Zabi's brother, Obaidullah—Obi—appears at the gates of Bagram Air Base and is escorted to his brother's bedside. After some discussion with doctors and soldiers, Obi signs a form, and they pay him $7,500 in compensation for Zabi's injuries. But at some point in the process, in that best hospital in Afghanistan, the only level-three trauma center for thousands of miles, Obi freaks out. He tells the Americans he's going to return to Bagram a suicide bomber, avenge his brother. The Americans decide to let him keep the money, but throw him off base. When Zabi wakes up thirteen days later, he tells me, they put him off base, too.

Obi, however, never gives him the money, and Zabi wants it. It won't cover much first world rehabilitation, but that's what Zabi says he wants it for. In the meantime, he's paralyzed below the waist.[211]

"I think there is a chance for me to get better," Zabi explains, pointing at his withered legs, "because I can feel the cold on my feet. My nails grow."[212]

His children argue over the privilege of handing their father's papers to me. Zabi raises a callused hand to quiet them.

"Do you wish," I ask, "the Americans had never come?"

"No, I don't think so. It was destined for me."

Tired from sitting upright, Zabi lies down on his thin pallet. He tells me he's gone to Bagram to explain the problem of his brother to the Americans several times, but each time has been turned away. The men he served with and knew best, the men in the pictures, have all rotated out. In Zabi's telling, his brother has always been crazy, trouble since they were children.

"I talked to the police chief and the district chief and asked them to help me enter the base. And they said, 'Your brother has already signed, we can't do anything.'"[213]

A few days later, I find Obi. He has all of Zabi's strength in the old pictures and a bright, unsettling gaze. As we drive around Parwan he fidgets beside me in the back of the fixer's blue sedan. When I ask him what he does for work, he tells me that he makes money "by tricking stupid, illiterate, gullible people into believing I am a fortune-teller."

"Do you ever feel bad about that?"

"Would you rather I robbed you, or kidnapped you?"

Obi laughs. He is quick to laugh, has much to be grateful for. Unlike Zabi's house, Obi's is warm, thickly carpeted, with heavy locks on an uncracked door. Safe behind it, over tea and tiny cigars, Obi admits he did indeed take the solatia payment—but only to *help* Zabi. He spent it, he insists, on his brother, doesn't know why his brother would say otherwise. He does confirm another part of the story, though:

"I told the translator that if they don't provide us with financial support, I'll become a suicide bomber and kill myself."

"Why did you say that?"

"When they brought me the money, I refused to accept it, and I said that either they should *treat* my brother, or I'll blow myself up. I said that because I wanted them to treat my brother. Why would a person kill himself?"

Obi is laughing again as he says this, and so I ask:

"Do you think they understood that was a joke?"

"I don't know, but I had heard from different people that if I didn't sign the paper they wouldn't give me a single penny."

I ask Obi if he has any record of the payment, anything with names of Americans involved that might help his brother seek further compensation or treatment. He only shrugs, as if the matter is closed. By the end of the interview I think him an unstable crook. We finish the plastic pot of tea. Then, as I am standing up to go, Obi asks me to sit again. He sends his large-eyed little daughter, who has been watching us, out of the room. He wants me to know, he says, that he does some good with his fortune-telling, too. I sit back down. Obi leans close, his pores enormous, gentle, and begins a story.

"Once," he tells me, "a lady came to me, and told me that her daughter had lost her virginity to one man, but then married another. To hide

U.S. GOVERNMENT
PURCHASE ORDER–INVOICE–VOUCHER

| DATE OF ORDER 11MAY15 | ORDER NO 20150508161037 |

PRINT NAME AND ADDRESS OF SELLER (Number, Street, and State)*
P. Obaidullah, brother of Zabi, son of Gul Musk
Bagram District, Parwan Province, Afghanistan

PAYEE

Furnish Supplies or Services to (Name and address)
CPT Burton McCarthy
TF Solid
21 EN BN, 3 BCT, 101st ABN DIV (AASLT)
Bagram Airfield (BAF)

SUPPLIES OR SERVICES	QTY	UNIT PRICE	AMOUNT
Claims	1	total disbursement (AFN)	same as unit price
Damage to personally owned vehicle	1	140,400 AFN	140,400 AFN
Condolence Payment	1	200,800 AFN	200,800 AFN
exchange rate 56.16			

AGENCY NAME AND BILLING ADDRESS*
PAYOR
Bagram Airfield
Finance Office
APO AE 09354

| TOTAL AFN 421,200.00 |
| DISCOUNT TERMS .... %. .... DAYS |
| DATE INVOICE RECEIVED 11MAY15 |

ORDERED BY (Signature and title)
CPT Burton McCarthy (Project Purchasing Officer)

PURPOSE AND ACCOUNTING DATA.

PURCHASER – To sign below for over-the-counter delivery of items
RECEIVED BY

CPT Richard Young (Pay Agent)

TITLE
Paying Agent

DATE 11MAY15

SELLER – Please read instructions on Copy 2

| PAYMENT RECEIVED AFN 421,200.00 | $ | PAYMENT REQUESTED 7500.00 |

NO FURTHER INVOICE NEED BE SUBMITTED

DATE 11MAY15

Signature

I certify that this account is correct and proper for payment in the amount of
AFN

DIFFERENCES

ACCOUNT VERIFIED CORRECT FOR

Paying Agent
Authorized certifying officer

BY

| PAID BY | ☐ CASH | DATE PAID | VOUCHER NO. |
| OR .... (Check No.) | | 11MAY15 | |

*PLEASE INCLUDE ZIP CODE

1. SELLER'S INVOICE
(See instructions on Copy 2)

STANDARD FORM 44A (Rev. 10-83)
PRESCRIBED BY GSA
FAR (48 CFR) 53.213(c)

U.S. Government Purchase Order–Invoice–Voucher

the loss of virginity from her husband, she was saying she was possessed—as an excuse, for not giving her husband sex. The lady asked me to find a solution to this problem, and I thought of a plan. I asked her to bring her daughter and son-in-law with her another day, and to bring a bottle of blood as well. The day they came, I talked to the husband in private. I told him that there were two ways the djinn could be made to leave his wife's body: through her mouth—which would make her completely mute—or through her private parts—which would make her lose her virginity. Her husband chose the second way. So I asked him to leave the mother and daughter and me alone. Then the mother spilled the blood on the daughter's legs. And this"—Zabi croaks with laughter as he reaches the punch line—"showed her husband that the exorcism was the cause of losing her virginity!"[214]

I laugh along with the joke. And then, just before I go, Obi hands me a much-folded sheet of paper. It's a voucher for the money the Americans who shot his brother paid him.

In the following weeks I put together a file on Zabi's case—pictures and certificates, the voucher, confirmation of the incident with various local officials and witnesses, a one-page summary.

"It is my hope in writing this letter," I conclude, "to bring his case to the attention of the relevant authorities, so that they might explore the possibility, pending appropriate investigation, of further medical treatment for Mr. Zarifi."

I also write, via Facebook, to the officers who signed the receipt, but they do not respond. They are back in the United States. Their Facebook profiles feature barbecues, weddings, and smiling reunions with their Army comrades.

When I am next at HQ in Kabul, I bring up Zabi's case with a colonel named Scott, who runs the Commander's Emergency Response Program in Afghanistan, the program responsible for solatia payments. He's worked in personnel at the Air Force Academy for most of his career and he speaks with tentative care. It's his first conflict-zone deployment.

"Why they would have given a payment to his brother," he wonders aloud, "I don't even know. . . . Do powers of attorney exist in Afghanistan? I don't know if the brother would have had a power of attorney that they . . . I can tell you that in the condolence payments that I have seen, we are very careful to make sure that the person that we are paying is the appropriate person."

"Gotcha," I say. "Well, anyway, if you are amenable to it, I'll just give you this file that I put together."

"Sure. We can certainly take a look at it."

I move on, hoping to get him on my side.

"And the CERP fund," I say, "it's used for other stuff besides condolence payments, right?"

"That's correct."

"What other stuff is it used for?"

"So it's the Commander's Emergency Response Program, and so, it is used to meet urgent humanitarian needs. And so, we have done things like wells. . . . We have provided desks and other supplies to schools in a local area. . . . There was a school in Kandahar that was shot up by the Taliban. We have contracted to try to fix that school up, to allow students to get back in there. . . ."

"Speaking of the Taliban, do you think the Taliban pay condolence money?"

"I don't know."

"Do you think they should?"

"I think they shouldn't kill people in the first place."

"Amen. But if they do kill people by accident, do you think that they should? Hard question."

"I guess, in my view, they don't kill people by accident."[215]

I never hear back from him about Zabi's case.

Governor Mohammad Asim of Parwan is likewise unresponsive, initially. He says he's heard of the case but didn't follow it closely. I'm sitting to his left, in an arc of supplicants in the Charikar district office. The windows cast amber Panjshiri light on their bearded faces as they stare at the governor. He is a humorless, balding engineer in black waistcoat and tinted spectacles. On his right sits the local director of intelligence, who, later, will confirm to me that an American airstrike killed civilians in a Taliban prison in the nearby Ghorband valley. The prisoners were kidnappers and, in his opinion, an acceptable loss. Colonel Nicholas, the American senior legal adviser, disputes his use of the word *prison*, but the Afghans refer to it as such in this case.

Around the room, men wait their turn to ask for money or favors.

The governor was appointed by the president of Afghanistan, who was formerly a senior official at the World Bank. "The number of civilian casualties," he tells me, keeping them all waiting, "has decreased a great deal compared to the casualties in 2007 to 2014!"

The opposite is true, but I don't contradict him.

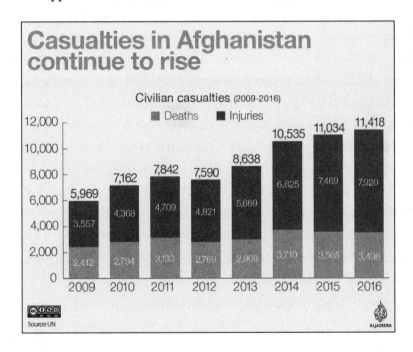

Instead, I ask his opinion about the value of innocent lives in war.

"Well," the governor responds, "the Americans have their own views on this based on their war tactics." He softly clicks his prayer beads. "But for us, killing even one person deliberately is a great trouble, as we are not allowed by our religion. Our religion tells us killing one person is the same as killing the whole humanity."

I am waiting to get back to Zabi, but before we address him again, the meeting breaks up. A week later, when I get the governor alone in his office, his position is different. In Afghan–U.S. clearing operations, he tells me, "not much care is given to civilian casualties. In such operations we try not to give time to enemies, we try to defeat them as soon as possible. In some cases we may have the numbers of casualties as fifty civilian and five enemies. . . . You can't distribute candies in a war."[216] And as for Zabi, the governor is skeptical.

"Most of these incidents, they say they don't get warnings, but they do."

And there he leaves it.

P rovincial governors are appointed directly by the president, but parliamentarians—members of the Wolesi Jirga—are directly elected by the Afghan people, closer to their constituents. At the capitol building in Kabul, I meet one of Zabi's representatives, Zakia. Over the phone, she claims to be working on compensation claims for several cases like his, though not his in particular.

"There were so many incidents," she tells me, bag-eyed but straight-backed on a heavy wooden bench. "They create hatred toward the Americans. Last year there was an incident in which the U.S. killed two hunters near Bagram. I complained about this and asked them to give the money to the family directly, but they gave it to the governor, and half of it did not go."

Zakia is thirty-eight, formal and indignant.

"I tried to speak with the foreigners," she says, "and they do not meet with me."

Her colleagues, mostly men, stand in clusters across the marble floor. The room echoes with conversation; daylight reflects up into the rotunda. Insurgents attacked this building a year ago, detonated a car bomb at the gate. The Kabul police chief announced an investigation into how the Taliban penetrated the outer layer of security, but in a general sense there was no mystery. The city is porous, deadly feuds exist within the government among ostensible allies. Zakia has herself been accused of threatening to kill a woman running a domestic abuse shelter, not far from where Zabi lives. Zakia insists she is only trying to reform the shelter.[217] But that's not what we're meeting to discuss.

"The foreigners do not care about causing civilian casualties," Zakia tells me.

She has examples. She knows about the imprisoned kidnappers killed in the Ghorband strike and believes that alternatives to bombing it existed. As she explains, the heavy doors to the hall open, and more men emerge from the National Assembly hall in embroidered *shalwar kameez* or pinstriped suits, tapping smartphones, swinging prayer beads, as they stroll across the echoing chamber. The scene is different in scale and style from America's Capitol, but the men walk and talk under their breath the same way, just like they do in stony, gray Whitehall, and at the honey-colored Luxembourg Palace, and across the broad flagstones of the Kremlin.

"I called the interpreters many times," Zakia concludes, incredulous, "but they are only the middle men. I got the sense that [the Americans] do not want to speak with me!"

She considers for a moment, quiet.

"Also, I criticized them in Parliament, and maybe that is the reason they do not want to speak with me."

The U.S. Army manual describing the use of CERP funds as condolence payments is titled *The Commander's Guide to Money as a Weapons System*. It does not use the word *solatia*, which has gone out of fashion in counterinsurgency circles. This came up one evening in Helmand as I was talking about Zabi's case with Bobby, the milk-drinking lawyer in the tactical operations center.

"Why isn't it called 'solatia payment' anymore?" I asked him.

"I think it really has to do with just the culture of it, and what the payment is actually for. The payments don't take—they don't necessarily imply responsibility, it's kind of a condolence payment, a 'We're sorry this has happened at all.'"

That is, the U.S. military sometimes makes condolence payments when it causes injury—but insists payments aren't admissions of guilt. This echoes the distinction between crimes and torts in the U.S. justice system. A crime is a wrongful act against society, while a tort is a wrongful act committed against a person or property, and so requires a lower burden of proof. The state prosecutes criminals, while plaintiff citizens bring suit against tort-feasors. Murder is both crime and tort. This is why a man acquitted of murder—unproved "beyond a reasonable doubt"—may, in civil court, still be held liable for wrongful death, given a "preponderance of evidence" that he did the killing. The distinction depends upon a system strong and capacious enough to encompass both civil and criminal law. Such a system does not exist internationally, though many U.S. soldiers instinctively feel responsible for innocent people they've killed, even if their country won't admit guilt.

As a species we've grappled with such problems throughout history. The Chinese philosopher Mozi, advising emperors to restraint in the fifth century.[218] European nobles in the Middle Ages, forbidding the killing of clergy and farmers. General Winfield Scott, promising the protection of civilians before he marched into the Plaza de la Constitución in the Mexican War in 1847. All the treaties. Imagine the room, Geneva, 1949, in which diplomats gathered from across rebuilding Europe, from as far afield as Burma and Afghanistan. The heavy wooden furniture, again. Gathered to write laws to stop the killing of innocents, to bridle wars in the name of rights, and their own ends. Who could imagine laws for war? And yet. Paul Ruegger, then president of the International Committee of the Red Cross, described the treaty that would emerge from Geneva that summer as a "miracle."[219] He was a Swiss diplomat, a Mussolini sympathizer under whose watch the Red Cross granted transit papers to Adolf Eichmann and other Nazis in flight. He pushed for the treaty. An agreement among flawed men, only glancing down over the edge of the cliff, realizing that violence is not like the rising of the sun. It is more like the weather. For a long time it seemed we could not influence it, but now we know otherwise.

I haven't heard anything lately about Zabi's case, though, in fairness, I haven't followed up in months. My last exchange about him was with Mark, the British lieutenant colonel who headed the Civilian Casualty Mitigation Team in Kabul, before being replaced by the chief of targeting. On the patio of the Green Beans coffee shop at Operation Resolute Support, Mark shook his head.

"Let's be really honest about it," he said, over the whirr of generators. "If the two of us are that concerned, we'd pay it ourselves."

22.

Theories

T he study of war is usually divided between *jus ad bellum* and *jus in bello*—the justice of going to war, and the justice of conduct in war. This dichotomy works better the further you get from the fighting, because *a war* is general (*ad bellum*), while *a killing* is specific (*in bello*). Movement between specific and general is treacherous, but finally the only way to deal with the blooming mass of our collective life. When, on September 14, 2001, the U.S. House of Representatives and Senate passed the Authorization for Use of Military Force, those chambers set in motion America's latest wars abroad, and so the attendant civilian casualties. They passed the resolution in response to the attacks of September 11, 2001, which, al-Qaeda claimed, were executed in response to American foreign policy. The notion that such politics or history must analytically precede or remain separate from the study of civilian casualties benefits the powerful, around whom such histories are usually woven. Far beneath state-centric history, however, every killing can be traced, walked in sandy footprints around the structures of our time, back to the birth of the dead, or up the steps of the Capitol building, just as the proper noun *American* can be traced to each of that country's citizens, *we*. Connection between individuals, however tenuous, is the essential hope of literature, politics, and life, from the moment of birth, when an infant, placed upon mother's belly, wriggles to the heartbeat, in the constant and never-ending struggle to close distance between an *I* and a *you*.

23.

Rescue of a Child from an
Islamic State Massacre

Dumuo, perhaps six, pink T-shirt, at the base of a cinder-block wall chipped by gunfire, in a tangle of bodies, sitting with her back against an adult female corpse, possibly her mother. She hides beneath the corpse's black abaya, peeks out right, then left, blank-faced, no longer flinching at the noises of the battle. The air is particulate and hot on this afternoon in Mosul, on the edge of Zanjili, about a mile from the Abajis' house, beyond the shadow of Shifa Public Hospital but within range of the snipers in its windows. Dumuo has been in the pile of bodies since they were shot and fell, two days before.

About 150 yards down the street, among Iraqi soldiers holding the front line, stands a fifty-six-year-old Texan named Dave. He didn't see the ISIS fighters shooting down the crowd as it ran for liberated territory, but now he's spotted Dumuo. Dave is the clean-shaven founder of the Free Burma Rangers, a Christian organization that for twenty years has provided medical and logistical support to insurgents in the Burmese jungle, and which has recently expanded operations to northern Iraq, joining the battle against the Islamic State. The Iraqi army officers on the front line know Dave, and after some hours of negotiation agree to send an M1 Abrams tank ahead of him for cover on a mission to rescue the girl.

Dave and four of his team walk low behind the tank as rounds ping off its armor. The newest member of the team, Ephraim, who turned twenty-five two days before, is a thickly bearded Wisconsiner in a backward baseball cap. When the tank stops, Dave grabs Ephraim by the elbow, gathers himself, then lets go and sprints into the open. Ephraim and a second Ranger step out behind him and open suppressing fire at the ISIS line. When Dave reaches the bodies, he plucks Dumuo, takes her under his arm like a football, and sprints back. As he makes it behind the tank, he's panting, groaning, a sound like sex or pain, exhausted. He's seen two more men alive in the pile.

Ephraim and the other Ranger make the next run and manage to drag the wounded men back to where Dave crouches with the little girl. She's in shock, her mouth hanging, her eyes wild and confused. It's a hundred yards through no-man's-land back to the front line; mortars are landing around them. ISIS machine-gun fire intensifies, sounds loud enough that all the violent attention of the caliphate seems focused on these few bodies, huddled behind the Iraqi-owned, American-manufactured tank.

"Stay with me," says Dave, holding Dumuo close. "Stay with me."[220]

The tank shifts heavily into gear and begins to roll back.

There's footage of all that, which I see later. On the day, though, I meet Ephraim as he lies on a cot, wide eyed and bleeding in the aftermath, just behind the front line in a makeshift medical station. Inside, medical officers of the Ninth Division of the Iraqi army have been treating refugees and soldiers spilling from ISIS territory, but at that moment a relative quiet prevails over the occasional rounds cracking nearby.

"We put the oldest man, he was on a stretcher," says Ephraim. His voice is low and washed out, "we tried to drag him, we couldn't drag him fast enough, and he fell off the stretcher, and the tank was backing up, we had no way to communicate with it, so he almost ran over the guy. Luckily he turned at the last second and—we had to leave the guy, there was no way to get him. Right after that I got shot. I think it's through and through, it'll be fine, it didn't hit the bone or anything. Then we ran about two hundred yards back, and, uh, got out of there. And I think the two civilians are all right. I just texted my buddy, he was out there with me."

A blond sixteen-year-old girl in a baggy T-shirt—FREE BURMA RANGERS SURF TEAM—leans over him. Sahale is Dave's daughter, and has been living above the aid station with him, her mother, and two younger siblings (Suuzanne, fourteen; Peter, eleven). She has the alert cheerfulness of a resilient transfer student.

"They're on their way in," she tells Ephraim, poised.

"They're on their way in right now? Yeah, he just responded, so we'll see if they're alive."

"Are you ex-military?" I ask Ephraim.

"Yeah, I was a SEAL."

"And were you in Iraq, Afghanistan?"

"I fought in Iraq," he says, then shakes his head. "I'm sorry, no, Afghanistan."

"That's okay. I'm confused and I'm not even shot in the leg."

Ephraim laughs. "Yeah so I'm just here as a civilian. I got out of the military back in April. So it's been just over a month."

"You ever been shot before?"

"No."

"How'd it feel?"

"Ah, it felt like just somethin' hit me, felt like I just, felt like a dull thud. I real—I knew immediately what it was."

"You said you got out a month ago from the military? And did you come straight here?"

"Yeah. Yeah. I got out 'cause I wanted to do more. I wanted to do more. Yeah. So here I am."

"Do more, like, you felt the American military needed to go kind of another step while you were out there?"

"Not necessarily. Actually, so, I'm a conservative Republican, not a huge fan of Obama, but I completely agree with his policy of having the Iraqis handle this and providing as much support as possible. We don't need more boots on the ground. The Spec Ops guys can help out. I felt like I should do more though, so I ended up getting out of the military and comin' here. Yeah."

"Quite a story."

"I was just thinking I was gonna be doin' medical work, like front-line medical work. I wasn't plannin' on gettin' shot, obviously. But it is what it is, so. Saved their lives and . . ."

"So, what do you think you're gonna do now?"

"Take a day at a time. See what happens. I have no idea. 'Cause right now I'm a homeless, jobless veteran, so . . . That's a joke."

"Yeah, no, I got you."

"Yeah, so, get healed up and . . ."

"What were you doin' before you joined the Navy?"

"High school. Joined right out of high school."

"What was the name of the high school?"

"I graduated from Ronald Reagan High School in Milwaukee, Wisconsin."

Ronald Reagan High School in southern Milwaukee lies on the inland side of General Mitchell International Airport, so named for Billy Mitchell, a World War I fighter ace and father, in part, of the U.S. Air Force, which by the end of the summer will bomb West Mosul into near total destruction. Wisconsin will remain the same, her gross domestic product nearly twice Iraq's, her population only a seventh as large, and the smell of the breeze coming off Lake Michigan in spring, compared to the body rot blown along the banks of the Tigris that day, still fresh, blue. Ephraim's gear will remain stronger than the Iraqis', his training superior. Even shot, he is so much sturdier than most of the men around him as to seem cartoonishly healthy by comparison.

"So is it a faith-based thing for you?"

"Principle-based for me. Yeah. I consider myself a Christian, but this, to me, is not religious at all. It's just the right thing to do."

On the other side of the clinic, an Iraqi major is yelling at his subordinates, but Ephraim and Sahale don't understand about what.

"You have any idea what's gonna happen to this city after it's all clear?" I ask.

"I've asked a lot of people about that," Ephraim says, "and they say it all depends on how the occupying police and"—he points a thick finger—"that's the little girl right there."

Dave runs in, cradling Dumuo, trailed by a crowd.

"The whole family shot," he announces, as more onlookers gather. "Her family all dead. Shot by ISIS. We go in Abrams, and we get her."

Something about the incident seems to have short-circuited Dave's language—he's dropping articles and prepositions. He points at Ephraim. "He got shot helpin' her. Whole family shot. Only her alive. One more guy, where's the guy?" Dave spots the civilian Ephraim rescued, walleyed on a cot in the corner. "This guy." Dave deposits the little girl on the room's remaining examining table and turns to me.

"Who are you, you a journalist?"

"A writer, yeah."

"Can you carry somebody?"

"Sure," I say.

But there is nobody, just then, to carry. Dave kneels down on the ground before the little girl, all the while holding on to her soft, brown ankles. The whole medic station is watching, soldiers, civilians. A Burmese[221] cameraman, whom all call "Monkey," films. The Free Burma Rangers have a thorough social media team.

"Oh, I'm so glad," Dave says. "Thank you. Thank you, little girl," and then his voice drops, and you can hear him talking about Jesus but not exactly what he's saying, until he lifts his head to the little girl and says: "So sad for you." Then he stands up and relates the story of the rescue again, in greater detail. A nurse in a nun's habit hands crackers to the little girl, which she eats between gulps of orange juice. She hasn't eaten or drunk anything in at least two days. On the next cot over, the wounded man Ephraim dragged out lies dazed and unattended. Shouts go up around the girl when the juice runs out.

"Juice!"

"Abu Ali," someone yells, "do you have more juice?"

Trying to impose order, the yelling major—Mohammed, forties, the commanding doctor for the medical station—confronts a pair of soldiers hovering around the spectacle. It is difficult to imagine someone looking more tired than Major Mohammed, but his mustache remains sharply cut across his lip. His tone is fierce but fatalistic.

"What are you doing here?" he yells at the lingerers. "Have you got something to do here? Don't crowd here!" He banishes them and calls a guard from the door, a pimpled youth in fatigues and ragged T-shirt.

"Why did I put you there?" Major Mohammed demands. "Don't let anybody come in here!"

The pimpled door guard, unresponsive, is staring at Sahale's friend, Madeline, another long-legged, teenaged blond. Her dad is an old friend of Dave's, so Madeline has joined the expedition for a few weeks.

Major Mohammed snaps at the pimpled guard.

"Sit there with your gun. Don't let anyone come in!" He tips his forehead at the soldiers he banished. "Did you ask them, 'Why are you coming in?'"

"No, sir."

The soldiers, it's clear, are coming in to look at the girls.

"Sir," one of the soldiers interrupts, "we came here in the morning. We brought two martyrs."

"No." Major Mohammed silences him. "It's not about you. I'm asking *him*."

The pimpled guard says nothing.

"Then put down your gun," explodes Major Mohammed. "Don't be a guard there!"

And the pimpled guard walks off.

Dave, meanwhile, has gotten to the part of his story where the American military drops smoke, allowing him to rescue Dumuo.

"I have no power, authority, or anything," he's saying. "I'm an old Special Forces Ranger officer, and I told 'em what I saw. I had no—I didn't call an airstrike. . . . I don't want to get them in trouble. I just said, 'If you don't give us smoke now, we're gonna die, and the kids are gonna die, please drop smoke,' and they did it, *boom boom boom boom boom*. I gave 'em the coordinates, and they talked to the Iraqis—'cause that's the way it has to work—and then the Iraqis sent the tank, ran in behind the tank, they called the smoke in, we got 'em out."

Later in the week, a reporter friend of mine will write a story about Dave for her newspaper. The piece will receive a lot of comments, some of which are highly critical of Dave, even accuse him of child abuse for bringing his kids to a war zone. But reactions vary; many applaud his heroism, the rescue of Dumuo. That night my fixer will post her picture to a Facebook group for displaced Muslawis, and eventually an uncle will find her and take her to Diyala.

"You know," I say to Dave, that day in the clinic, when it's quieted. "I bet you're gonna be a really interesting person to ask this question I've got for you."

"You're a good question asker," he says, with manic cheer.

"This book that I'm writing, is partly about the civilian protection policy, and one of the things that has developed over the last, sorta, ten years is called the non-combatant cutoff value."

"What the heck is that?"

"The NCV. Which is a number that goes onto a target package. Dynamic packages too. And, it's the upper limit of civilian casualties U.S. forces will tolerate in an airstrike. So, at the bottom of an airstrike packet, for example, you got a sheet of paper like that."

I outline a strike packet in my notebook for him.

"You got your intel, your weaponeering, and at the bottom, you got a casualty estimate, which is how many they expect, civilians to die, and then the NCV, which is the limit, before it has to go to sec def and the president. And for this country, as of December, it was ten. So, as some-body who is actually risking his own life, you know, you see it's kind of a weighing of that thing, and I was curious what you make of that num-ber, ten, as of December?"

"Never heard of it. . . . You mean, they'll accept ten dead people to accomplish a mission?"

"Ten would be the cutoff. And you know, some people think it's a good thing to have this number, some people think it is a bad thing. You know there are arguments for it on both sides."

"I don't believe in any numbers or fixed values on people. I believe you do your best to help people with whatcha got, and me, I rely on God. And I, you can't measure that, people use his name in vain and do terrible things, that's the only way I could do it. Like today, we had a chance to rescue her all day. I kept looking at it and praying and thinking, there is no way we're gonna get there without getting killed, and if we did, we'd get her killed, and us, on the way back. And then finally we got enough pieces in place that I felt I could do it, but it wasn't based in numbers or nothin'. It was based on gut feeling of what was what. And I was willing to risk my team, five guys. If they all died, they all died. They didn't wanna die. I never do numbers. So I don't understand it."

"You think the government should do numbers, or you think that number should be zero? Or do you think . . . ?"

"I don't think you do numbers! I think you just do the best you can do. I don't understand it. You can't guarantee nine, ten, seven, one, with that. That's beyond me. That's trying to quantify the unquantifiable."

"That is an original answer; I'm glad to get it. Thank you."

"It's my answer. America's bogged down in risk assessment, blame, litigation, just a bunch of baloney, to cover your rear end."

There are eighteen Free Burma Rangers in Iraq that day, working in the tide of four hundred thousand Muslawis fleeing the city.[222,223] A stream of refugees freshly spilled from ISIS territory ebbs and surges past the clinic as Ephraim recovers. Leaving for the night, I get to talking with one of them. Ayman,[224] twenty-one, bloodstained VINTAGE SUPER DRY T-shirt, black eye rising, bandage at his waistline, shrapnel still beneath. Ayman is green with injury and malnutrition. Unruly sideburns sprout, wolfmanesque, from his jaw. Next to him, Iman, his mother, black abaya, beige headscarf, forty-six and thin as a radio antenna. She's yelling at an ambulance driver, twenty-one, who slouches like young Brando, arms up and palms out, in the universal sign for *Look, lady, I hear ya but what do you want me to do about it?*

"He was with his dad and brother," says Iman, tears on her craggy face, "he's the only one who survived. And when we reach the army, instead of welcoming us, helping us, they *hit* him!"

Ayman, swaying in shock, twirls a sideburn between thumb and forefinger, says to no one in particular: "My last cigarette cost forty thousand. I shared it with two of my friends."

"Ma'am," says the ambulance driver, "maybe this is because of his name. They told us his name is similar to an ISIS name."

"No, no, no, they didn't check my name!" says Ayman, snapping out of it. "Once I reached them, a guy shouted, 'This guy was fighting us.' They hit me, and I told them, 'How can I fight, I'm wounded!'"

"This was your mistake," says the driver, "to tell them you're wounded. Because now, they're using families who escape to hide themselves. You saw the ISIS guys with you trying to escape. The army caught them. . . ."[225]

"I brought them from the front line and the fighting," the ambulance driver[226] explains, turning to me. "When they tried to come, there was a suicide car, and it blew up on other families, and the army, a lot of them got killed, civilians and army."

"When that car exploded," Ayman adds, "we immediately decided to get out from the house, and we escaped."

"One hundred and fifty civilians are still stuck there in the Pepsi factory. They don't let them out, they're using them as human shields."

"I told them, 'I'm wounded, can I go?' They said, 'You die with us. You are Muslims, don't go to non-believer areas.'"

Ayman details further horrors of his escape but soon is distracted. He points at my recorder: "Did you get this from the States?" Then, showing off, he says in English: "How much?"

Just escaped, dripping blood, he wants to know about the recorder. Before Mosul fell, his father traded in electronics.

"See my T-shirt?" says Ayman, of his VINTAGE SUPER DRY. "It's *haram* when ISIS is here, because it's written in English. And your pants must be like this." He taps his shin. "I never wore short pants because of my surgery, and they were always threatening me, 'Go, this is your last time.'"

Iman interrupts with her own story, how she led the escape. "When the mosque called for midday, we decided to go. We said, 'If we stay here we will die.' We were some families together. I said, 'I'm going out with my children. Whoever wants to come, I'm going.' Everyone came with us, and ISIS started shooting us, and that guy in the red T-shirt"— she points to an adolescent just beyond earshot, who appears to be pleading with another ambulance driver—"his father got shot. We don't know what happened to him, but he doesn't know, don't tell him."

"His father is still there," says Ayman, shaking his head.

Eventually Iman looks around, asks the usual escapee question.

Where can we get a taxi around here?

It's hard for her to know where she is with all the landmarks destroyed, but some taxis follow the front line every day, waiting a few blocks behind to pick up refugees. Iman and four of her children—Ayman, his little brother, and two little sisters—lead the crowd to the taxis, guided by my fixer. Across a block of rubble we see three American MRAPs bumping down a parallel street, unmistakable as Hannibal's elephants in the Alps.

The taxi driver Iman approaches looks her over, then the small crowd she's leading, then me.

"Madam," he says, "what are you doing here? Because the army is here, and I'm afraid they might inspect us for no reason."

"It's okay," says Iman, opening the back door.

"What if they come to me and ask, what would I tell them?"

"Tell them that you are a taxi driver and you're taking this family from here to another place," says my fixer, then offers to pay for the taxi, producing the money. This calms the driver. Iman stuffs her children into the car. We give Iman our water and a can of potato crisps from a Classy Hotel minibar. She opens the can and hands it through the window to the smallest girl, who shoves chips into her mouth faster than she can chew. The smallest boy glugs the water. They trade.

Thank you for liberating us, Iman says, crying again.

Behind her, a column of refugees stretches down the block, out of sight.

S oon my fixer and I get a taxi, too, a yellow Kia Rio. The middle-aged driver appears of a piece with the vehicle, belly beneath his tan dishdasha like a cyst grown from the tan driver's seat. We ask him about airstrikes and civilian casualties.

"ISIS, they collect families and civilians." He points. "They put them in this house, for example. And the pilot knows there are families."

"Usually how many civilians are in there?"

"As many as ISIS can get, they collect people and put them in the house. In my neighborhood, more than fifteen families died because of the airstrikes. And this is only *airstrikes*." He waves dismissively. "The *mortars* are like sunflower seeds, we're having them all the time."

"What do the Muslawis think?"

"Muslawis, they want to live. When Saddam was alive, we were clapping for him." He takes his hands off the wheel and brings them together. *Clap.* "The Americans came, we clapped." *Clap.* "Then the army came, we clapped." *Clap.* "ISIS came, we clapped." *Clap.* "Now the army has come back, we clap." *Clap.*

"People," he says, hands back on the wheel, "they want to live."

We keep talking. The federal police stole the truck of his friend, he tells us, and repainted it. No authorities can be trusted. Eventually, the driver says, "I'll ask you a question. This plan of surrounding ISIS in the old city—is it good or bad?"

"I don't know," my fixer says.

"If this was the best plan, they should have started from the west, not from the east, because the east is an open place, the streets are open. In the Old City, you have some streets a bicycle can't go through. If they continue like this, it will be like putting the Old City through a sifter. . . . If they fight continuously, like this, it will be like a sifter."

When we arrive, my fixer takes a ten from me to give to the driver.

"No, no," he says, "you guys keep it, it's on me. I enjoyed talking to you."

"No, you keep it."

And he does.

VII.

Arguments for Reform of the Non-Combatant Casualty Cutoff Value

24.

The Morning Brief

It is morning in the palace and the colonel and I are discussing your life and death. "We have a very good sense of any civilians that we, our airstrikes, have killed," says the colonel, "and we announce them." The colonel is a particular man, he is reading this, but you are not specific. You are general, still unannounced. We're in Baghdad again and the temperature is ninety-seven degrees, the dust yellow-white and formerly packed down by thousands of U.S. soldiers but now under Iraqi control—except in these few places, in these most secure locations, where we haven't left. And this is American: We don't leave. And we can be anywhere tomorrow. The briefing room is air-conditioned. Sometimes the colonel points to a large map. Sometimes he rocks on his feet in front of a rack of assault rifles. He is well liked by the press corps and valiant according to a system of rules widely believed to be the most righteous in history. He is from Virginia.

"We're much less concerned," he says, "about public relations, I think, than we are about just not wantin' to hurt civilians. I mean, we take our values with us when we go to war."

I ask the colonel how many civilians America has killed in this war.

"I can't remember," the colonel says, "what our CIVCAS number is up to. Do you recall, Captain? Do you remember?"

The captain is enormous, towering at ease by the door. He doesn't know, either, how many innocent people the United States has apologized for killing.

"I wanna say, we're in the sixties, maybe? Fifties? Forties?"[227]

But our chief spokesman can't recall.

That day, the number of innocent people the United States acknowledges killing in its campaign against the Islamic State is forty-one.[228] The number is incorrect. I've met the widows, orphans, and fathers of more than forty-one innocents killed by American airstrikes in that war by then, none of them counted among the dead. I've walked around the rubble, collected interviews, documents, and photographs. And though I've read about the emptiness of intent, when I listen to the colonel I can't help but think him a reasonable man, and my country decent, even honorable. It's only later, as it's always later, beyond the blast walls, away from power, that I remember the specificity of violence, and turn against that honor, again.

Perhaps a state must keep some secrets. Mine obscures the killing of civilians, now and then justifying their death as means to an end. We act often in good faith, and do not kill so many innocents as some others, nor so many as in the past—but kill them we do.[229] Within American leadership some know this is grotesque and struggle with the inconsistencies. They have told me so, walking in light rain outside the Pentagon, close to tears on a combat outpost in Helmand province. Then, often, they remind me of progress, like an old executive order that civilian protection is a core national interest—even if, according to that order, civilian casualties are an "at times unavoidable consequence of the use of force."[230]

And yet we often calculate the civilians expected to die in our strikes. We make the Casualty Estimate, set Non-Combatant Casualty Cutoff Values, and decline to investigate repeating catastrophes. If you know an accident will happen, it isn't an accident.[231] Our wars are not accidental. No civilian casualty is "unavoidable." All are the result of choices made by people in positions of authority. Many of these choices reflect the idea that certain lives are more valuable than others, which is contrary to the American axiom that all men are created equal. Eventually, such choices will be viewed as criminal, tragic, and peculiar to their time.

O r so I hope. We live, as usual, in a period of uncertainty. America's president, a real estate mogul turned television star, has condoned the killing of civilians rather than elide, obscure, or denounce it, reversing a trend of decades in American foreign policy.[232] Progress is not assured. It never has been.

Like me, the president is of the establishment, a man for whom hope should come more naturally. He is protected by the myth of his race, privately educated, never wanting. His life is so distant from a little girl killed in Tikrit as to appear unreal, extraplanetary, invincible, to her community. But in Iraq, Afghanistan, and other countries where our country kills innocents to advance our aims, families know that no one is invincible. Peaceful societies succumb to violence. Empires deteriorate and collapse. We are more like these countries than we know. Today, some of America's opponents believe it necessary and correct to kill people who mean no harm, like children, in order to advance their particular vision of the world. In our willingness to sacrifice foreign civilians, we mirror them.

The reflection is not exact, and I do not wish to forget what is good in our ongoing experiment, nor rein hysteria for the benefit of essay. There will not be revolution in New England tomorrow. Species-wide, there is evidence that violence is in decline, that lives are longer and richer than ever, and that our energies are best spent on local decency and protecting the natural world. But I also know that, most days, America does mortal damage abroad, to actual innocent people, with actual teeth and tongues and hair and skin and fingernails.

Usually the government attempts to sell, rather than hide, the process. It adapts old propaganda to new technology, co-opting intellectuals and entrepreneurs. We call this public diplomacy and hold *ideas festivals* to celebrate the union as the U.S. Departments of State and Defense ignore questions, obfuscate, and omit. The foreign policy establishment depends unabashedly on lies. Off the record, senior officials, some of them former journalists, confirm the killing of innocents with a nonchalance that is chilling.

These officials are not always great salesmen and their wars often turn unpopular. But they've never needed to sell us on our own value, the superior worth of American lives. The belief that we, here, are more valuable than them, there. It is this belief which allows us to look away from the ongoing destruction of particular people, any one of whom would be too many, none of whom need to die for our immediate protection.

It is normal that Americans should care more for their countrymen than foreigners. Devotion to family, neighbors, and friends define a life. One cannot love a stranger, a little girl in Tikrit, as much as a daughter. But neither should we be willing to kill that little girl, or risk killing her, to save our own. Killing innocent people to increase our own security is cowardly. This idea does not require an understanding of classified intelligence, cosmopolitanism, sovereignty, utilitarianism, or geopolitics. It requires only a little courage.

25.

Strikes Through History

That this account relies upon, perhaps exploits, the stories of so many who will never read it remains troubling, but not so troubling as to foreclose more of the reporting that has brought me to this point. As I write I am waiting for another visa to Afghanistan, where I will continue interviewing the families of civilians killed by Americans. The narrow focus of the mission is also sometimes troubling, brings to mind the definitions of *selection bias* and the Ivy League university where I learned them.[233] But for all the rigor that university encourages, the clearest imperative, it still seems to me, is to maintain a suspicion of power. The world's undisputed disparity was reason enough then, and is now. Its relevance to civilian dead in wars is a grim and complex topic but also intuitive and fascinating, being as it is a hallmark of the human condition thus far. Or at least I have to think that way, sometimes, and set it aside, so we aren't paralyzed in political economics, and the colonel and I are ever able to have a drink together at the embassy bar, the Duck and Cover, or back at the Classy Hotel.

Eventually conversation among expatriates in such places always lands on *local colleagues* and these are as important as any philosophy, here at the end. I am referring particularly to my *fixers*. They tell me they don't mind the word, which stands in for interpreter, guard, driver, researcher, strategist, partner. The intimacy that arises between *fixers* and *foreign correspondents* can be as intense as love and must anchor any understanding of their peculiar relationship. It is a relationship which colors, like invisible ink, much information about foreign wars and all the information in this book. I know a fixer who married and bore the child of her journalist. At the other extreme is the legendary fixer who shoots his journalist to prove a more pressing loyalty, but that's intimate in its way, too.[234]

The fixer with whom I first saw a civilian casualty was a Pashtun from just outside Kandahar. He has since found refuge, I hear, in Australia with his numerous children and wife, to whom he frequently referred, in our time together, as "the general." His awareness and concerns back then were intensely local and he worked with curiosity, unhinged courage, and apparent certainty of wrong and right in his part of the world. I never doubted his compass and still don't, even though the civilian we saw die together did not figure, not once, in our conversations about the events of that particular November afternoon.

I write *saw*, but in truth the gunfire was overwhelming for a novice and the situation confusing enough that I struggle to remember what exactly I did see. Certain moments are hyperreal in the mind's eye. I can see puffs of dirt rising in a line where bullets strike the ground in front of me. I can see a smooth-cheeked soldier, the jacket of his uniform unbuttoned and a cigarette in his lips, feyly firing his Kalashnikov from the hip into a stand of poplar trees. I can see the fixer briefly covering his eyes with a scarf so as not to see the mayhem, as though to protect himself in blindness. And I see, perhaps twenty meters from the wheel well of the Humvee where I am crouching, a man supine in the road. A correspondent who mistakes knowledge of combat is hollowed and undone,[235] but what harm to tell a detail, even if memory flickers. For how, at twenty meters, taking cover, could I have seen so clearly his yellow toenails? Soon a squat border commander, Rasul, was sprinting toward me, shouting that we must get in the truck and go, and I cannot see the man anymore.

And still in mentioning the toenails I am uneasy. Where are the man's sandals? Do I remember more vividly what is convenient, years later, now that certain thoughts have worn a grooved track in my skull? Without these keystones of private history, ever more weight falls on secondhand information, on books, and the arguments bleed white.[236] And can I prove I was not looking down into the rubber of a tire, rather than watching the life ebb from this man, years ago? I can't, I can only try, and keep to skepticism, to transparency, to better record keeping since that afternoon, to the pursuit and accumulation of facts. Some miles down the road, after we cleared the ambush, Rasul noted with a dark chuckle the rounds which had pierced our car during the escape and told me that the old man on the side of the road was dead. Rasul claimed to have run through the fighting in hopes of saving him, but arrived too late.

It was the clearest kind of civilian casualty—caught in a crossfire. We were driving in convoy with the Afghan Border Police from a town called Sangin, in Helmand, seventy kilometers south to the provincial capital of Lashkar Gah. This was among the most contested stretches of territory in a civil war and everyone seemed to take for granted that people would die along the way. Such deaths are the ultimate surprise, but in another sense no surprise at all. In Sangin that morning a slouching intelligence agent had correctly predicted the location of the ambush through a haze of cigarette smoke. And what was there to say about that single civilian casualty, save it was a tragedy?

On the way back to Kabul, that fixer told me he would fast for three days. It was around the time of the holiday Ashura, and he observed that we had much to be grateful for, having survived that ambush and another besides. I fasted with him the first day, but didn't feel obliged to continue. Religion didn't matter, so much, between us.

What mattered, the essential difference, was that I could leave.[237] I could always depart, quickly, for the safety of American power, which

extends deeply into that country and every other I have visited. It is manifest not only in military outposts where colonels brief, but in four-star
hotels and the residences of well-rewarded proxies. Sanctuary in such
places for an establishment-accredited reporter, which I was at the time,
is almost guaranteed, since we are often proxies ourselves, or seen to be.

Exceptions occur, and these sanctuaries will reject a supplicant on
the basis of perceived threat, or whim. It was during those days in Helmand I began to learn about that. The difference between reading it and
learning it in person was substantial and is at the root of passing desires
I have to put people who don't know about it in difficult, even dangerous
situations, to slap them and worse, though in the end I am always
ashamed of the desire, contrary as it is to the diminishment of violence
for which several men I've known have now given their lives in one un-
necessary way or another. Much is clarified in the obituaries, but it's
wise to be as skeptical of them as the rest of the news.

Because it's true: Deals are cut with the press. Arriving in Sangin we
were under the protection of the district governor, but on learning of a
U.S. military base nearby, walking distance, the fixer and I decided to
visit. The young sentries were surprised that an American should appear
at their gate dressed in *shalwar kameez*, but on radioing for permission
they cheerfully invited us in for lunch. I was enjoying a hot dog and the
temporary but intense relief of American military security when a major
arrived and demanded to know who I was and what I was doing. He told
me it was illegal to report in Helmand without American permission,
and ordered a captain to escort me off base. I told the major he was
mistaken about permission and that an escort wouldn't be necessary,
that I could show myself back to the district governor's compound,
where I planned to spend the night. The major, however, said I was not
allowed there, either, since it was within his security remit. This put me
in a precarious position: an American in Sangin at sunset with nowhere
to stay, and no car. Our driver had refused to come with us. The major
told me I should have thought about that beforehand.

We were shown off base to a street on which the fixer and I agreed we had been identified by Taliban while working that afternoon. We ended up, by chance meeting in the dusk, under the protection of an Afghan Special Forces unit, and spent the night on a nearby rooftop, listening, via captured radio, to Talibs plot car bombs and complain of the cold. On returning to Kabul I received and accepted an invitation from the communications director at the U.S. Embassy to discuss the incident. She claimed to be shocked that a Marine had thrown an American citizen off base into a combat zone, and afraid of the way it would play if I wrote about it. I told her I wouldn't, if she would help me with my story. A small deal, but a deal cut nonetheless.

You know how much bigger they get. I later heard a rumor, almost certainly false or exaggerated, that a newspaper reporter was using the incident for leverage, too. The press corps liked to gossip, even, especially, at the height of the killing. It wasn't that we forgot, but we couldn't hold all the trouble in our heads at once, even if we'd wanted to. I couldn't, anyway. The biggest deals were the ones we cut without meaning to, without thinking, with ourselves. It took me a long time to realize that, to begin disaggregating the tangled, pulsing world into a series of actual deaths that stop you ever feeling the cheek of a person you were beginning to love, the freckled skin. Sometimes when I think of the dead, I mourn the work they will never do, all the potential lost, but more often I mourn that.

And I wish the dead could've met that fixer. They could've, almost, if they'd been in California. For a brief period he was headed to Hollywood, to work on a television program I wrote about politics in Afghanistan. The bus he rode from Kandahar to Kabul to apply for his visa was struck by an IED, though, delaying and discouraging him, and the production would not wait, and finally wouldn't release money for plane fare, though the director and we producers often flew business class on short notice. The man sitting behind him on that bus, the fixer later told me, was blinded by shards of glass. The trip would make a good movie, but such stories have a hard time finding their way onto the screens where we play the way we see the world.

S o much of what we tell one another about violence comes off those screens. That my grandfather the fighter pilot was a good man when, at twenty-six, he crashed his deadly machine and became another corpse, dead as however many Japanese he'd killed. Or at least, his was a good war. Especially now that most who fought it are dead, America recalls World War II with nostalgia, though like all wars it depended on an array of lies. We know this and yet we don't. "The world will note that the first atomic bomb was dropped on Hiroshima, a military base,"[238] announced President Truman immediately after that attack, in which between 70,000 and 80,000 civilian city residents died, instantly.

The story on-screen and in the classroom is that the bomb, and its brother in Nagasaki, ended the war in Asia, thereby forestalling continued suffering and an even greater death toll. But the story isn't so simple. Would Americans be willing to lay down arms, after such flashes of light over Boston, or Phoenix?[239] The Japanese weren't, for eight days—days in which the Soviet Union joined the war against them, their military attempted a coup d'état to prevent concession, and Emperor Hirohito, who the year before had ordered his subjects to commit suicide rather than surrender, received assurances of personal postwar security. President Eisenhower later rejected the necessity of the bomb and said it wasn't the decisive element in victory. And you'll find this, reading about the *necessary sacrifice of civilian life*: those who say it is not, in every single instance. The notion that Tokyo's incineration made the destruction of Nagasaki superfluous only raises questions about that prior inferno.

Burn injuries were the most frightening. Exposed entrails were too alien to understand, sliding the living quickly as they did into inconceivable death, but I could identify with burns, living burned. Once in a refugee camp a woman pushed through a crowded tent and deposited her ten-year-old daughter on the ground at my feet.[240] The girl was criss-crossed and patched with laceration and burn scars, silent, her legs bent uselessly before her. Her name was Hidran Ali Abdullah, and according to her mother she had been holding her five-month-old brother Saif at the time of a strike, and so saved his life, but nearly died herself. She'd awoken three days later, paralyzed. The attack had come during what is sometimes called the Third Battle of Fallujah, and as in the First and Second Battles of Fallujah great numbers of civilians were expected to perish and did so, at the hands of U.S. and Iraqi forces that, in uneasy partnership, secured the city.

"We were not scared of airstrikes," Hidran's mother told me, "because people in the area told us the Americans have mercy. They don't attack civilians."[241] In the weight of her paralyzed daughter she had learned the opposite. And while it is true that U.S. policy has improved over the years, the physiology of burns has not, and the skin of Hidran's legs in that tent was puckered, pink, and shining.

Hidran knew only the ground level of what had happened, burns but not flight. She had never flown. Living in that camp, she probably never will. So she could imagine a plane, but not remember one, as many can, cramped or reclining, comfortable in wealth or glancing to see who sits in the $10,000 seats as they walk past. Almost as soon as we flew we weaponized flight. The first hot-air balloon launched on the outskirts of Paris in 1783, and within a decade France's revolutionary government had established a corps of balloonists dedicated to directing artillery fire. By the middle of the following century, Austrians were floating armadas hundreds strong over Italy armed with bombs designed to explode upon the *fondamenta*s of Venice.[242] It was surely a strange and beautiful sight against the Adriatic horizon, but most days I don't take much pleasure in imagining it, or in Ferdinand von Zeppelin, or even in the irony of Russia's proposal, at an international conference of Great Powers in the Hague in 1899, to outlaw "any kind of projectile or explosive from balloons, or by other methods of similar nature."[243]

Soon thereafter the airplane was invented, and Europeans began bombing the Middle East and Central Asia. In November 1911, Italians dropped hand grenades on Turks in what is now Libya. In 1912, the French bombed Moroccans outside Marrakesh, destroying villages and markets. In the next decade the British bombed "rioting Bedouins"[244] in Egypt, rebels in Yemen and Punjab. Bombing runs in Somaliland in 1920 were seen to be such a great success that Winston Churchill, soon-to-be colonial secretary of Britain, articulated a new idea: "air policing" for the Middle East. He went on to propose that the Royal Air Force take ultimate responsibility for ongoing uprisings in Iraq, in co-ordination with four thousand or so troops there deployed. This is at least superficially identical to the current U.S. strategy against the Islamic State. And in Afghanistan in 1919, when King Amanullah launched a war on the British forces occupying the Hindu Kush, the Royal Air Force bombed Kabul. The following year in Pakistan, it targeted the Mahsud and Wazir tribes of the North-West Frontier Province, dropping tons of ordnance. The tribal fighters firing their Enfield rifles into the sky in retaliation were ancestors of the men who fear strikes and lay IEDs today. They were Pashtun, like the fixer I worked with in Helmand.[245]

And what of this to an American? As she walks in the sunshine to her coffee this lonely Sunday. Perhaps in our era of data only physical contact assures true investment. Perhaps one needs to be drinking tea on the main drag in Tikrit to care, or mourning a daughter's once smooth and brown legs. But I don't think so. I choose to believe that our phones expand our vision and that in remembering moments of joy in our own lives we feel what is lost when America destroys another's. The coffee is cold, the sunlight is past, we are another, sheltering in Kadisiya, holding a daughter's body. Listen with me to a president, our forty-fourth: "I've said to my staff and I've said to my joint chiefs, I've said in the Situation Room: I don't ever want to get to the point where we're that comfortable with killing. It's not why I wanted to be president, to kill people. I want to educate kids and give people healthcare and help feed the hungry and alleviate poverty. So do I think that the critiques are fair or fully informed? Not always. Sometimes they are. Much of the time they're not. To give you the most basic example: People, I think, don't always recognize the degree to which the civilian-casualty rate, or the rate at which innocents are killed, in these precision strikes is significantly lower than what happens in a conventional war."[246]

Precision here means killing fewer innocent people to achieve our ends. That president is right about the rate of innocent deaths in conventional war versus air campaigns. And he speaks within an accepted frame. Today, killing civilians is legal, and America operates according to the doctrine of proportionality, wherein the number of innocents killed is "proportional" rather than "excessive" in relation to military benefit. But in a deeper sense, that president is wrong, there, and contradicts his stated allegiance to equality. Proportionality is not a dignified doctrine for a superpower. Though arguably legal, and perhaps even just in its arithmetic, it is not courageous or morally ambitious. Everywhere, America enjoys unapproachable military advantage, maintaining over eight hundred bases and spending, roughly, the combined budget of the seven next largest militaries, as the famous comparison goes.[247] It need not take innocent lives for military benefit or protection, nor set a tolerable limit for the innocent dead. Such a number is inconsistent with truths we hold to be self-evident.

The only non-combatant casualty cutoff value consistent with our values is zero. This is also the instinct of our soldiers, who kill far fewer civilians than the NCV permits, and remain haunted by the dead. We cannot reduce the columns of those dead, but it is within our power to stop adding to their ranks. To set a limit of zero in good faith requires a radical reduction in our use of force, a rejection of violence equal to the full measure of devotion that many of our citizens have given throughout history, in defiance of cruelties at home and abroad. It is to recommit ourselves to equality, and so to a difficult moral truth: that Americans should be more willing to risk death, so that others might live, because those others are our equals.

Insistence on equality, despite its piercingly slow entry onto the rolls of law, is the most powerful aspect of our experiment. America has always been hypocritical and violent and still is, every time a white cop shoots a black child, every time an airstrike dismembers an Iraqi child. But we have progressed, and perhaps even finer ideas can take root and grow around the central hope. There is no reason why *advanced nonviolence* can't have its seeds on the wind, now. Why the turning of the cheek need be religious vacuity or naiveté, rather than wobbly next step in a world where it is possible to translate languages instantly and yet remain skeptical of techno-utopia. If Americans are willing to accept greater risk in place of killing, others will take note, and follow, just as they have for two centuries of stumbling toward ideal and impossible equality.

26.

Origins of This Account

A nd yet, at night, I sometimes believe it is too late, that America's essence is racial exploitation, that secular humanism is a religion, that vengeance is as real as peace, that most will always disagree, that techno-utopia is a ridiculous phrase, that violence is in us all. But the stories we tell each other make the world. If I have any religion that is it, though like all religions it is finally personal. The specific reasons I'm talking with that colonel and quoting that president are mine alone, and everyone else has particulars, too. You can't escape them when you join the militia or the White House or the network. Structure is not all. There are no men or women without personal history and those who ignore their own are most frightening.

F or some years, I believed I shared responsibility for the death of several innocent men in Iraq. It came about like this. I'd arranged an interview with a basketball team, and then, by chance, hadn't been able to go. I was emailed soon after by one of the players that three of his teammates had been ambushed and killed at the appointed place and time. The man who'd helped set the meeting, cousin to one of the victims, confirmed the story, and added that a note had been discovered at the scene, laying responsibility with an American journalist—me. *This is what you get for working with foreigners*, essentially. My colleagues at the time agreed there were no coincidences and that my request, spoken of too freely in a dangerous city, had precipitated the ambush. One called a friend in the security services, he told me, and confirmed the killings. It was a tragedy but *just a drop*, as he put it, in the bloody story of those days. I never saw the bodies, but believed what I was told, and carried the weight of those deaths heavily.

The essayist Joan Didion once wrote of transforming the white flag of defeat at home into the brave white banner of battle away from home, and I was guilty in that way of displacing the anxieties of my own life onto these deaths, for which I could never have borne as much responsibility as the killers. But there was, nonetheless, a problem. In certain vertiginous moments I could see it. That I was connected, even if I was innocent. That I was part of a chain, that my actions, my good intent, my careerist gambling had contributed, however minutely, to deaths. And here was the brutal thing: Mostly, I did not care. Mostly, life is not vertiginous moments. Mostly, I forgot. Because the reality of being an upper-class white American man is near endless opportunity for pleasure, security, and an organically corrupted meritocracy which insists that the satiation of your own desires cut with the commonest drop of discipline and decency increases justice. Three men were dead, but I was just doing my job. This connection between death and work had the unnerving hum of truth for every anglophone foreigner I knew in such places, even those too practical to abide a paragraph such as this, with no time for unsolvable problems like what in our own lives might justify the end of others.

I thought about it all for seven years before returning to Baghdad to figure out exactly what happened. I was in for a surprise. Over the course of several months, I discovered that the story was false, there had been no ambush, that the basketball players had never existed. That ultimately I had failed as a reporter, been manipulated and lied to by the man who'd arranged the meeting—the "cousin." There were no records, no witnesses, no recollection in the basketball or law enforcement communities, no real names. The "cousin," I found, had left behind a series of angry, distrustful colleagues and confused stories. He was a serial liar, and the details of his life are not worth recounting here except to say that whatever drives a man to such fictions is itself terrible, and in this case likely connected to growing up amid dictatorship and violence.[248]

This was the path that brought me to civilian casualties. The unreality of the basketball incident renders less meaningful its application to the real systems of destruction that result in airstrikes and old men dying on the side of the Sangin road. But there it is. I do not have nor wish for anyone any perfect clarity or peace of mind about third-order consequences, or even believe such possible. Most know, well as I, it is not. But this knowledge will not stop the orchestration of the next editorial meeting, wedding, or attack authorization in Iraq. And it will not stop me from noting: our limited ability to know the past only illuminates the profound cruelty of killing innocent people in the name of an unknowable future.[249]

Which is not to say that plans are impossible, or that it is wrong to assign a dollar figure to lives, which of course we do. From report 07-699 of the U.S. Government Accountability Office: "Solatia payments: Iraq: Up to $2,500 for death; up to $1,500 for serious injury; and $200 or more for minor injury."[250]

Such numbers are ugly, but progress that has brought us into a world where death is more common by diabetes than homicide demands the valuation of abstractions. This is not righteous, and without deference to mystery, even love, it is rarely even effective. But it is not properly the sole burden of those blown apart to accept that paradox, or conceive a better path than we now tread. It is also for those in power, Americans, with the greatest accumulation of resources and knowledge in history, to imagine how Hidran's legs did not have to burn, how to operate without killing innocents.

My own imagination with regard to Hidran depends upon the facts of the day we met, what I saw for myself. I came of age in a time when the answer to any question—or at least, the history of any debate—began to download faster than I could name my elementary school teachers. But such answers are presented in dialogue boxes. There is no wiki yet for the children we pass on the Bzebiz Bridge connecting Baghdad to Anbar over the Euphrates, en route to Hidran. They could make one on their phones, if they ever get phones, and upload themselves into the wider consciousness, but they probably won't. At least, they won't in any way that penetrates the psychic unease characterizing life in the Western capitals, which demands, like a ravenous hangover, entertainments, repeating rewards, sexual partners vetted and swiped on a phone while defecating in a bistro bathroom.

Abroad, the unease took different forms. When I'd woken up that morning in Baghdad, the office was empty, the house cat named for a war criminal[251] was asleep, on television the news was muted in three languages. Beyond the iron gates I met a fixer who had recently adopted his niece because her father, his younger brother, had died in a bombing on a foreign journalists' compound. There was little traffic and we sped to the clinic of an Iraqi charity which had agreed to smuggle us into a camp outside Fallujah.[252] And at the Bzebiz Bridge those children waited, looking for work as porters. But we had nothing for them to carry.[253]

The silver of processed food bags flashed in the ditches, the streams of people thickened. The charity's director parlayed with an army officer. The bridge was crowded. Women pulled bursting suitcases over its uneven planks. Small boys stood shirtless on the pilings and dove off, screaming. On the far side a denser crowd waited in a holding pen. This crowd of refugees grew even in the moments we walked by, looking for a ride onward. The sun was overhead at that point, the color draining from the desert as we drove toward the camp. Originally we'd been invited to spend the night, but the situation had changed, the director of the charity told us.[254] We would have to recross the bridge before the army closed it at dusk. Soon tents appeared on the horizon. They were white or off-white, marked with the blue type of aid agencies, and to varying degrees their residents had tried to make them into homes. Economies spring up in these camps, some grow as large as cities, generations are born and die within. Sheets printed with cartoon characters; a football of wadded-up cardboard and masking tape; colorful plastics in a repeating field of rags. The camp, like each I have visited, was sad, low eyes everywhere.[255] News of a foreigner taking names spread, and soon the tent I sat in was full of people who wanted to talk.

Well before Hidran and her mother pushed through, Noor Najem Abid, who didn't know how old she was, told me that on the morning of the twenty-fifth or twenty-sixth of April, nine months pregnant, she had stepped into her garden to bake bread when a missile landed on her street and two pieces of shrapnel pierced her belly; at the local hospital she delivered dead twins. She also said that the day she returned home her street was attacked again, and in that second strike her thirteen-year-old cousin Yakin Jamal Abid died. The neighborhood agreed that F-16s had carried out the attacks, but Noor herself, it must be said, had no way of verifying this, just as I, for the moment, could not verify any of these stories, or that she'd escaped, as she claimed, with the help of a merciful member of ISIS. An interruption: Omar Abdel Qader, approximately six years old, shoved to the front of the crowd in that tent by his mother, had suffered shrapnel wounds, as I could see. But since Omar was not dead I politely asked his mother to take him away, and send someone whose child had been *killed* in an airstrike.

Eventually more people crowded the tent with stories of their dead than I could take down. Kamila Sabar Jassim, forty-five. In the early morning of November 21, 2015,[256] a Saturday, her son was struck in the skull by a piece of a missile. She took him to the hospital, where he died seven days later. His name was Mohammed Musab Ahmed, seventeen, and at the time of his death he was working in a garage. Earlier in the year airplanes had dropped papers warning of airstrikes and instructing residents to flee, but Kamila and her five children couldn't escape the occupied city and anyway had nowhere to go. There's a phone number[257] in the endnotes on which she used to be reachable—I have numbers for almost all of them, and some had smartphones. If they make it into Baghdad we'll all be able to stream the same songs, and can talk about that, prepare for the concert we wanted to organize: The conductor of the Iraqi National Symphony Orchestra told me we could use the National Theater and guarantee their safety, but OutKast rarely perform together anymore, according to their agents,[258] so there will be no performance of "Bombs over Baghdad." But maybe 3 Stacks could come and drop a guest verse anyway, *So low that I can admit / When I hear that another kid is shot by the popo it ain't an event.*[259] Next: Nohad Adnan, four, and Sumaye Adnan, three, killed in al-Kharma, northeast of Fallujah, on July 14, 2014, at approximately three in the morning, according to their father, Adnan Saad, thirty. He said he had a strong house and many in the neighborhood were sheltering with him, but the missile came through the kitchen window, not only killing the girls but injuring his sister, Hana, as I could see from her leg, and his cousin, Mariam, as I could see from her arm and throat. Another man was pushing to the front of the crowd at that point, and we had to tell him that I did want to hear his story about his daughter, Reem, nine, who lost her leg and whose "lip is cut open to her ear," but again, for now, we were only speaking with people whose relatives were dead, ideally those with documentary evidence, like Bashir Ahmed Abdullah of Nainlia, of the Zoba tribe. He and his brother were construction workers.[260] In the early days of Ramadan in 2015, they had just walked outside the house when it was destroyed by an airstrike. Both of their wives and daughters, a brother, and a niece were killed, he claimed. Their mother, other brother, and sister-in-law survived with burns. Bashir recalled being "pushed into the air" by the explosion. "When I woke up I was surprised I couldn't see the house." He said he found body parts. He admitted to me there was an ISIS house nearby, but swore he was not ISIS himself. "We don't understand what's going on in the sky," he told me.

All that, before Hidran. But she is only one, and they are only seventeen and though I have implied that she, and the rest, were injured or killed in American strikes, I have not yet provided comprehensive evidence. Despite some documents and photographs, everyone in that camp could be lying, or exaggerating. The strikes could have been Iraqi, perhaps some were, merely supported by Americans, which would shift the conventional and mostly reasonable assignment of responsibility. And lack of cooperation from official players doesn't justify unverified accusation, which can be bad as many crimes and lead to worse.

Quickly, then, pass the crowd of children pressed against the chain-link fence fighting for a few bottles of water; see only briefly the link impressing a red line on a small boy's cheek, and the white of his wide eyes. See the dust behind us as we leave and the desert rushing past and the sweating hour spent in that holding pen, and the smiles on our faces when we are safely back over the bridge and they have chained the pen gate closed behind us, pushing back the crowd. Our colleagues weren't detained long, either. And once those images have passed, on to verification, to the full process of a single strike, just one more. This one happened in Tikrit, rather than Fallujah, and concerns a little girl about Hidran's age rather than Hidran, and so cannot stand in for her story or all others, is only itself, however it might cast colonels as liars, if every life is deserving of individual account.

27.

The Unavoidable Question

Sara Mohammed, seven, cheerful problem child, black pigtails, dimples, eldest daughter. Since toddlerhood, she's suffered difficulty breathing and bouts of fever and lethargy. Her trim and adoring father, Nazhan, thirty, an accountant at the Tikrit University College of Nursing, has taken her to doctors in Tikrit, Baghdad, and Erbil; asked favors at the College of Nursing on her behalf; even appealed to the governor of Baghdad province for help—but no one has been able to diagnose or treat her. Eventually, Nazhan sells half his house to afford a flight and consultation at a hospital in Delhi. Indian doctors diagnose a hole in one of Sara's heart valves, perform surgery. She improves immediately and is enjoying the best health of her life on the June day ISIS arrives in Tikrit. She doesn't understand exactly what's going on, but knows her father is afraid of the new men in the neighborhood, coming and going from the big house across the street.

Nazhan keeps the news of that grim summer from his children, best he can. Beheadings in the square, crucifixions. Two of Sara's uncles are police officers, and both are shot dead. ISIS doesn't shut down the College of Nursing, but Nazhan is too frightened to go to work and leave his family alone. He goes out only once a month, to buy food. And three times that summer, ISIS fighters knock on his door. The first time, Nazhan freezes, is silent, pretends no one's home. The second time, the same. The third time, fighters shout that they want water, and keep

shouting. So Nazhan opens the door. He tells the masked men, We don't
have any water. They push him out of the way and try the tap—but nothing comes out. To Nazhan's relief, they leave—but now Nazhan feels
more trapped than ever. Every day there are food shortages, price spikes.
He's worried about Sara's health. His wife, Sundus, says they should
flee, and Nazhan wants to flee, too—but he's afraid ISIS will catch
them, and anyway he doesn't know where to go. His whole family is
from Tikrit, and he doesn't have money to rent a place somewhere else.
He considers following a friend who's fled to Kirkuk—a nearby city that
escaped ISIS's onslaught—but when he calls to ask about conditions
there, the news is bad. His friend can't find a place to stay, refugees are
filling the city. Nazhan decides to stay put.

Then, in early September, the first good news for months. A colleague asks Nazhan to return to the College of Nursing to perform an
audit, and Nazhan, screwing up his courage, does. He goes to work and
comes home without incident. Perhaps life can return to normal, or at
least improve a little.

Two days later, Nazhan is finishing lunch in his living room, and the
kids have just gotten up to play, when an enormous explosion blows out
the windows.

S ara's story is as dense as the resources we commit to investigating
it, to hearing all sides and imagining what her life might have been.
But even for her parents there is an upper limit of investment. From an
evolutionary perspective that upper limit exists for each of us, given
fertility or multiple children, each of whom if healthy would be capable
of imagination. Did Sara ride Nazhan's shoulders like Calamity Jane
upon her horse, or steal his glasses and hide them, or play any game a
daughter might play with a father? According to Nazhan, she was "playing in the garage" when the American missile struck.

N azhan didn't know it, but when Tikrit fell, there was an Iraqi Coalition spy living in his neighborhood, a slender, hot-eyed young

woman named Sabrine. When ISIS occupied the big house across his street, she reported their presence up her chain of command.

A year and a half later, in her dark and dusty living room,[261] Sabrine tells me that she was concerned about hurting civilians with the strike her intelligence would precipitate, but that she couldn't warn anyone about it "because then I would become a target." So she didn't. She relayed the target to a major in the Ministry of Interior—a heavily scarred Tikriti major named Talat.[262] Sabrine chose Major Talat in particular because, in addition to being an intelligence officer, he was the owner of the occupied house in question. He should know, she thought, and have the opportunity for vengeance.

When Major Talat and I walk around the rubble of his house, he confirms Sabrine's story. He also tells me, dismissively, that "of course, civilians die in war," and that he never had any doubt about requesting the airstrike, and so immediately passed the information on to a young operative working with the Americans.

That operative goes by the pseudonym Fat Mike, and was recruited by the United States as a teenager. He speaks in a slangy, hip-hop-inflected English, and has a tattoo across his forearm in the gothic style favored by U.S. soldiers: *No one jajing of me exipt my god.*[263] When he and I meet in the lobby of a shabby Baghdad hotel, he tells me that yes, he checked for civilians in the area, "called people," but was satisfied there were none in danger. So he, in turn, passed the target on to his handler, an American named Marius who "works with the Company."[264]

Then Marius and the Americans, Fat Mike tells me, called in the strike.

Freeze the moment, glass in the air, a long second, before the dust blocks the sunlight and the debris falls. Many things have happened quickly, but they are not mysterious. Gases have expanded, exerting pressure on their container—a warhead, which has shattered. The pieces have flown outward, becoming shrapnel. The pressure has pushed outward, too, become a blast wave. This wave, faster than sound, has compressed the surrounding air. Your ears popping, multiplied a hundred

thousandfold. The wave has pulverized all the nearby concrete and created a vacuum, sucking debris back toward the zero point. The initial
interaction of chemicals has also produced heat, which has caused
fire.[265] All this was planned for and expensively engineered.[266]

Nazhan is stunned and thrown to the ground. When he regains his
senses, the dust is so thick he can't see anything. As the ringing subsides, he hears his wife's screams, and in the choking gloom finds her
and his three youngest children, but not Sara. He runs outside and finds
her sprawled in front of his garage. Major Talat's big house across the
street has been turned to rubble. Nazhan kneels to examine his daughter.
She doesn't seem to be bleeding, but she's unconscious, barely breathing, and he can't wake her. He picks her up and loads her into his car,
shouts for the rest of the family to get in, too. He gathers all their ID
cards and drives for Kirkuk. He is determined to save his daughter.

N o litany of sufferings will reduce our tolerance for violence. Only
life can do that, not death alone. And so for my part I am grateful
for swimming in the ocean, and for the desert, too, and for bats over
rubble. For iron, which is found not only in missile fragments but Paris's
wrought railings. For everything, really. When I was perhaps fourteen
my school class visited the Capitol and shook the hand of an elderly
senator, a conservative, who had supported foreign wars and segrega-
tion, and I am grateful for him, too, for that complex and wretched old
man wheeled out in the warm shadow of the Senate offices, all around
him columns of wealth, risen from a history of terror, rape, and robbery.
Still, I am grateful for a suit cut gracefully enough to hang in a wheelchair. And I can't deny that I am grateful because I enjoy some of these
pleasures, because of what they fire chemically. But I am also grateful
because they are elements of our universal but as yet scientifically un-
articulated shared consciousness, representing grace, which makes need-
less death all the madder. Maybe the point is irksome, obvious, and it's
better to swivel the lamp back to the horizon. Sara's T-shirt was printed
with the words HAPPY FOOD.

Finally even lighthouses disintegrate. The material pleasures fail to fire chemicals, and I am left only with the people to whom I had access. Other sets of chemicals, consciousnesses. At home, many were conflicted about the system they lived in, but many were not, simply operating in their chosen field with the full weight of our age behind them. Young men and women who learned to speak eight languages, who invented quarters of the Internet, who went to the Olympics, who repurposed mausoleums for art. All of this hums in American society and serves— whether one takes on the country's ideals naively, or for the sake of imminent critique—to remind what can be achieved and felt, given time to live. Recall the morning, a single cup of black coffee in Central Park, in flanneled light across the Great Lawn. Recall the clarion singing in the Cathedral of St. John the Divine. And recall that in all literature the more we learn, the more suspicious we become of the accumulation of wealth which demands deadly protection. It is, like the most terrible clichés, simple. Singing and confessions are everywhere, books know no barriers but literacy, and so a life ended, ended to protect my own. . . .

All writing is argument but I wish sometimes it were not. I wish I could simply draw your attention to the shadow of Sara's eyelashes without attendant thought, without implicit demands: for rage at lives taken, for you to survive, for knowledge of death's constant presence, for reform within Congress and the tactical operations center, for everything and anything but the twisted logic of violence enacted in my name, as an American.

Sara dies in the hospital.

Some will contend her death was tragic but necessary, inseparable from the retaking of Tikrit, the defeat of the Islamic State in Iraq. Others might trace it back to the U.S. invasion, or the Sykes-Picot Agreement, link it in a chain of colonial crimes. Choice of context is the writer's most powerful weapon, as choice of battlefield is the soldier's. If you're fortunate enough to choose what to look at and study, to choose what's normal and what's not in your own life, you probably know this already.

It's not just a question of money, though, of time and leisure to read books. To stand in other shoes is a truer fortune. The habit can't be bought, it must be given, taught, and earned through experience, and maybe it's incompatible with empire. Our worst crimes stem from a failure of imagination rather than any evil particular to our kind or time or nation.

Fat Mike tells me he doesn't know about Sara. He does tell me, however, that Marius the CIA officer knows about me.

"He said, 'Don't give [you] nothing.'"

Central Command, CENTCOM, does not grant my requests to meet with any Americans who might have been involved in the strike. Officially, there is no strike on the house across the street from Sara.[267] A public affairs officer for CENTCOM writes me that "there were no strikes conducted in Tikrit during September 2014."

And yet it's in this period that Sara's mother, father, their neighbors, Sabrine, Major Talat, Talat's superior officer,[268] and Fat Mike all say Americans destroyed the house. It's possible they came to lies or confusion independently, that Fat Mike and Major Talat and Sabrine never requested an airstrike. But I believe them.[269] Major Talat had dated notebooks and was an active-duty intelligence officer in partnership with the Coalition; Fat Mike had dozens of documents—contracts, recommendation letters from generals—proving a long relationship with U.S. forces. And while Sara's parents know nothing of the military, they have dated medical records, cause of death translating as "full stop of the heart."[270]

These are facts. It is also factual that mistakes occur, that sometimes I wish she were my daughter, or America's, generalized—daughter of the ambassador without time for sentimentality, of the tourist in a hurry to have breakfast and drive north to see the leaves change, of the commentator enraged by disrespect shown Muslim families, writing op-eds on the architecture of choice. Someone who is *offended* or perhaps thinks *Islam needs to get its house in order,* or someone who breaks

Sara Mohammed

campaign promises. The Americans never say it aloud, they write it down. The locals never write it down, but they say it aloud: Our life is cheap. But she can never be some American's daughter. She was Nazhan's daughter. He's thirty-three now but looks older when I meet him at the Babylon, a highly fortified hotel overlooking the Tigris River. He's calm, carefully shaved, still an accountant.

"Didn't they know," Nazhan asks me, "that families were living in that area, and in that house? How could they bomb that house, knowing many families live in houses surrounding?"[271]

I recount what I know, the non-combatant casualty cutoff value, systems, the mitigation team, a little about America's tolerance for civilian casualties.

"So," I tell Nazhan, "people argue about how high this number should be—should it be five, should it be ten, should it be twenty?"

The fixer begins to translate, but Nazhan interrupts.

"I understood what he meant," Nazhan says, "like, two civilians and one hundred ISIS members are in the same area, right?"

"Yes," says the fixer.

"So they favor killing the hundred ISIS members over saving the two civilians?"

"Yes."

"Why then, in their normal life, if a group of terrorists took over a place and held one hostage, would the entire world try to save that one hostage?"

We speculate, keep talking. Soon Nazhan asks me the unavoidable question.

"Is one life worth more than another?"

VIII.

Notes, Sources, and Additional Context

I. THE CLASSY HOTEL

1. ". . . incomprehensible, incomprehensible the multitude of visible things." Czeslaw Milosz, "An Honest Description of Myself with a Glass of Whiskey at an Airport, Let Us Say, in Minneapolis," *The New York Review of Books*, December 20, 2001, http://www.ny books.com/articles/2001/12/20/an-honest-description-of-myself -with-a-glass-of-wh/.
2. "'I don't want to bother you much with what happened to me personally,' he began, showing in this remark the weakness of many tellers of tales who seem so often unaware of what their audience would best like to hear." Joseph Conrad, *Heart of Darkness* (New York: Modern Library, 1991).
3. Bertelsmann, the majority shareholder in Penguin Random House, has its own dark history regarding civilian casualties and war crimes. In 2002, given the findings of a commission it organized, the company acknowledged and expressed regret for its involvement with the Third Reich, and its probable profits from Jewish slave labor. According to *The New York Times*: "'We cannot prove that those 50 Jews were specifically printing the material that Bertelsmann shipped to the eastern front,' said Saul Friedländer, a historian from the University of California at Los Angeles who led the four-member commission. 'But we can assume that during that period, some of them did.'" Bertelsmann did well to organize the commission to investigate the issue; the more companies do likewise, the better. Mark Landler, "Bertelsmann Offers Regret for Its Nazi-Era Conduct," *The New York Times*, October 8, 2002, http:// www.nytimes.com/2002/10/08/world/bertelsmann-offers-regret-for -its-nazi-era-conduct.html.

4. Then, one day, the bars close or change hands, and certain correspondents approaching late middle age, who risked their lives for
information on the plight of illiterate children, trade stories of sexual conquests and campaigns waged in the bathroom. Here's some
methodology for violent language: Swap out the expatriate press
corps for worse criminals. By *bearing witness*, many journalists
hope to catalyze change, and sometimes it works. But such work
requires identification with the perpetrators of the crimes, so that
in understanding them one might deter or solve the problem.
American journalists, American crimes, but what about the *bad
guys? How can you criticize the United States in a war against
ISIS?* Fair enough, let's return to that bathroom, in one of these
bars, let's drag in Abu Bakr al-Baghdadi, or one of his human
shields–using lieutenants. Let's turn away from understanding for
a moment and grind his face to the concrete for every single kid
killed by an airstrike. Let's hear what his scalp sounds like when it
tears. Let's smell his funky armpits when they're covered in blood.
Let's rape the motherfucker. Is it possible for you to imagine pleasure in such action? The waiters at the Classy never make anyone
leave, and in the darkest hours one often finds reporters in the dim
lobby, a duty-free bottle on the table. Imagine sitting with them.
Some of them are writing what it is like to be a slave of sadistic
fighters for three years. The girls who are liberated at the very end,
from the Old City, who have been held the longest in the heart of
ISIS's stronghold—after they escape, they are immobile, silent,
nearly unconscious, for weeks. Is that you? Or are you instead a
scholar, wishing no jump cuts between Iraq and Afghanistan, that
accounts of civilian casualties were perfect gemstones, rather than
crutched-up remixes of all the authors whose names you can read
in the notes? Because there's no time, with all the suffering, as if
anyone needs another lyrical American war story, when Michael
Herr's *Dispatches* is in every guesthouse from Kerada to Taimani.

You have been grown since the salting of Carthage, and books are entertainment. Give you the statue any day, the empire, never mind "Ozymandias" and the passage of time. Become powerful. Perhaps you are.

II. CIVIL DEFENSE

1. Attempt to Reach Civilians Trapped in West Mosul

5. Author recordings, Mosul, June 2016. Here and throughout, where I have elided, I use ellipsis points; choices of diction were made in concert with interpreters to maintain pace and clarity at the same time as fidelity to what was said. Those interpreters—fixers in the highest sense—include Walid Fazly, Sangar Khalil, and others who prefer to remain annonymous. In addition, Jennifer Rasigade-Marchand and her company, Word For Word Language Services, provided top-notch translations and transcription throughout, and Yasmine al-Sayyad provided careful independent fact-checking.

6. "Mosul is an ancient and prosperous city, whose fortress, known as al-Hadbá' ["The Humpback"], is famous for its strength. Next to it are the sultan's palaces. These are separated from the town by a long and broad street, running from the top to the bottom of the town. Round the town run two strong walls, with close-set towers. So thick is the wall that there are chambers inside it one next the other all the way round. I have never seen city walls like it except at Delhi. Outside the town is a large suburb, containing mosques, baths, hostelries and markets. It has a cathedral mosque on the bank of the Tigris, round which there are lattice windows of iron, and adjoining it are platforms overlooking the river, exceedingly beautiful and well constructed. In front of the mosque there

is a hospital, and there are two other cathedral mosques inside the town. The Qaysaríya [walled market] is a fine building with iron gates." Ibn Battúta, *Travels in Asia and Africa 1325–1354,* trans. H. A. R. Gibb (1929; Abingdon, England: RoutledgeCurzon, 2005), p. 103.

7. The competing arguments of these powers are not equally valid, but better addressed elsewhere.

8. Important to note, for this book and generally, are the implications of Steven Pinker's argument that violence has been declining globally and is at its lowest point in human history. While the explanatory power of Pinker's older evidence can be contested, the intuitive power of his argument cannot. The decline, he argues, is partly due to the growth of liberal democracies such as the United States and their improving norms. This is likely. However—while the absolute number of civilian casualties caused by the United States has declined over the past hundred years, it may be that continuing hypocrisy on the topic—the collective cognitive dissonance—presents a threat to the sort of liberal democratic progress that, in Pinker's work, is responsible for violence's decline. See Steven Pinker, *The Better Angels of Our Nature: Why Violence Has Declined* (New York: Penguin, 2012). For ongoing conversation on this topic, and much else besides, I am grateful to Dr. Anand Gopal.

9. Tal Kopan, "Donald Trump: I Meant That Obama Founded ISIS, Literally," CNN Politics, August 12, 2016, http://www.cnn.com /2016/08/11/politics/donald-trump-hugh-hewitt-obama-founder -isis/index.html.

10. At this point in the book, I am removing myself from the narrative as much as possible and so elide some of this conversation. This is an instance of a greater good/absolutist compromise on the page, if absolutism here calls for transparency.

11. Or *moai*, made by the Rapa Nui, in the indigenous language.

12. The attraction is ancient, as Philip Gourevitch, discussing Plato, notes in his study of the Rwandan genocide: "Like Leontius, the

young Athenian in Plato, I presume that you are reading this because you desire a closer look, and that you, too, are properly disturbed by your curiosity." Philip Gourevitch, *We Wish to Inform You That Tomorrow We Will Be Killed with Our Families* (New York: Picador, 1998).

13. But not ivy, really. Everywhere you look, all is man-made, nothing green or organic save the soldiers and the men of civil defense themselves, pressed against their cars or the pocked walls, and the corpse. The idea behind leaving the ISIS corpses to rot in the sun is twofold. They are the enemy and so do not deserve sympathetic treatment. Resources are thin, so cannot be spared for their removal. But what, I wonder, if we buried each of them, according to their religion? What if we did so without broadcasting the burials for the sake of influencing potential ISIS recruits, of winning the propaganda war? What if we did so simply because we believe such action correct? No consequence save the burial itself.

14. "Cowards die many times before their deaths; the valiant never taste of death but once." Julius Caesar in William Shakespeare, *The Tragedy of Julius Caesar,* act 2, scene 2, http://shakespeare .mit.edu/julius_caesar/full.html.

2. Correspondence (I)

15. There is an argument to be made that this letter is taken out of context. It is dated from three years before the events in the surrounding chapters. In the interim, the president announced his authorization of expanded strikes. However, this letter marks the official start of the latest American war, the point at which unclassified airstrikes began again in Iraq. Subsequent authorizations expanded them in the similar spirit.

Elided from the president's letter:

In addition, I have authorized U.S. Armed Forces to provide
humanitarian assistance in Iraq in an operation that commenced

on August 7, 2014. These operations will also be limited to
supporting the civilians trapped on Mount Sinjar.

I have directed these actions, which are in the national security
and foreign policy interests of the United States, pursuant to my
constitutional authority to conduct U.S. foreign relations and as
Commander in Chief and Chief Executive. These actions are
being undertaken in coordination with the Iraqi government.

3. Excavation of Bodies off Pepsi Road

16. One of the best and earliest of the stories about the White Helmets:
    Matthieu Aikins, "Whoever Saves a Life," *Medium*, September 14,
    2014,   https://medium.com/matter/whoever-saves-a-life
    -1aaea20b782.

    A more recent, also excellent piece—particularly about Rabih
    and his men—is by John Beck, "The Men Who Rescue Mosul's
    Dead," *GQ*, December 28, 2017, https://www.gq.com/story/men
    -who-rescue-mosul-dead.

17. All of this could seem normal, especially if you were tired. This
    night was one of several times I fell asleep in the back of military
    vehicles; soldiers did too, occasionally.

18. Before we reach the red van . . . in the predawn ISIS breaks through
    a federal police line and regains enough territory to land mortars
    on al-Jadida market, close to Rabih's station. Pink morning rises
    from her rumpled bed to the vacuum rush of jets. The heat is al-
    ready tangible, the sort of heat in which almost anyone would be
    grateful for a tall, cool glass of water or, better, a pitcher of lemon-
    ade by a pool, perhaps tiled in blue, plush cotton towels across teak
    lounge chairs, dune grass whispering beneath salt breeze. But bar-
    ring all that, even the shade of a civil defense crane is welcome. An
    improvement, it may be said, on certain refugee camps in the area.
    For in Rabih's station lot, in the shade of the unit crane, Ayman,
    thirty-five, is a valuable person, not to be left behind in endnotes or
    in the station by the men of civil defense. He admits to me he's

scared. He's the unit crane mechanic, and today he's going to Pepsi Road.

"Now we're all scared," he says, throwing his hands up. They are gnarly with calluses and motor oil. "The police are telling us that ISIS took back some land."

This is much more worrying to Ayman than American airstrikes, which, in his view, "are all because of ISIS!" He is therefore of the opinion that "if you capture an ISIS fighter and kill him, God will not punish you, even if you bury him alive."

Still, his relations with the God are not great.

"I don't pray anymore," he says, "because ISIS was forcing us to pray."

Ayman doesn't even pray as he rides the crane out of the station, though he is highly aware of the casualties suffered by civil defense and Iraqi security forces in the previous days. Perhaps his mind is elsewhere. There's much to occupy attention along the way. The destroyed city is dense with unusual sights: a double-decker bus flipped over, a bare leg sprouting from a pile of concrete, graffiti of a heart transfixed by a drawn arrow and real bullet holes, a corrugated roof opened like a tin of sardines, a university library split to the sky. Every part of the destruction is personal for someone. Ayman notices, on the sunny drive, that the building where his sister lived is on fire. Smoke rushes from a second-story window devoid of glass. Fortunately she's with other relatives, elsewhere.

19. The driver of Ayman's crane is his cousin Amjad. His side of the family is substantially wealthier, though—Amjad actually owns the crane, and several others besides, even if some remain in ISIS territory. Prior to the takeover, he had a subcontract with an American construction and logistics company to work on the oil fields outside Mosul. This made him rich by local standards. But he was still local to West Mosul and so subject to ISIS rule until he and his wife and children managed to escape a year or so before. His two brothers and sister living nearby with their spouses and children,

twenty-two in all, weren't so lucky. They were liberated only a month ago. By then Amjad had volunteered the services of his crane to Lieutenant Colonel Rabih, and so was able to ask a favor— that the red van retrieve his relatives from their newly liberated neighborhood, which was still treacherous and closed to civilian vehicles. Rabih obliged, and the reunion was a happy one. In this spirit of collegiality Amjad also got cousin Ayman taken on as unit mechanic, though neither of them are, officially, civil defense.

Amjad's crane isn't the most agile vehicle and takes the left turn onto Pepsi Road wide, more slowly than a reasonable passenger might like. The only covered compartment contains the driver's seat. Ayman, perched on the yellow chassis—so as not to burn the back of his legs on its hot metal—rides fully exposed to a block controlled by ISIS snipers the day before. Their flag still flies a block distant, the body of a fighter still rots in the intersection. But finally, to Ayman's relief, cousin Amjad's crane comes safely to the Abajis' street.

20. To illustrate the kind of elision that I am engaged in, some of the elided dialogue:

"Abdul Mohsin, fetch a hammer."

Civil defense worker Abdul Mohsin often acted as gofer and wasn't integral to the chapter. He ran off to fetch a hammer.

But everything elided is part of some other story.

Later that day, resting, I watched Abdul Mohsin examine a bird in a cage that he'd found in a bombed-out house across the street.

"I will take these birds," he said, "the house owner is not here. I will feed them and bring them back to the owner."

Ahmed the guard replied, "No, one of the Baghdad guys said he would take them."

Other men, whose names I do not have, were talking in the room at the time: "Baghdad, Baghdad guys."

"Yeah?"

"Who said he'd take these birds? He'll bring them back later to the owner?"

"Yeah."

"Who will bring them back?"

"Where you gonna bring them?

"I'll bring them to Hamam Ali."

That evening I noticed the birdcage in the front seat of a Baghdad fire truck, not with Abdul Mohsin.

21.

Adil's T-shirt

22. Plastic memory: I vividly recall him scraping grime from his stubble in this conversation, but do not remember at which moment *exactly* in the dialogue he did so—I think it was here, at the beginning, but have no proof. And so inserting the detail here, without total certainty, is a kind of epistemological compromise I make, now and then, for the sake of pacing. But I can't think of anywhere else I do it, without an in-text warning, in the book.

23. Martin Pengelly, "Defense Secretary Mattis Says US Policy Against Isis Is Now 'Annihilation,'" *The Guardian*, May 28, 2017, https://www.theguardian.com/us-news/2017/may/28/james-mattis -defense-secretary-us-isis-annihilation.

24. Regarding this business of phone calls to and from the rubble. I never heard one, but the men of civil defense said they happened regularly, and in this case my fixer had received a call from an activist friend who maintained a Facebook page for people searching for missing family in Mosul. He said he'd gotten a call from a

girl named Najah who was trapped under some rubble in Zanjili, though it was unclear which pile of rubble in particular. My fixer reported the call to Colonel Rabih, but no action was taken.

25. Qusay al-Saadi, interviews, Mosul, June 2016.

26. The destruction is clearly too complete to have been caused by mortars. I ask the question just to get the conversation started, not knowing what else to say, in the moment, to the bereaved brothers Abdulilah.

27. Other families were identified in my recordings by onlookers, family, civil defense workers, and subsequently by the invaluable monitoring organization Airwars. Their complete assessment of this strike—https://airwars.org/coalitioncivcas2017june/—is as follows:

JUNE 10TH, 2017
(I569) Borsa Area, Centre of Mosul,
Nineveh Province, Iraq

Summary: Local sources reported that 18 civilians from four named families—mostly children and women—died under the rubble. An airstrike reportedly hit their homes in the Bursa area in the centre of Mosul. It is presently unclear who was responsible for the airstrikes.

Sawlf Ateka, a local Facebook page, launched an appeal to save the families from under the rubble. It said that those affected were the families of **Khalis Ahmad Hamed Abaji** and his brother **Dr. Banyan Ahmad Hamed Abaji.** They used to be the owners of Al Hadba analytical laboratories. The destroyed homes were located near the Bursa area, close to the Central Preparatory School and Fawaz Library. Sawlf Ateka said that as many as twenty civilians were under the rubble.

Other sources also said that the house near Borsa Street, opposite the school, was bombed. Iraqyoon Agency said that 18 members of four families were killed—the families of Dr. Banyan Abaji, the family of his brother (as mentioned above), as well as **the families of his sister-in-law** and his **neighbour**. And the local Syndicate of Pharmacists reported the deaths of **"Dr. Anfal Karim Ismael Al-Hamdani** and her **family."** All of the bodies were later recovered.

Civilians reported killed: 21–23, including women and children

Civilians reported injured: Unknown

Sources: Sawlf Ateka [Arabic] [Archived], Nineveh Media Center [Arabic] [Archived], M.N.N [Arabic] [Archived], Iraqyoon Agency [Arabic] [Archived], Iraqyoon (2) [Arabic] [Archived], Sawlf Ateka (2) [Arabic] [Archived], Urgent News Mosul [Arabic] [Archived], Iraqyoon Agency [Arabic] [Archived], Radio Alghad [Arabic] [Archived], Yaqein Agency [Arabic] [Archived], Iraq News Center [Arabic] [Archived], El Mosul Official [Arabic] [Archived], MNN [Arabic] [Archived].

Quality of reporting: Contested—unclear who carried out the raids.

Coalition position: For June 9th–10th the Coalition publicly reported: "Near **Mosul**, three strikes engaged two ISIS tactical units; destroyed seven fighting positions, three ISIS-held buildings, a command and control node, a VBIED, and a VBIED staging area; and suppressed an ISIS tactical unit and a mortar system."

For June 10th–11th: "Near **Mosul**, three strikes engaged two ISIS tactical units; destroyed five fighting positions, two mortar systems, two VBIEDs, a supply cache, and an explosives cache; and suppressed a mortar team."

III. ALLIES

5. Iraqi Special Forces and the al-Jadida Airstrike

28. This T-shirt, though one of the most popular souvenirs of the war, is not as highly coveted as the ISIS flag, which at least two

correspondents I know bring across the increasingly tense U.S. border. The desire for artifacts of battle remains mysterious to me, though it's salted through the study of history. For example, the former targeteer who appears in chapter 11, "Revelation in Pleasantville of Anticipated Civilian Casualties," is reported to have a grotesque interest in Nazi paraphernalia, which led to controversy in the press and eventually his resignation from Human Rights Watch, though he subsequently returned to work for the Center for Naval Analyses and the United Nations.

29. See, for example, James Verini, "The Living and the Dead," *The New York Times Magazine*, July 19, 2017, https://www.nytimes .com/interactive/2017/07/19/magazine/mosul-battle-against-isis .html?mcubz=0&_r=0.

30. Ma'ad said something else in this conversation that stayed with me; he talked about the possibility of negotiations with ISIS: "Let's go back to Fallujah," he said. "In Fallujah in the first three days, all the army was mixed and the advancing was so hard, but after three days, I don't know, maybe political dealing, or business dealing with ISIS, and then our advance was like: We're running. After those three days, in one week, we liberated Fallujah. But in those first few days, like from here to the school, we were only advancing a few meters."

Excellent work exists on negotiating with such groups. See, for example, Ashley Jackson, "Negotiating Perceptions: al-Shabaab and Taliban Views of Aid Agencies," Policy Brief 61, Humanitarian Policy Group, Overseas Development Institute, August 2014, https://www.odi.org/sites/odi.org.uk/files/odi-assets/publications -opinion-files/9104.pdf.

31. This reference to Lawrence is deserving of explanation but not here, where my hope is that, as a well-known figure, he may draw readers into a shared understanding of a colonial past and forward through this particular narrative simultaneously. For a brief on what Lawrence was doing in Kut, see "Kut 1916: How the Otto-

mans Defeated the British Army," Al Jazeera, https://interactive
.aljazeera.com/ajt/2016/kutul-amare/en/kut-siege.html.

32. They are a striking pair: Jordan and Pippen, Butch and Sundance,
Bonnie and Clyde, to use a few American touchstones.

33. I can't find the recording of the exchange with the old fireman who
conferred the honor on me.

34. Rafe Said, interview with the author, May 2017.

35. President Obama said there was a plan, but none was ever made
public: "Obama said there has been extensive planning for the day
after Iraqi forces win control of Mosul, saying that there is a 'strategic as well as humanitarian interest in us getting this right.'"
Nicole Gaouette, "Obama: We'll Defeat ISIS in Mosul but It Will
Be a 'Difficult Fight,'" CNN Politics, October 18, 2016, http://
www.cnn.com/2016/10/18/politics/obama-well-defeat
-isis-in-mosul-but-it-will-be-difficult-fight/index.html.

36. Nsikan Akpan, "Antarctica's Larsen C Ice Shelf Finally Breaks,
Releases Giant Iceberg," *PBS NewsHour*, PBS, July 12, 2017, http://
www.pbs.org/newshour/rundown/antarcticas-larsen-c-ice-shelf
-finally-breaks-releases-giant-iceberg/.

37. *Greek* myth, here, though the unsolved question of who *you* are
suggests that we might be better off looking at myths from other
traditions.

38. "Female Kurdish Sniper Cheats Death at Hands of IS," BBC News,
June 28, 2017, http://www.bbc.com/news/av/world-middle-east
-40430552/female-kurdish-sniper-cheats-death-at-hands-of-is.

39. Perhaps we should have sent a battalion of women. Or perhaps we
should have sent no one, and we should leave immediately, look
critically and constantly at the history and myth of our own excep-
tionalism, and dedicate ourselves to nonviolence and the redistribu-
tion of the vast fortunes of our oligarchy.

40. Matthew Isler, "Executive Summary of the Investigation of the Alleged Civilian Casualty Incident in the al Jadidah District, Mosul,"
Operation Inherent Resolve Media Office, May 8, 2017, http://

www.inherentresolve.mil/News/News-Releases/Article/1193707
/executive-summary-of-the-investigation-of-the-alleged-civilian
-casualty-inciden/. The full report is still not available online.

41. A piece in *The Guardian* notes:

    "Mattis, who has been nicknamed 'Mad Dog' because of his
    preference for aggressive tactics, was also asked: 'What keeps you
    awake at night?' 'Nothing,' he said. 'I keep other people awake at
    night.'" Martin Pengelly, "Defense Secretary Mattis Says US Pol-
    icy Against Isis Is Now 'Annihilation,'" *The Guardian*, May 28,
    2017, https://www.theguardian.com/us-news/2017/may/28/james
    -mattis-defense-secretary-us-isis-annihilation.

42. For what are we *used to*, what do we *predict*, if not a "fact of life"?

43. The series of conditions leading us to the conclusion that Saif's life
    is expendable is based on a constructed international order, rather
    than immutable facts.

44. The slamming of dominoes in Saif and Allawai's abandoned ISIS
    safe house suggest the cracking of teeth and bone in the corpses
    excavated by Colonel Rabih and his men, which decompose all
    around them.

45. Office of the Secretary of Defense, "Justification for FY 2018 Over-
    seas Contingency Operations (OCO) Counter-Islamic State of Iraq
    and Syria (ISIS) Train and Equip Fund (CTEF)," Washington,
    D.C., May 5, 2017, http://comptroller.defense.gov/Portals/45/Docu
    ments/defbudget/fy2018/fy2018_CTEF_J-Book_Final_Embar
    goed.pdf.

6. Crazy Horse

46. "By July 2008, as the Democratic nominee for president, Mr.
    Obama had embraced Afghanistan as a priority over Iraq—the
    'good war,' in a phrase that he never actually used himself but that
    became so associated with his approach it was sometimes wrongly
    attributed to him." Mark Landler, "The Afghan War and the

Evolution of Obama," *The New York Times*, January 1, 2017, https://
www.nytimes.com/2017/01/01/world/asia/obama-afghanistan-war
.html.

47. I made the same promises, too, wherever I went. And had the same
daydreams. One in particular, every time I was in a tented camp
for the displaced. The tent vibrates, the fabric groans, rises off the
ground, the pegs snap out of the dirt, ropes crack. Through the
flaps I see the displaced crowding below, and on rising the whole
of the dry camp, the strewn trash and peeling banners of the aid
organizations, and higher still the roads and checkpoints, and then
Mosul in the distance, then all the shapes of wrecked farmland and
charred villages, and the tent is getting cold, cloud moisture coming in, and we are speeding away, south along the rivers, silver
lines beneath us, until Baghdad and the slums, then Basra and the
Persian Gulf and the sparkling Indian Ocean and the sunrise-
colored flesh of a dorado pulled upon the shore. And everywhere
we fly, we know we might run into an American drone, but, lucky
for us, we don't.

7. The Afghan National Army
and the Security of Outpost Shamalan, Helmand

48. "Seen from the air, the thin, twisted thread that is the Helmand
River meanders through southern Afghanistan, representing 40
percent of the country's water resources. It rises from the snows of
an extension of the Hindu Kush mountain range just south of Kabul
and flows in a southwesterly direction where it finally is submerged
and lost in the vast deserts and series of marshes along the Iranian
border. . . . In Helmand Province (the largest province in the country, with 10 percent of the land area), the river passes through dry
mountains; rocky outcroppings; and brown, rolling foothills that
abruptly demarcate the green areas of cultivation along the narrow
strips of flood plain; and between the southern shifting sands of

the Registan Desert and the gravel-strewn clay flats of the Dasht-i-Margo (Desert of Death). This was the site of the winter capital of the Ghaznavid Empire, and the breadbasket of Afghanistan." U.S. Agency for International Development Special Study No. 18, December 1983.

49. Men like Mujahed were often deployed far from their home provinces. This stopped the army bonding with the population they were meant to protect. Such deployments were done in the name of a unified Afghanistan, which is a questionable project with a long history that is inseparable from civilian casualties in the country.

50. My hope is that the accumulation of such exchanges between Afghan and American soldiers—unbalanced, violent, erotic, comic—is as valuable in its way as the regular cleaning of a weapon.

51. In this, Mujahed echoes U.S. military and sympathetic commentators who assert that journalists do not bring the intellectual rigor to CIVCAS reporting that they should, i.e., that ISIS and enemy combatants are using civilians as shields, and so real responsibility rests with them, so what's all the fuss, the Coalition is doing its best. The brutality of the insurgent groups is not in doubt, but does not excuse our own.

52. This whole conversation was tricky, because the interpreter was working for the U.S. forces with whom I was embedded at the time. His allegiance was clear: to them. But in almost every instance like this one, I was afforded great courtesy by the interpreters and American military, and the lower down the chain, the less spin I encountered.

53. See, for example, George Crile, *Charlie Wilson's War: The Extraordinary Story of How the Wildest Man in Congress and a Rogue CIA Agent Changed the History of Our Times* (New York: Atlantic Monthly Press, 2003).

54. Ryan Jeschke, Matthew Manoukian, and Sky Mote.

55. We are more vivid in tragedy, even commonest tragedy: his uni-brow, acne, his illiteracy and absent father, the death of his platoon-mates.

56. Turn of phrase borrowed from the opening pages of F. Scott Fitzgerald, *The Great Gatsby* (New York: Scribner, 2004): "for the intimate revelations of young men or at least the terms in which they express them are usually plagiaristic and marred by obvious suppressions."

57. Specifically, civilian casualties at the hands of the Americans, and their *apostate dog-washer* allies.

58. This practice of banning cellphones and making rule breakers eat the SIM cards was novel, and I did not confirm it.

59. Lieutenant Nate Combs does the Army proud. One imagines he'll become a general if he stays in, rather than apply to Harvard Business School, as is his plan. Extended quotation for context:

    "I personally have not [called in an airstrike]," he says. "As a ground force commander, that is something we have, that we can use. It's not as common around here, I don't think. It will be used on the eastern part of Helmand, by the river. Do I think we tactically need it over there? Probably not."

    Playing devil's advocate, I ask him:

    "[But] wouldn't that be safer for your guys and for the ANA and all that?"

    "I think it would," he tells me, "but from an aspect of collateral damage, the structures out there, there are civilians out there, there are kids there that used to go to school and be able to walk out at night and not worry about it. If you continue to call air support, yeah, the ANA will like it, and they love the air support, and it'll show our support for them—but I think we can effectively accomplish our mission without it as well as if we continue to use air support. You heard yesterday—you may have asked about the Afghan air force, how much have they helped, right?"

"Right."

"And they said, 'None.'"

"Not much."

"So if we continue to bring in these air assets, how much are we really helping the ANA . . . ?"

"So is the implication of that—you are more willing to accept risk to achieve your mission without collateral damage?"

"I think so. I think that's what you have to do as a ground force commander. You understand the rules of engagement, the escalation of force needed to accomplish the mission."

"Well, let me push you on this idea for a second. Why should you accept more risk? Why should you, Nate Combs, from . . . where are you from?"

"Louisville, Kentucky, sir."

"Louisville, Kentucky. And you have a father and mother, and are you married?"

"No, sir."

"Girlfriend?"

"No, sir."

"Children?"

"No, sir."

"Sisters? Brothers?"

"Yeah. Yes, sir."

"How many sisters and brothers?"

"Older sister, younger brother."

"Anyway, so why should you accept more risk?"

"I guess that's why when you raise your right hand and swear the oath and go in the Army and say you want to be in infantry and lead the men, you take a risk already. You take a risk, say you're gonna lead men, whether it be a combat deployment or into Kuwait just hanging out. But I think you accept and mitigate that prudent risk by putting your guys in the right places or training your guys back in the rear so they're ready. That they don't need enablers such as that. Would it be nice to have enablers every time we went out? Yes. Would it be awesome to walk out and be like, 'Oh, is CAS [close air support] online?' Yes. But we can still accomplish our mission without it. Now, to answer your question why do I accept that risk, I guess, I don't know. I just do. I feel like it's my duty."

And later:

"I don't know. You feel like you have to do something bigger than yourself at one point in your life. I needed to go to West Point at the time. I felt like I needed that. And then to choose infantry was a whole 'nother ball game. I could have done aviation or a quartermaster, but at that time, I lost a lot of friends over here and felt like, if they were doing it, to put their lives on the line for me, and I could have an influence on twenty-five, twenty-six young guns, then that's what I'll do."

60. Lieutenant Nate wasn't the senior-most American present.

61. We're all tilted, in whatever station we happen to occupy, toward the status quo. By advertising, or the academy, or the government launching the jets that turn blocks of Mosul into concrete and bone dust. By a press half dependent on the whims of oligarchs. By elites who pay lip service to diversity and refuse dissent, even as they possess the canon, our wisest predecessors readily available on their devices as a commencement address, delivered at Lieutenant Nate's alma mater, West Point, by the latest American secretary of defense.

"We do everything humanly possible, consistent with military necessity, taking many chances to avoid civilian casualties at all costs." (Martin Pengelly, "Defense Secretary Mattis Says US Policy Against Isis Is Now 'Annihilation,'" *The Guardian*, May 28, 2017, https://www.theguardian.com/us-news/2017/may/28/james -mattis-defense-secretary-us-isis-annihilation.)

The secretary of defense speaks from a grand stage, there at West Point. Shakespeare's plays, perhaps one of them, perhaps only an abridged version, are sometimes taught in the upper grades of

American high schools; it is likely Shakespeare appears on some syllabus at West Point. Almost certainly, Nate has read some Shakespeare, though it seems unlikely Mujahed has. I imagine he would like it, might identify with the sentries, who, in dealing with Hamlet, contradict the secretary.

Approaching the guards at West Point, in the Hudson spring, the dappled light:

"Let me question more in particular: What have you, my good friends, deserved at the hands of fortune, that she sends you to prison hither?"

If West Point is a prison that day, it's a comfortable one, green and gold.

The grass cut carefully as a starlet's hair.

So the sentries reply:

"Prison, my lord!"

And Hamlet, whose very name stands for such drama as is not welcome by most scholars of war, who would not have the study disrespected, replies:

"Denmark's a prison."

"Then is the world one," Rosencrantz tells him back, still sore from PT.

"A goodly one"—but Hamlet won't give up the point—"in which there are many confines, wards and dungeons, Denmark being one o' the worst."

"We think not so, my lord."

"Why, then, 'tis none to you; for there is nothing either good or bad, but thinking makes it so: to me it is a prison."

"Why then, your ambition makes it one; 'tis too narrow for your mind."

Adapted from William Shakespeare, *The Tragedy of Hamlet, Prince of Denmark*, http://shakespeare.mit.edu/hamlet/full.html.

62. Outpost Shamalan lies on the edge of an imaginary circle. At this circle's center is another, smaller American base. This one is built

around a hangar and runway for CIA drones. The circle's radius is just longer than the maximum known Taliban mortar range, and to protect the drones, a few platoons patrol the circle every day, keeping it clear of any Taliban who might cross the invisible circumference. To this end, they visit their local allies, including, at one point on the circle's edge, the men of OP Shamalan. This is another reason the Americans are present. Officially, American combat engagements in Afghanistan ended years ago, but these patrols take and return sporadic small-arms fire. When I am there an American officer tells me the men are *glad to be where the action is.*

IV. OPERATIONS

9. The Targeting and Killing of a Helmandi Combatant

63. "So I mean there were times, and I haven't done it with this group, but with the old group, there were times where guys would cheer, and it would infuriate me. And I'd be like, 'Hey, we just literally just fucking killed a guy, so for you to cheer about it, it's not a video game.' And it's not their fault; they haven't walked through one of those compounds." General D. A. Sims, interview with the author, Helmand, December 6, 2016.

64. "We always establish pattern of life, meaning we don't just go 'Okay, well, this looks good and I don't think we're gonna to hit anything around it.' We—mandatory are . . . we call it soaking a target and you've watched, meaning you've watched that target for days sometimes. And then you know there's no women or children or non-combatants in that." Colonel Sean McClay, interview with the author, Kabul, November 10, 2016.

65. The dining facility was staffed by a variety of Africans and South Asians, often hoping to immigrate to the United States. For an excellent story on this topic, see Sarah Stillman, "The Invisible

Army," *The New Yorker*, June 6, 2011, https://www.newyorker
.com/magazine/2011/06/06/the-invisible-army.

66. *Snaps to* from, for example: banter, video game playing, Internet
video watching, fishing-magazine reading, the tossing of empty
water bottles over a wall into a trash bin.

67. In my interviews with U.S. military, this no-strike list comes up
often, with a kind of pride. Hospitals, mosques, orphanages, and so
on, all are meant to be on it. I am shown maps covered in red
no-strike dots. There are about twenty-eight thousand buildings on
the list in Afghanistan, according to one of the targeteers.

68. How high depends on an administration's delegation policy.

69. Factual but particularly manipulative end of a paragraph.

70. When packages are complicated by, say, the arrival of a woman
on-screen, the men are obviously and profanely frustrated. Often
they have invested days, even weeks, soaking a compound, building a packet.

71. Michael J. Sandel, *Justice: What's the Right Thing to Do?* (New
York: Farrar, Straus and Giroux, 2010).

72. Lieutenant Colonel Mark Goodwin-Hudson, interview with the author, Kabul, November 2016.

73. At guys like Asadullah, maybe, or the guy in his platoon who killed
those Marine special operatives, or someone like Mujahed, conducting recon by fire. I wanted to visit the OP that digger-shooter
fired on; the Marines took me elsewhere—to OP Shamalan.

74. Olympic gold medalist Jamaican sprinter. Also, regarding race:
only one black person in this room, just then.

75. But the slant is not always so clear. In the week I'm present, if it
changes to reflect a woman or a child present, Captain John and his
team have to start soaking all over again, to establish a local pattern of life minus any civilians. This happened once that week,
because a drone-feed analyst located elsewhere claimed that someone in a targeted compound was carrying water:

"So there's been a lot of carrying back and forth of what appears to be water," the night-shift captain, Kirk, explained to me. "There will also be people pulling kettles and things of that nature, which is typically, within this culture, a female job to do—household chores, carrying, cooking, using the water or possible bathing. So when someone is carrying a kettle it's likely that that's a female. In this situation . . . it's not likely that that is. However, we can't prove specifically that it's not a female doing these, and that really throws a wrench into our ability to attack." Captain Kirk Landon, interview with the author, Helmand, December 10, 2016.

76. "Oh, back to Kill TV. So the Zangabad PTZ camera, it probably had more viewership than whatever the top show in the United States was at the time." General D. A. Sims, interview with the author, December 6, 2016.

77. I asked Captain John if he thought the right number of people were watching the feeds.

"I don't think so," he said.

"How? Should it be more, should it be less?"

"I think it should be less."

"How many less?"

"Really it's just being the chain. . . . But our videos are shared through a secret system where anybody could watch the feeds."

Captain John Fridlington, interview with the author, Helmand, December 7, 2016.

78. The swagger reminds me of a couple of Special Forces guys I stop, one day, outside the TOC. SF has its own TOC one building over, and two of the operators, bearded and wary, agree to have a tiny cigar with me in the mid-morning sun, provided our chat is off the record. They don't give anything away, but in recent years the Special Forces community has become porous enough that you may not be surprised to read they wage war under different rules and at higher tempo than the men to whom I am officially granted access.

"Special Operations command here," General D.A. tells me, "they're making these decisions much more than I am, right? So in my time here, just under thirty strikes in three months. NSOCC [Nato Special Operations Component Command], I don't know what their numbers are, but . . ." General D. A. Sims, interview with the author, December 6, 2016.

79. Though the embed had been cleared through CENTCOM, a general somewhere in Rob's parallel Air Force chain of command forbade/didn't provide permission. Kay said it was all the same chain, but Rob wouldn't risk it once a general said no. And so I do not have an interview with him, but can report that he appeared to be guiding the planes precisely toward their target and seemed well liked by his peers.

Aside from Special Forces and CIA, the only other person I request to interview who will not speak—or is not permitted to speak—is said to be the most knowledgeable intelligence contractor on-site, said to know the local tribal structures, said even to know some Dari and Pashto. I never even see him, though I request both official interview and off-the-record conversation.

80. For further poetic chatter between pilots and ground control, and stories of air war, see James Salter, *Burning the Days: Recollection* (New York: Random House, 1997); and Patrick Cockburn, *Kill Chain: Drones and the Rise of High-Tech Assassins* (New York: Henry Holt, 2015).

81. For more on lock-in, see Jaron Lanier, *You Are Not a Gadget: A Manifesto* (New York: Alfred A. Knopf, 2010); and Matthew Crawford, *The World Beyond Your Head: On Becoming an Individual in an Age of Distraction* (New York: Farrar, Straus and Giroux, 2015).

82. My opinion, based on the right to vote, flawed though it is, disenfranchised though a great many are. Are you, for example, in your wheelchair, beaten by the police, in the projects, really owning a

piece of all this? Are the subalterns (that's what some academics call you) *empowering* guys like Captain John?

83. Population figures are based on U.S. Census estimates.

84. He has the quiet intensity of a water buffalo.

85. Extended quotation for context, file under "Don't hate the player, hate the game": "You can still achieve effects on the enemy without civilian casualties. And you say, 'women and children,' I got four kids at home. If this was back in the U.S., I wouldn't want something to happen to them because someone just says 'Fuck it,' you know?"

86. For detail on this process, see General Counsel, "Joint Targeting Cycle and Collateral Damage Estimation Methodology," Joint Staff Targeting, Department of Defense, November 10, 2009. Via American Civil Liberties Union, https://www.aclu.org/files/dronefoia /dod/drone_dod_ACLU_DRONES_JOINT_STAFF_SLIDES _1-47.pdf.

87. Fort Sill is where the Apache chief and medicine man Geronimo is buried.

88. The whole process is full of acronyms, jargon, and legalese. The word *collateral* itself comes from the Latin *com*, meaning "together with," and *lateralis*, meaning "of the side." In common usage as a noun, it refers to anything provided as security for a loan, to be forfeited in the event of default. As an adjective, it means "next to" or "beside."

89. The menu he was using when I visited is currently classified, but it's similar to this unclassified version, made available by the American Civil Liberties Union and forwarded to me by a commander at HQ in Kabul.

90. Just as Facebook, in the beginning, categorized its users into one of five relationship statuses, so, too, does the collateral damage software prescribe a limited number of functionalities for any structure.

91. Recurring contradictions in the occupation at the dinner parties of the internationals, from memory, unattributed, to be considered for atmosphere:

     Afghan solutions to Afghan problems are best, but the Afghans run the zoo, and the zoo is fucked up!

     The Afghans' constitution mandates to have more women in its legislature than currently serve in the United States Congress!

92. The paths that brought journalists to that bear and amplified coverage of the zoo were twined with the emphasis of media on *clicks* and so on animal memes and stories.

93. All of Chief Ron's choices become variables in the equation of the collateral damage estimate, which eventually produces three numbers marked *day*, *night*, and *episodic*. So, for the zoo, *day* might be 50, *night* 0, and *episodic* (a holiday, say) 150. Each describes population per thousand square feet. Episodic events are unspecified but include, at command's discretion, "unique cultural practices and periodic events (i.e. religious holidays) that may influence the population density." General Counsel, "Joint Targeting Cycle and Collateral Damage Estimation Methodology," p. 37.

94. "So when we start talking about casualty count, that's classified, so I can't talk about that. . . . But yeah, when you get up to CDE-5 High is when you start estimating body counts and stuff like that. . . . And these are not the hard numbers, these are just giving you an example. But it's estimated that in a grocery store in the middle of the day, there's a safe assumption to be approximately thirty people. So striking near that with a particular mission is gonna affect it; it will estimate the body count being higher. Where opposed to at night a store is probably closed then it's expected that maybe one to two people." Sergeant Albert Carpenter, interview with the author, Helmand, December 7, 2016.

95. I have found no other study of the etymology of this word; if I am mistaken, I would welcome a correction, as about everything else,

in the spirit of collaboration rather than as the final word on any of these subjects.

96. See the opening pages of Evan Wright, *Generation Kill: Devil Dogs, Iceman, Captain America and the New Face of American War* (New York: G. P. Putnam's Sons, 2004).

97. "Would you ever want to be in a position where you'd be making the call?" I ask him.

   "No." Chief Ron is certain. "I like having the responsibility and authority, but not that much, to be honest with you." Chief Warrant Officer Ron Feasler, interview with the author, December 9, 2016.

98. Author observation, Mosul, March 2009.

99. The term *haj box* is derogatory slang for the retina scanner Americans used on Iraqis; it derives from the honorific *hajji*, meaning one who has made the pilgrimage to Mecca.

100. HUMINT is information you learn from people directly, as opposed to imagery intelligence—IMINT—or signals intelligence—SIGINT—like a hacked email account.

101. Specifically, she thinks Afghanistan needs a leader like Singapore's Lee Kuan Yew.

102. Her appeal to anticorporate solidarity and personal struggle rings, in the moment, both evasive and unconscious. Here on the page she cannot respond, but I look forward to further discussion if she, or any of the men in this TOC, are so inclined.

103. For background, see Georges Nzongola-Ntalaja, "Patrice Lumumba: The Most Important Assassination of the 20th Century," *The Guardian*, January 17, 2011, https://www.theguardian.com /global- development/poverty-matters/2011/jan/17/patrice -lumumba-50th-anniversary-assassination; for extensive background, see Tim Weiner, *Legacy of Ashes: The History of the CIA* (New York: Anchor, 2008).

104. "I was having a conversation with the general the other day," Callie tells me, cheerfully. "It's hard to see either side die, because at the

end of the day in Afghanistan, women are not allowed to work. And so essentially you have a guy on either side with two wives and six kids. What happens to that wife and those children? They become destitute. They're not allowed to work, they may have to sell themselves, and sell their children, and that's a bigger question for me and my morality is, in this society, when the men die, what happens to the other side of the population? I don't know what the right answer to that is. And then I hurt [the general's] feelings because he's like, 'You trying to make me feel bad?' And 'No,' I told him, 'I'm sitting in there with you. I'm right next to you when you make that decision. I'm right there.'

"And that's our moral dilemma, is, what point are we going over that line of becoming our enemy? Or being good? But when you're good and you don't take a stand on something that may be bad, what does the world come to? And that's essentially what World War Two was about."

And:

"History is written by the winners," Callie sums up, at one point. "I don't know if there's gonna be a winner in this one." Callie Lentz, interview with the author, Helmand, December 7, 2016.

105. Most of the wall is undamaged, the bunker, untouched, though we may imagine the wash of heat that blew over it. You prefer simplicity, and insist that tenured and highly paid thought leaders, merchant bankers who want only one boat, have no need of that second Hinckley—that these men will not take our argument under advisement unless presented starched like the Savile Row shirts acquired on your most recent European weekend. Perhaps, for pleasure, these ambassadors will read a book of history, or perhaps, like this new breed of president, they will not read at all.

106. The Kuchis—estimated population two to three million—are mostly Pashtun nomads living across Afghanistan and Pakistan.

107. General Westmoreland to the filmmaker Peter Davis: "The Oriental doesn't put the same high price on life as does the Westerner. Life

is plentiful, life is cheap in the Orient. As the philosophy of the Orient expresses it, life is not important." Via the essential Nick Turse, *Kill Anything That Moves: The Real American War in Vietnam* (New York: Metropolitan Books, 2013).

108. "Do you think," I ask the general, "that it's legitimate to kill Iraqi civilians to stop ISIS?"

"Yeah," he tells me. "I mean, again, if . . . I mean I hate to keep going back to the fact that it's probably situation-based, right?"

"It's situation-based," I agree, "but also, there is policy for a theater. So in this theater [Afghanistan] it's zero, in that theater [Iraq] it's greater than zero. My question really is, do you think that it's correct that it's greater than zero?"

"I do. I mean, I do. Again, the situations are different, right? And it would be very difficult in Mosul, having been there, too, to use munitions and not understand that you're probably gonna have some civilian casualties. . . . But the way we're fighting in Mosul, I've gotta believe, is different than the way the Syrians are fighting in Aleppo. And our view of civilian casualties in Mosul is much different, morally, ethically, and application-wise, than the way that Assad's forces are fighting in Aleppo."

By the time the general and I are having this conversation, we've elected an American president who speaks sympathetically of Bashar al-Assad, the Syrian dictator and war criminal.

"And do you think," I ask the general, "the institutions you represent will maintain that kind of strength, even if politically you become aligned with somebody like Assad?"

"Yeah, I do. I've got this faith in our country, right, that it is really a moral country. I mean the Russians bomb a convoy, and we're all up in arms about it. We have civilian casualties in Kunduz . . . and we're gonna investigate the shit out of it. . . . I don't know what the Russians did to the convoy that they hit, probably nothing, right? Hey, the world, they don't even think about it anymore. But they expect more of our country, and we expect more of our country."

109. Echoing Taylor Swift et al., "Shake It Off," *1989* (Big Machine, 2014).

110. Referencing directly Swift's purported antagonist Katy Perry et al., "Firework," *Teenage Dream* (Capitol, 2010).

111. As of the 2010 census.

112. "Growing up, you always sit down at some point in your life and you're like, 'Man, I'm gonna play soldier,' and you run around and you fake guns, and fake gun noises, stuff like that. And it really just came down to . . . I said to myself, 'I'll maybe join the service some-day.' And then high school came around, senior year, just goofing around senior year, and I didn't really have any . . . I wanted to go to college but, at the same time, I'll admit I didn't take my senior year very seriously, and that didn't help anything but . . . And then it came down to college, job, military. And I didn't have any money for col-lege. Didn't earn really any scholarships, none of that stuff, so noth-ing really to help me. Didn't really have a job either throughout high school. And then I said, 'I need to get away from here. This place is . . . all the jobs are going away,' stuff like that." Corporal Ryan Erdek, interview with the author, Helmand, December 10, 2016.

113. Separately, each man involved tells me he shares responsibility for the killings, but also that authority is carefully circumscribed and informed by rank and task. No one bears responsibility alone.

114. This practice was well reported by Matthew Cole, "The Crimes of SEAL Team 6," *The Intercept*, January 10, 2017, https://theinter cept.com/2017/01/10/the-crimes-of-seal-team-6/. He addresses the SEALs' response in Matthew Cole, "SEAL Team 6 Responds to *The Intercept*'s Investigation of Its War Crimes," *The Intercept*, January 18, 2017, https://theintercept.com/2017/01/18/seal -team-6-responds-to-the-intercepts-investigation-of-its-war -crimes/.

115. I never confirmed with the fiancée, or verified whether he had one.

116. From *U.S. Field Manual*, 1956, via the International Committee of the Red Cross, "Practice Relating to Rule 154: Obedience to Supe-

rior Orders," https://ihl-databases.icrc.org/customary-ihl/eng
/docs/v2_rul_rule154.

117. "Also above and beyond that we go and we help to ensure that the
soldiers' well-being and thought processes are protected, because
as a chaplain we are afforded one special right that, well, basically
nobody else in the United States have, is we have non-disclosure.
Anything that's told to me as a chaplain can never . . . I can't tell
anything. It's above classification. I cannot be ordered to break,
like a priest in confession, same concept. And ours is legally bind-
ing all the way to the Supreme Court." Chaplain Sidney Aaron,
interview with the author, Helmand, December 7, 2016.

118. Correct understanding of evolution is anathema to policies of co-
ordinated violence.

V. NUMBERS

12. The U.S. Civilian Casualty Mitigation Team

119. Samuel Oakford, "For First Time, Coalition Now Killing More
Civilians than Russia," Airwars, February 10, 2017, https://airwars
.org/news/for-the-first-time-the-coalition-is-now-killing-more
-civilians-than-russia/.

Up to this point I regularly told American soldiers, as a way of
reassuring them, that we were "better than our Russian brothers and
sisters," when it came to civilian casualties, "the best in history," let
alone compared to the Taliban and ISIS. After this, I stopped.

120. Political change came slowly, then all at once. As his administration took power it delegated authority for strikes, relaxing the rules
of engagement.

For early reporting on this, see Michael Gordon, "Trump Shifting Authority over Military Operations Back to Pentagon," *The
New York Times*, March 19, 2017, https://www.nytimes.com/2017

/03/19/us/trump-shifting-authority-over-military-operations
-back-to-pentagon.html?mcubz=0.

121. There were, however, some excellent posters; "When Does Marty McFly Arrive?" was the caption on one, referring to the *Back to the Future* films. The author of this poster had drawn the head of one of the trilogy's stars, Christopher Lloyd, in the character of Doc Brown, next to the text. As it happened that night I had dinner with Lloyd's cousin, the great American magazine editor Lewis Lapham, eighty-three years old at the time. When I asked when if ever it was acceptable to kill civilians to achieve your goals, he replied, "whenever the mission requires." As a child, he went on, he had shaken the hand of Admiral Chester Nimitz, who commanded the American Navy during World War II, and he himself had wanted to become a fighter pilot. He was color-blind, though, and received a 4F designation when he lost his toes to an amputation following a blood infection. "I personally couldn't do it," he said, of ordering the deaths of civilians to achieve goals. "But it's war, you can't be cute about it."

122. The black masks of anarchists often resemble those of Shia militiamen.

123. Email correspondence to the author, January 2017.

124. George Orwell, "Pacifism and the War," *Partisan Review*, August–September 1942, http://www.orwell.ru/library/articles/pacifism/english/e_patw. For discussion of the uses of this quote (and Orwell's revision of it), see "'Pacifism Is Objectively Pro-Fascist,'" *The Atlantic*, February 26, 2010, https://www.theatlantic.com/daily-dish/archive/2010/02/-pacifism-is-objectively-pro-fascist/189950/.

125. This concurrent with the protection of U.S. oil interests. See Steve Coll, "Oil and Erbil," *The New Yorker*, August 10, 2014, https://www.newyorker.com/news/daily-comment/oil-erbil.

126. That is, in every case that I am aware of. I use the definitive rhetoric in good faith here, but welcome any new information.

127. In addition to this scene and quotes—which reveal a self-interested bureaucracy made up of decent men and thereby provide justification for a cautious enlightenment humanism and mature attention to detail—don't forget:

> *Sometimes I go about in*
> *pity for myself,*
>   *and all the while,*
> *A great wind carries me*
> *across the sky.*
>   —*Ojibwa prayer,*
>   *as told to the author by Peter Matthiessen, 2005*

128. Members of the CCMT do not typically visit the sites of allegations; Sergeant Roger, for example, has never visited any of the sites, as of our interview.

129. Margaret Hartmann, "Trump Says U.S. Should Have Stolen Iraq's Oil, and 'Maybe We'll Have Another Chance,'" *New York*, January 22, 2017, http://nymag.com/daily/intelligencer/2017/01/trump-u-s-may-get-another-chance-to-take-iraqi-oil.html. See also "Trump's Talk of Keeping Iraq's Oil Sparking Concerns," Fox News, January 25, 2017, http://www.foxnews.com/us/2017/01/25/trump-talk-keeping-iraq-oil-sparking-concerns.html.

     "'To the victor belong the spoils,' Trump told members of the intelligence community, saying he first argued this case for 'economic reasons.' He said it made sense as a counterterrorism approach to defeating the IS group 'because that's where they made their money in the first place. . . . So we should have kept the oil,' he said. 'But, OK, maybe you'll have another chance.'"

130. For some theory on how, see, for example, Vincent Ferraro, "Dependency Theory: An Introduction," *The Development Economics Reader* (London: Routledge, 2008).

131. Some of this passage appeared, in different form, in the online edition of *n+1*.

132. Regarding Abdul Manaf's grace, I had taken to carrying a string of plastic *tasbih*, prayer beads, as good luck, and as an icebreaker. Afghans sometimes thought my affectation was amusing and would ask me about it, or tease me. After one meeting in Abdul's district office, an older journalist snapped at me about playing with the beads. It was disrespectful, he said, patronizing of the Afghans, he said. But Abdul approved of the beads.

133. Mirwais Adeel, "Helmand's Nawa District Chief Shot Dead by Taliban Militants," *Khaama Press*, May 18, 2015, http://www.khaama .com/helmands-nawa-district-shot-dead-by-taliban-militants-943; and Frank Biggio, "An Afghan Death: Haji Abdul Manaf Was My Brother," War on the Rocks, May 26, 2015, https://warontherocks .com/2015/05/an-afghan-death-haji-abdul-manaf-was-my-brother/.

134. The Marines have since returned to Helmand in greater numbers. See, for example, Mujib Mashal, "Marines Return to Helmand Province for a Job They Thought Was Done," *The New York Times*, April 29, 2017, https://www.nytimes.com/2017/04/29/world/asia /marines-return-to-helmand-province-for-a-job-they-thought-was -done.html?mcubz=0.

135. This has been reported for nearly a decade; for example, David Ariosto, "U.S. Trucking Contracts Funded Taliban, Source Says," *CNN World*, June 26, 2011, http://www.cnn.com/2011/WORLD /asiapcf/07/25/afghanistan.us.funds.taliban/index.html; Dexter Filkins, "U.S. Said to Fund Afghan Warlords to Protect Convoys," *The New York Times*, June 21, 2010, http://www.nytimes.com/2010 /06/22/world/asia/22contractors.html?mcubz=0; Sune Engel Rasmussen, "Afghanistan Funds Abusive Militias as US Military 'Ignores' Situation, Officials Say," *The Guardian*, December 26, 2016, https://www.theguardian.com/world/2016/dec/26/afghanistan-us -military-militia-funding-human-rights.

136. Imagine a class of students, "double-hatted" as graders for their own exam papers. Whatever the rigor of the process, there's a conflict of interest, an internal contradiction. Such a process is not so

useful to civilians at risk. Systems of review favor their founders, and achieve justice only by dispersing power. This is the essence of American government, the reason for separation of the legislative, executive, and judicial branches. The targeteers should not be expected to police themselves.

In my interview with Sergeant Roger (Staff Sergeant Rogelio Hernandez, November 17, 2016), I don't say all this. Nor do I point out that forensic work and local interviews are forgone in favor of force protection and money spent elsewhere—for example, on missiles.

137. The one I remember best was a profane, vocally homophobic second lieutenant named Max, who happened to be paired with a gay Yazidi interpreter. I thought Max was going to get us killed, driving around Mosul late at night, spoiling for a fight.

138. The bombing of the MSF hospital in Kunduz, for example. See BBC Staff, "Kunduz Hospital Bombing: 16 US Forces 'Disciplined,'" BBC News, April 28, 2016, http://www.bbc.com/news/world-us-canada-36164595.

13. Sar Baghni and the Deadliest Civilian Casualty Incident to Date

139. International Security Assistance Force, "ISAF's Task Force Reports on Alleged Casualties," press release #2007-585, ISAF Public Affairs Office, August 4, 2007, http://www.nato.int/isaf/docu/press releases/2007/08-august/pr070804-585.html.

140. I never get to this village myself. Now, in the writing, I wonder if perhaps I should have tried harder to do so, spent more money, insisted to my colleagues, taken the risk. I didn't, in favor of this less expensive, less hazardous path toward what I hope is nearly the same result. But in low moments I am troubled by what more could have been done.

141. UN officials, background interviews, April 2016.

142. Damien McElroy, "Afghan Governor Turned 3,000 Men over to Taliban," *The Telegraph*, November 20, 2009, http://www.telegraph.co.uk/news/worldnews/asia/afghanistan/6615329/Afghan-governor-turned-3000-men-over-to-Taliban.html.

143. Abdullah Safi al-Nur. I would meet him again, years later, on a shabby pleasure boat ride at the intersection of the White and Blue Niles, in the company of a number of Rizegat elders and Khartoum elites. He was attending, briefly, a conference about the future of nomadism.

144. Representatives Jan Schakowsky of Illinois, Mark Sanford of South Carolina, Bennie Thompson of Mississippi, and Marcia Fudge of Ohio.

145. The Corinthia Hotel, Khartoum.

146. "If that this simple syllogism will serve, so. If it will not, what remedy? As there is no true cuckold but calamity, so beauty's a flower. The lady bade take away the fool. Therefore, I say again, take her away." William Shakespeare, *Twelfth Night, or What You Will*, act 1, scene 5 (New York: W. W. Norton, 2015).

147. "Americans don't have the right," Akunzhada insists, "to kill even one innocent civilian." Sher Mohammed Akunzhada, interview with the author, Kabul, October 28, 2016.

148. Giving Akunzhada's assistant an envelope of cash to pass on to the men making the list feels a lot like paying for information and was not good practice—a mistake, in fact, as I am reminded at the time by conscientious journalist friends, particularly Ali Gharib and Anand Gopal.

149. And others, though you cannot tell from the list, are related. Mohammad Wali, Mohammad Lal, and that first Gul Zaman, for example, are brothers, sons of a man named Khawaas. The second Gul Zaman's father was Noor Rang.

150. Interviews with the author, Kabul, October–November 2016; phone interviews with the author, Helmand, October–November

2016. The key witness, fearing retribution, does not wish to be identified.

151. Identified as "mosque" in classified U.S. report.

152. In *A History of Bombing*, the Swedish historian Sven Lundqvist breaks the problem down like this:

"The laws of war have always answered two questions: When may one wage war? What is permissible in war? And international law has always given two completely different answers to these questions, depending on who the enemy is. The laws of war protect enemies of the same race, class, and culture. The laws of war leave the foreign and the alien without protection. When is one allowed to wage war against savages and barbarians? Answer: always. What is permissible in wars against savages and barbarians? Answer: anything." Sven Lundqvist, *A History of Bombing* (New York: New Press, 2000).

153. "Afghans 'Wounded in Airstrike,'" BBC News, August 3, 2007, http://news.bbc.co.uk/2/hi/south_asia/6930292.stm; Abdul Waheed Wafa and Taimoor Shah, "U.S. Airstrike on 2 Taliban Commanders in South Wounds at Least 18 Civilians, Afghans Say," *The New York Times*, August 4, 2007, http://www.nytimes.com/2007 /08/04/world/asia/04afghan.html; "Up to 300 Afghan Civilians Wounded in NATO Air Strike: Report," CBC News, August 3, 2007, http://www.cbc.ca/news/world/up-to-300-afghan-civilians -wounded-in-nato-air-strike-report-1.648756.

154. "On 2 August 2007, international military forces carried out an air attack in the area of Baghni in Baghran District of Helmand province. The strike resulted in numerous casualties, though so far it has proven extremely difficult to verify how many of these civilians were in fact [*sic*]. Most of the available evidence supports that the strike targeted a large gathering of Taliban, many of whom had traveled in from surrounding districts and are thus likely to have been armed. This suggests that [a] substantial majority of the up to

200 people reported killed were in fact combatants and as such a legitimate target of attack."

UNAMA Human Rights Unit, *Civilian Casualties During 2007*, United Nations Assistance Mission to Afghanistan, https://unama.unmissions.org/sites/default/files/poc-civilian-casualties-report-2007.pdf.

155. At the same time, we should remember the power of the Taliban disinformation campaign, and their interest in a higher civilian casualty count, and their controlling influence in the province.

156. UN official, Skype interview with the author, April 24, 2016.

157. IWPR Trainees, "Helmand, Precision Strike or Reckless Bombing?" Institute for War and Peace Reporting, August 9, 2007, https://iwpr.net/global-voices/helmand-precision-strike-or-reckless-bombing.

158. Here and in the documents below, Haji Salim Din's name has been changed.

159. There is, I am told, an American assessment of the precise number killed, but I have been unable to obtain this final document.

160. I am not reproducing images of the classified documents here. The source is concerned that any reproduction might allow a trace of the documents to their origin, and this concern is legitimate; see, for example, the case of whistleblower Reality Winner; Charlie Savage et al., "Reality Winner, N.S.A. Contractor Accused of Leak, Was Undone by Trail of Clues," *The New York Times*, June 6, 2017, https://www.nytimes.com/2017/06/06/us/politics/reality-leigh-winner-leak-nsa.html. In this light, rather than reproduce the documents, I have retyped the relevant portions of them here in full—with the exception of certain names whose publication, in my opinion, could jeopardize the safety or freedom of concerned parties.

DOCUMENT A

SECRET//REL TO USA, ISAF, NATO

STABILITY OPERATIONS INFORMATION CENTER

VICTORIAM PER SCIENTIAM

RCSW

Overall Classification: SECRET//REL TO USA, ISAF, NATO

SOIC Report on the 2 August 2007 Baghran (BGN) Air Strike

Date: 20110109

DECL ON: 20360109

UNCLASSIFIED//FOUO: Background on the Baghran Elder who brought SOIC the details of the air strike: Haji Salim Din (HSD) is an Alizai-Hassanzai from Baghran. He is thought to be a large landowner in the area. He was chosen by the elders in his district to be a candidate for the 2005 Helmand Provincial Council (HPC), which he won. He chose not to run in the 2009 HPC elections due to security concerns for his family in Baghran. He has worked with the coalition before in coordinating high-level meetings with Baghran elders and is happy to do so in the future. He currently lives in Lashkar Gah [LKG] and has met with the SOIC on three occasions.

UNCLASSIFIED//FOUO: Details of the Air Strike: On Thursday 2 August 2007 in Sar Baghni village (41R PR887310) at the Abraham Shah Baba Shrine the TB paraded two local nationals out to be hanged in front of hundreds of Afghans who had gathered for a picnic. A local elder, Bashir Khan, implored the Taliban not to hang these "spies" at the shrine. HSD claims that the people know not to kill snakes or cut down trees near the shrine because the snakes won't bite and the trees are sacred. Adding emphasis to his plea, Bashir Khan brought his holy Koran. HSD states that the airstrike occurred while the elders were negotiating with the TB. According to HSD, there were about 500 people killed and 250 injured in the strike. He stated that three tractors (flatbed trucks) full of body parts were removed from the area.

UNCLASSIFIED//FOUO: Claims Settlement: HSD claims he gave the list of families to Rais Baghrani to take to Kabul but does not know what happened afterward. He says he did not give the list to the British or any other ISAF forces. He did present the list to the Helmand Provincial Council, of which he was a member, who then placed their seal of acknowledgement and legitimacy upon it. To this day, HSD claims no one affected by the strike has received compensation or an apology. According to HSD, the former Afghan Interior Minister, Esmarai Bashari, claimed that only Taliban were killed in the airstrike.

HSD claims that Helmand Provincial Governor Mangal knows about his concerns and has ignored him. HSD asked that the people affected receive some support and to inquire if any monies were paid to officials that should have gone to the victims.

SECRET//REL TO USA, ISAF, NATO, GIROA: Implications: According to HSD, the survivors were more upset with the Taliban for bringing alleged spies to the shrine than they were with ISAF for conducting the strike. The widows and orphans are a major concern for influential Baghran elders such as HSD. Failure to satisfactorily resolve this issue will make any potential peace settlement in north Helmand difficult.

SECRET//REL TO USA, ISAF, NATO: According to ——, the Department of State local national cultural advisor in Lashkar Gah, President Karzai's government did pay a claims settlement to Senator (and former Helmand Governor) Sher Muhammad Akhundada [sic] (SMA) in the sum of 36 million Afs ($836,722). This amount can possibly be confirmed by IJC in Kabul. HSD, the man who brought SOIC the airstrike documentation, probably knows that SMA was paid the settlement claim although he claimed ignorance at our meeting. SOIC suspects that HSD wants ISAF to uncover the truth for themselves and somehow get the claim re-started or demand that SMA hand over the money he received back in 2007. In any case the effected [sic] families most likely never received compensation. From all local accounts the casualties suffered in this one airstrike were enormous and left a lasting scar. Therefore, any outreach to Baghran elders prior to operations or a political settlement should involve resolving this issue.

DOCUMENT B

SECRET//REL TO USA, ISAF, NATO
FRIC/20110115
15 Jan 11
NATO SCR
COM RC(SW)
HQ ISAF DCOS (Ops)
HQ ISAF DCOS (Intel)
Copy to:
HG IJC DCOS (Ops)
HQ ISAF SOF COMD
CFSOCC-A CDR
TF5-35
UK-OISG for DIS ——

NORTH HELMAND: ENGAGING THE ALIZAI SENIOR ELDERS

Reference:

A. FRIC-SCIF/s0101228 dated 28 Dec 10. F-RIC Engagement EXSUM—
Helmand Provincial Governor Gulab Mangal.

B. CJIOC-A ——— dated 10 Jan 10. Opportunities and Risks in Sangin
(US Read Book).

C. UK DIS Report dated 14 Dec 10. North Helmand Political Engagements.

D. FRIC-SCIF/20101223 dated 23 Dec 10. F-RIC Engagement EXSUM—
Rais Baghrani

ISSUE

1. I am seeking your concurrence for supporting an "Alizai Elders Deep Dive"
for COM ISAF (date tbd), and offer a number of engagement issues to be
developed for this deep dive.

DEEP DIVE

2. The RC(SW) operation to support the Alikozai-Sangin Agreement and along
rte 611 to the Kajaki Dam will cross into Alizai Tribal area. On Dec 26 (Ref A)
PG Mangal requested Dir FRIC support in engaging Alizai Senior Elders in order
to set the conditions for provincial level negotiations with the Helmand-based
Alizai Tribal Elders, leading to an outcome that reduces Alizai tribal support to
the INS. . . .

a. **Aim.** The aim of the deep dive will be to cross-level the HQ ISAF, HQ IJC, and
HQ RC(SW) understanding of the situation, and to seek COM ISAF direction
and guidance on the way forward.

b. **Methodology.** The CJIOC-A is requested to set the scene presenting on
Ref B (15 minutes). UK DIS is requested to brief on Ref C. DIR FRIC will outline
the engagement strategy concluding with recommendations for the COM ISAF
direction and guidance.

c. **Coordination.** The FRIC point of contact ———, will ensure that all briefs
are synchronized with HQ RC(SW).

ISSUES

3. There are number of policy issues requiring Command Group agreement
with the engagement of Alizai Senior Elders:

a. Alizai Baghran Elders—see Enclosure 1. In Ref D, Rais Baghrani raised this civcas event. On Thu 02 Aug 07 an air strike killed civilians in front a mosque [*sic*]. It would appear that the eventual claim settlement (Approx USD800K) was paid to Sher Mohammed Akundzada (SMA) and did not subsequently find its way to the effected [*sic*] families. Any outreach to the Alizai Baghran Elders need to resolve this issue first. **IDAF DCOS (Ops) is requested to research this incident and the payment of the claim.** FRIC proposes that the settlement of USD800k is repaid in a PG Mangak shura in LFK with Rais Baghrani and the Alizai Baghran Elders in order to open the way for the negotiation of a local agreement (akin to Sangin). . . .

14. Official Spokesmen

161. "When there are casualties," he says, "we do not conceal them from the Afghan people. Whenever there are casualties we inform the press and media and we also tell them the causes." Lieutenant General Dawlat Waziri, interview with the author, Kabul, October 25, 2016.

162. Why do some lie, or forsake truth? We know and we don't. Why Galileo sacrificed so much, while Descartes, safe in Holland, noted his peer's censure by Inquisitors, renounced heliocentricity, and wrote that "to live well, you must live unseen."

163. According to the United Nations Assistance Mission for Iraq [UNAMI]:

"In analyzing civilian casualties, UNAMI utilizes as wide a range of sources and types of information as possible, which are analyzed for reliability and credibility. Attempts are made to cross-check and verify such information from other sources before conclusions are drawn and published. Sources include, for example, testimony of victims, victims' relatives, witnesses, and evidence provided from health personnel, community elders, religious and civil leaders, local, governorate and central Government departments and officials, UN and other International Organizations, the United Nations Department of Safety and Security (UNDSS) and UNAMI Security Section (SSI), media reports, members of the international community, civil society, and NGOs. Where security does not permit direct access to the location of an incident, UNAMI relies on a range of techniques to gain information through reliable networks.

"Every effort is made to ensure that data contained in UNAMI reports is as comprehensive as possible; however, the data presented is not exhaustive. Where UNAMI is not satisfied with the evidence concerning a particular incident it will not be reported. In some instances, investigations may take several weeks before conclusions can be made. This also means that conclusions concerning particular incidents or alleged violations may be adjusted as more information comes to hand and is analyzed. However, if information is equivocal, then conclusions will not be drawn until more satisfactory evidence is obtained, or the case will be closed without conclusion and it will not be included in statistical reporting or analysis. As information is updated, and conclusions and statistics are modified, this can result in slight differences in reporting of the same incident or variations in statistics reported by UNAMI over time.

"In some incidents where civilian casualties are alleged, the status of the reported victim(s) as civilian is disputed or is equivocal. In such cases UNAMI is guided by all the information to hand, as well as the applicable standards of international humanitarian and human rights law in determining whether the victim should be classified as a civilian, as a person actively participating in hostilities, or as status unknown.

"In light of the above-noted limitations in methodology, UNAMI does not claim that the information it provides is complete, and it may well be that UNAMI is under-reporting the extent, nature or seriousness of the effect of armed violence and acts of terrorism on the civilian population."

UNAMI Human Rights Office, Civilian Casualties 2008–2012, United Nations Assistance Mission to Iraq, 2012, http://www.uniraq.com/images/documents/UNAMI_HRO_%20CIVCAS%202008-2012.pdf.

164. And old men drank tea on Mutanabbi Street, and traffic cops cursed their fate, and ISIS tried to send car bombs through the checkpoints to the markets.

165. Francesco Motta, director of the Human Rights Office for the United Nations Assistance Mission for Iraq.

166. Ali Omran, interview with the author, Baghdad, May 2016.

167. But who was I to know what he thought, from those moments in his office? I may be concerned with the tension between truth and power, but that is probably not a frame he'd use. As James Baldwin noted: The "line which separates a witness from an actor is a very thin line indeed; nevertheless, the line is real." James Baldwin in *I Am Not Your Negro,* ed. Raoul Peck (New York: Vintage International, 2017), p. 30.

168. The process by which bodies are collected in the morgue is fraught. The morgue is not simply the morgue, it is also a hospital, ghoulishly named the Institute for the Study of Forensic Medicine, and on passing the various checkpoints required one is confronted with a pair of waiting rooms. One is for the living, who come to visit doctors, but the other, smaller, room, located in a trailer, is for those seeking the dead. In the institute, as elsewhere in the public health system, economic crisis has resulted in the introduction of user fees to raise revenue, but it remains free to sit in that trailer and watch the large television upon which flash slides of unidentified corpses, and in front of which sits an old woman, blinking at one image after another of the murdered dead, in hopes of seeing her own.

15. Record Keeping in the Emergency Room of the Baghdad Teaching Hospital

169. The Baghdad Teaching Hospital has operated continuously through other treacherous periods. Since opening its doors in the early

1970s, it has seen as much war as peace. Wathiq al-Jabiri, the hospital's media director—and informal historian—recalls that on April 9, 2003, when the famous statue of Saddam Hussein came down in Firdos Square, he was one of only five staff in the whole facility. And in his opinion, it was a relatively easy day. But for all the bad days, Jabiri speaks with affection for the hospital. In an office down the hall from the ER, he recounted the occasions when patients had been moved to the facility's bunker; the mortars that had landed on the grounds; the months when staff refused to wear lab coats, in order to avoid targeting by kidnappers. In the larger context, he said—his office was about the size of an upright piano, and thick with cigarette smoke—the hospital was doing fine. Wathiq al-Jabiri, interview with the author, Baghdad, February 28, 2016.

170. Dialogue in this scene is taken mostly from Rafid al-Waly, interview with the author, Baghdad, February 29, 2016. And much of this chapter appeared, in slightly different form, in *The London Review of Books.*

171. Abdul Karim Khamees, First Division, Third Brigade, of the Iraqi army.

172. In 2010, the Iraqi parliament approved a draft law addressing this problem, increasing sentences for anyone convicted of threatening or attacking a doctor. It didn't seem to help. More than two thousand Iraqi doctors were killed between 2003 and 2014. One consequence of this violence is a continuing medical exodus. Fewer than thirty cardiac surgeons, for example, remain in the country of 37 million, according to Dr. Hillal Bahjet al-Saffar, a bespectacled professor of cardiology at Baghdad University's College of Medicine. Hillal al-Saffar, interview with the author, Baghdad, February 2016.

173. Shrapnel had entered between his ribs, and some is stuck.

174. "This country, we're always paying blood tax. I entered the army with black hair. I am seventy, should I be working [gestures down at his rough and dusty trousers]? We have the hopes of cats: eat,

shit, and sleep. He was at Abu Ghraib—I called him at the morning and he was fine." Karim Jawal Abbas, interview with the author, Baghdad, February 29, 2016.

175. Their uniforms are irregular but many wear the same patch, translating roughly to the Hassan Brigades, likely after Shia Islam's second Imam, one of the Prophet Muhammad's grandsons.

176. Bad record keeping is not confined to countries at war, and in some ways the Baghdad Teaching Hospital is like any hospital. Fluorescent lights, the smell of antiseptic, nervous relatives lingering. But just outside the ER doors, it was normal to hear the screams of women—high-pitched, shrieking—emanating from a nearby lot, where corpses were refrigerated as they awaited shipment to their graves. That was where the bereaved gathered, and wailed. Most people, coming and going, did not even turn their heads.

   I tried to count, but couldn't get a solid number because of the commotion, and lacked the authority to demand numbers and attention even in the quiet aftermath of the awful rush. No doubt many present had a personal count, very specific, not an estimate, refreshed by the stickiness and metallic smell. Blood all looks the same. As janitors mopped it into floor drains, it resembled the blood that dripped out beneath a detainee's head bandage, applied by an American First Cavalry medic (Specialist Adam Gade) in West Mosul, years before. He was in the care of local police, one of whom was cutting the air with a length of black polyethylene pipe even while the medic treated this detainee.

177. Though heart transplants are not performed in Iraq, cardiac care is highly advanced. Eight floors above the ER, another middle-aged female patient had, just that afternoon, been discharged after pacemaker implantation. The surgeon, Dr. Ghassan Mohammed Mahmoud—forty, with the beginnings of a paunch—had implanted the pacemaker's battery under her left clavicle and wired its tiny leads into her right atrium, via her subclavian vein. This

vein is about as wide as a pinky. Ghassan performed such operations regularly—he had performed three similar operations that very day—though he expected to stop soon. Given the government's new budget, he said, he would run out of stents and pacemakers in three months. The office of the health minister, Dr. Adeelah Humood, did not return my calls for comment, and figures are not readily available, but a senior ministry official said the budget had been cut by approximately a quarter for 2016. Like Ghassan, the official predicted a major reduction of equipment, drugs, salaries, personnel, and then "system failure. Like the 1990s, during the embargo, but it will be worse."

This is particularly troubling in the context of new user fees. There is growing consensus among public health experts internationally that user fees increase inequity and decrease utilization in developing countries. As fees rise, their studies tell us, the sick will be less likely to seek out medical care at all, or will seek it out later in the course of illness, when it may be too late for effective treatment. Many believe this leads to increased mortality. With new fees, the Iraqi government is pursuing a strategy that has been receding in healthcare development since the late 1980s.

178. Ninety-five percent is not ideal in academic statistical terms, but not bad given the obstacles.

179. Gilbert Burnham et al., "Mortality After the 2003 Invasion of Iraq: A Cross-Sectional Cluster Sample Survey," *The Lancet* 368, no. 9545 (October 21, 2006), http://www.thelancet.com/journals/lancet/article/PIIS0140-6736%2806%2969491-9/abstract.

The actual *Lancet* research is executed by Iraqi physicians. Another statistically significant investigation, though not peer reviewed, and focusing exclusively on Mosul, is Anand Gopal and Azmat Khan, "The Uncounted," *The New York Times Magazine*, November 16, 2017, https://www.nytimes.com/interactive/2017/11/16/magazine/uncounted-civilian-casualties-iraq-airstrikes.html.

180. David Brown, "Study Claims Iraq's 'Excess' Death Toll Has Reached 655,000," *The Washington Post*, October 11, 2006, http://www.washingtonpost.com/wp-dyn/content/article/2006/10/10/AR2006101001442_2.html.

181. "Politics," Rudolf Virchow wrote, "is nothing else but medicine on a large scale." Virchow was a German pathologist, writer, politician, and early advocate for the discipline of public health. Via J. P. Mackenbach, "Politics Is Nothing but Medicine at a Larger Scale: Reflections on Public Health's Biggest Idea," *Journal of Epidemiology and Community Health* 63, no. 3 (March 2009), https://www.ncbi.nlm.nih.gov/pubmed/19052033.

182. Which remain solid, present, often eager to be counted. The day after that Sadr City bombing one man, his feet and abdomen slit by shrapnel, is determined to sit up in bed in order to explain that during the "second explosion, a body flew and hit me, it only had a head and body, a guy I know came on a bike and took me to the hospital." He wants to talk about that other body. A friend at his bedside puts a hand on his shoulder and pushes him, gently, back down.

183. Max Bearak, "NATO and Government Forces Are Increasingly Responsible for Afghan Civilian Deaths," *The Washington Post*, November 3, 2016, https://www.washingtonpost.com/news/world views/wp/2016/11/03/nato-and-government-forces-are -increasingly-responsible-for-afghan-civilian-deaths/?utm_term =.d88d31 d06069.

16. Definition of the Non-Combatant Casualty Cutoff Value

184. Zabiullah Mujahid, phone interviews and correspondence with the author, October 2016.

185. "[The Taliban Civilian Casualties Avoidance Commission]," Zabiullah writes, "have a lot authority, and their job is to investigate the civilian casualties and inform the leadership. If there is a mistake

from Mujahedin side, they even ask for the court to reach out the family of the people killed in the attacks—and the Mujahedin should go to their homes for apologies."

186. Rod Nordland, "One Voice or Many for the Taliban, but Pegged to a Single Name," *The New York Times*, June 14, 2011, http://www .nytimes.com/2011/06/15/world/asia/15zabiullah.html.

187. See, for example, the reporting from Kate Clark, "Kafka in Cuba: The Afghan Experience in Guantánamo," Afghanistan Analysts Network, November 2016, https://www.afghanistan-analysts.org /wp-content/uploads/2016/11/20161101-Kafka-final-SV.pdf.

188. Committee to Protect Journalists, "32 Journalists Killed in Af-ghanistan/Motive Confirmed," *Committee to Protect Journalists Statistical Analysis*, 2017, https://cpj.org/killed/asia/afghanistan/.

189. "Do you think that people understand . . . ?"

"Which people?"

"Say . . . the American press?"

"No."

"Okay. So . . . What don't people get?"

Colonel Nicholas Lancaster, interview with the author, Kabul, November 16, 2016.

190. He added: "We just had a bombing at Bagram, and we reported right way that there were four U.S. killed, and the Taliban spokes-man reported that they attacked a training ground with hundreds of military officers and they had killed forty-four and wounded . . . or I think wounded twenty-eight and killed forty-four. Ludicrous. And yet you can read in *The Washington Post* or *The New York Times*, 'Taliban Spokesman reports that they control more of Af-ghanistan than anybody else.' I think it is laziness and lack of qual-ity control.'" Colonel Nicholas Lancaster, interview with the author, Kabul, November 16, 2016.

191. This damning and melancholy problem has been well docu-mented in accounts of our recent wars, as for example in Rajiv

Chandrasekaran, *Imperial Life in the Emerald City: Inside Iraq's Green Zone* (New York: Vintage, 2007).

192. Which five children would you choose?

193. See Ali Watkins, "The Numbers Game," BuzzFeed, February 28, 2016, https://www.buzzfeed.com/alimwatkins/syria-civilian-casualties -policy?utm_term=.gnnm0w4gb#.okx8arxG9.

194. "The fact is that many of these incidents are foreseeable, often foreseen, and the probability of death is sometimes calculated using computerized algorithms. The incidence of civilian deaths fluctuates depending on changes in rules of engagement or choice of weapons; it can be ratcheted up or down." Neta Crawford, *Accountability for Killing: Moral Responsibility for Collateral Damage in America's Post-9/11 Wars* (Oxford: Oxford University Press, 2013).

    For another useful work, particularly on perception of the phenomenon during earlier wars, see John Tirman, *The Deaths of Others: The Fate of Civilians in America's Wars* (Oxford: Oxford University Press, 2011).

195. Author email correspondence with Anand Gopal and Azmat Khan, October 25, 2017.

196. I felt rage at ISIS and the desire to bomb them to dust acutely on several occasions. One was the death of David Haines. I had met him on a plane from Kabul to Lashkar Gah when he was working for Mercy Corps. Within moments he had offered me a car, a place to stay, any help I might need in that unfamiliar place. When an Islamic State fighter eventually beheaded him and posted the video, it was consistent with their genocidal insanity and I thought, yes, go punish these evil men, even at great cost.

197. Iraqi official, interview with the author, Washington, D.C., June 2016.

VI. SOLATIA

18. Dirt Worship

198. Thomas Nagel, "War and Massacre," *Philosophy and Public Affairs* 1, no. 2 (Winter 1972), http://web.cs.ucdavis.edu/~rogaway /classes/188/spring06/papers/nagle_war.html.

19. Provision of Tents and Staples to the Bereaved

199. "Drones," *Time*, November 6, 2012, http://nation.time.com/2012 /11/06/12548710-60/.

200. "[We'd] talk about the difficult situation generally," Inizi recalls, "and all these calamities that God sent to us." Inizi Taha, interview with the author, Baghdad, May 19, 2006.

201. From fiscal years 2003 to 2006, the DOD has reported about $1.9 million in solatia payments and more than $29 million in condolence payments. U.S. Government Accountability Office, *The Department of Defense's Use of Solatia and Condolence Payments in Iraq and Afghanistan*, USGAO, Washington, D.C., May 2007.

202. Starting in 2005, an undersecretary of defense allowed that the program could be used for "condolence payments to individual civilians for death, injury, or property damage resulting from U.S., coalition, or supporting military operations." Ibid.

203. "CIVIC Amends Information Paper," Center for Civilians in Conflict, Washington, D.C., https://civiliansinconflict.org/. This paper is no longer available online but was sent to the author in email correspondence, April 24, 2016.

For background on solatia payments and CIVIC's arguments, with links, see Sahr Muhammedally, "Civilian War Victims Receive Recognition in US Law," *Just Security*, April 3, 2014, https:// www.justsecurity.org/8882/. See also Cora Currier, "Our Condo-

lences," *The Intercept*, February 27, 2015, https://theintercept.com
/2015/02/27/payments-civilians-afghanistan/.

204. Also, sometimes, a self-replicating structure of the industrial aid
complex.

205. CJTF-Operation Inherent Resolve Public Affairs Press Desk, email
correspondence, June 7, 2016.

206. Ali Musa, Media Office, governor of Saladin province, interview
with the author, Tikrit, May 21, 2016.

207. For a whole other set of reasons around the consolidation of Shia
power and demography in Baghdad, the Iraqi police won't let Inizi
come and go from the camp.

20. Notes on Security

208. Jean-Marc Mojon, Agence France Presse, "Iraqi Artist Imagines
Life in a Bomb Suit," *Al-Monitor*, February 22, 2016, http://www
.al-monitor.com/pulse/sites/almonitor/contents/afp/2016/02/iraq
-conflict-art.html; "Baghdad Artist Makes Statement in Bomb Disposal Suit," *Rudaw*, February 22, 2016, http://rudaw.net/english
/culture/22022016. For this piece, and much else, I am grateful to
the inimitable Jean-Marc Mojon.

209. The title is credible on account of circumstance, observation, reports from colleagues.

210. Greg Jaffe and Loveday Morris, "A Desperate Woman's Email from
Iraq Reveals the High Toll of Obama's Low-Cost Wars," *The Washington Post*, June 9, 2016, https://www.washingtonpost.com/politics
/a-desperate-womans-email-from-iraq-reveals-the-high-toll
-of-obamas-low-cost-wars/2016/06/09/3e572976-2725-11e6-b989
-4e5479715b54_story.html?tid=a_inl&utm_term=.75974147c219.

And on the reopening of the investigation: Greg Jaffe, "U.S.
Reopens Investigation into Bombing That Killed at Least 11 Iraqi
Civilians," *The Washington Post*, June 27, 2016, https://www.wash
ingtonpost.com/politics/us-reopens-investigation-into-bombing

-that-killed-at-least-11-iraqi-civilians/2016/06/27/0f8a5332-3c85
-11e6-80bc-d06711fd2125_story.html?utm_term=.8bc211ec17ad.

21. Compensation for Injuries Caused by U.S. Forces

211. Thirty-three vertebrae make up the spinal column, giving the hu-
     man body its form. The first seven—the cervical vertebrae—run
     from the skull to the neck's base and are the most delicate and
     susceptible to injury. They are also the most important. Nerves
     enclosed within control many of the involuntary processes by
     which we live. The phrenic nerve, for instance, originating be-
     tween C-3 and C-5, sends and receives information to and from
     the diaphragm, which in turn relaxes or contracts. On contraction,
     flexing, the diaphragm increases the volume of the chest, and this
     creates a vacuum. Air rushes into the lungs to fill this vacuum, just
     as it rushes into a vacuum created by an explosion. This is
     inhalation.

     The contraction of the diaphragm is also the cause of laughter,
     which is worth remembering along with the rest of the vertebrae:
     twelve thoracic, continuing to the bottom of the rib cage; five lum-
     bar, stacking down from there to the pelvis; five sacral; and finally
     four coccygeal. Those last nine are fused, and least exposed. When
     we notice them, it's often under great stress, or breakdown, bone
     rising out of skin, extraordinary circumstance in whose bereft in-
     stant even the most rigorous men and women are forced to give
     themselves over to evolution, instinct, whatever peace they've made
     in the world, or in the mind. Like many powerful structures, the
     spine is most durable where we notice it least.

212. Zabi is probably wrong about his chances for recovery. According
     to Dr. Tim Tan, a professor of emergency medicine at the Icahn
     School of Medicine at Mount Sinai, email correspondence with the
     author, December 4, 2016: "Growing toenails are completely unre-
     lated to nerve function. As for feeling cold, the part of the spinal

cord with nerves mediating temperature sensation (spinothalamic tract) is a little bit more anterior relative to the portion with nerves that control motor function (the corticospinal tract). It's possible that he only injured the back half of the spinal cord, sparing the part that senses hot/cold, which would explain his ability to feel cold—it's pretty rare, though, since bullets don't cause such precise damage."

213. The district chief confirmed the story. The two officers who signed the form for that money have not responded to my requests for comment, and various public affairs officers say they can find no record of the incident.

214. Obaidullah Zarifi, interview with the author, Charikar, October 26, 2016.

215. "You don't think the Taliban ever kill people by accident?"

"That's a very big generalization, right? But . . ."

"The way they . . . have you ever seen 'em fire a gun? Because they fire 'em like this. They're completely out of control."

"I don't know."

"I don't mean to laugh. It's, like, really not funny, but they . . ."

"I don't have an answer for that. I . . . Yeah."

"Okay. All right. I mean, these questions are not traps. I mean, really . . ."

"No."

"The way I learned anything about this is really just by . . . I mean, it sounds insane, but by shooting the breeze about all of this with people, it's like . . . Nobody has answers to these questions, really, you know?"

"Right."

Later in our interview, the colonel tells me that he is about halfway through *Black Hearts*, a well-known and highly regarded account of murders committed by Americans in Iraq, which highlights our indifference to populations of the countries we've invaded. When I ask him what he makes of the book, he tells me, "I think I probably wish I hadn't read it while I was here."

The colonel's incoherent statements stand in a long line of American self-deception. The current president regularly contradicts himself; so did his more stable predecessors. Johnson, for example, during the Vietnam War, insisted *in private* that American pilots never missed:

"Well, I don't think a single one of 'em, even when they were getting shot at. . . . I don't believe they missed their targets."

New Year's Eve, 1966. Johnson was on the phone with Arthur Goldberg, who had recently resigned his seat on the Supreme Court and taken up an ambassadorship to the United Nations, in his words, "to persuade Johnson that we were fighting the wrong war in the wrong place." On this particular call Goldberg struggled to get a word in. He and the president were discussing bombing runs over Hanoi. It was the height of Operation Rolling Thunder, the signature U.S. campaign of the wars in Indochina, and President Johnson was personally selecting targets. CIA estimates would later put the civilian death toll at 72,000.

"Mr. President," a reporter had asked at a press conference earlier that day, "what is your reaction to the reports by *The New York Times* from North Vietnam about the results of our bombing there?"

"I think the country knows," Johnson replied, "and I would like to repeat again—that it is the policy of this government to bomb only military targets."

Lieutenant Colonel Scott Heyler, interview with the author, Kabul, December 12, 2016. And see Lyndon Johnson, news conference, LBJ Ranch, December 31, 1966, http://www.presidency.ucsb.edu/ws/index.php?pid=28076; Arthur Goldberg, phone conversation with Lyndon Johnson, December 31, 1966, http://www.lbjlibrary.net/collections/on-this-day-in-history/december.html; "An Appraisal of the Bombing of North Vietnam (Through 15

March 1967)," folder 122, box 8, Central Intelligence Agency Collection, Vietnam Center and Archive, Texas Tech University, http://www.vietnam.ttu.edu/virtualarchive/items.php?item=04108122005.

216. Governor Mohammad Asim, interview with the author, October 23 and 26, 2016.

217. "MPs Trying to Shut Down Women's Shelter in Parwan," Tolo News, August 8, 2013, http://www.tolonews.com/afghanistan/mps-trying-shut-down-women%E2%80%99s-shelter-parwan.

218. "To kill one man," wrote Mozi, "is to be guilty of a capital crime. . . . To kill ten men is to increase the guilt ten-fold, to kill a hundred men is to increase it a hundred-fold. This, the rulers of the earth all recognize, and yet when it comes to the greatest crime—waging war on another state—they praise it! It is clear they do not know it is wrong, for they record such deeds to be handed down to posterity; if they knew they were wrong, why should they wish to record them and have them handed down to posterity? If a man on seeing a little black were to say it is black, but on seeing a lot of black were to say it is white, it would be clear that such a man could not distinguish black and white. Or if he were to taste a few bitter things and were to pronounce them sweet, clearly he would be incapable of distinguishing between sweetness and bitterness. So those who recognize a small crime as such, but do not recognize the wickedness of the greatest crime of all—the waging of war on another state—but actually praise it—cannot distinguish right and wrong. So as to right and wrong, the rulers of the world are in confusion." Via Mark Kurlansky, *Nonviolence: The History of a Dangerous Idea* (New York: Modern Library, 2008).

219. Via Philip Spoerri, address at the ceremony celebrating the sixtieth anniversary of the Geneva Conventions, December 8, 2009, https://www.icrc.org/eng/resources/documents/statement/geneva-conventions-statement-120809.htm.

23. Rescue of a Child from an Islamic State Massacre

220. This quotation was taken from video of the incident shot by the Free Burma Rangers; all the other quotations in this section are from my own recordings.

221. Specifically, Karen.

222. Total civilian casualty figures in the fight for Mosul are huge—Kurdish intelligence estimates forty thousand dead. Patrick Cockburn, "The Massacre of Mosul," *The Independent*, July 19, 2017, http://www.independent.co.uk/news/world/middle-east /mosul-massacre-battle-isis-iraq-city-civilian-casualties-killed -deaths-fighting-forces-islamic-state-a7848781.html.

223. UN High Commissioner for Refugees, *Iraq UNHCR Flash Up-date*, June 18, 2017, https://reliefweb.int/report/iraq/iraq-situation -unhcr-flash-update-18-june-2017.

224. Ayman Bashar Abdul Aziz, interview with the author, Mosul, June 1, 2016.

225. "Where you from?" I ask the driver in a quieter moment.

   "Me?" The ambulance driver smirks, "Tweal. West Baghdad. The neighborhood for fucking and dancing."

   Other drivers laugh.

   "He's recording."

   "Oh, really?"

   "He's trying to get people's life stories."

   More laughter.

226. "I joined as a fighter," the driver tells me, "but saw they needed an ambulance driver with experience in first aid so I told them I could do it, and they took me on. Before I was in the military I was in *Hashd*. I wasn't even an adult."

   "Which *Hashd*?"

   "Hashd al-Shaabi."

   "No, like, *Saraya al-Salam* or . . . ?"

"Saraya al-Salam."

The driver opens his shirt, pinches a medallion bearing the face of Muqtada al-Sadr from black chest hair. He's a jock, king of the locker room, mocking but winning.

Saraya al-Salam, or Peace Brigade, is the Iraqi militia loyal to Muqtada al-Sadr.

VII. ARGUMENTS FOR REFORM OF THE NON-COMBATANT CASUALTY CUTOFF VALUE

24. The Morning Brief

227. Colonel Steve Warren, interview with the author and Baghdad foreign press corps, May 9, 2016.

228. As a result of 13,121 official airstrikes, up to that point in May 2016; see "Daily Military Reports," Airwars, May 2016, https://airwars.org/daily-reports/.

229. Imagine one woman beside you, her smell. Imagine ten. Do you feel a hitch in thought, as I do? A hitch, then release: Surely we, here, cannot be responsible for that, there. A more legitimate estimate of the number that May morning is 1,500. "Civilian and 'Friendly Fire' Casualties," Airwars, May 2016, https://airwars.org/civilian-casualty-claims/.

230. Barack Obama, "Executive Order—United States Policy on Pre- and Post-Strike Measures to Address Civilian Casualties in U.S. Operations Involving the Use of Force," White House Press Office, July 1, 2016, https://obamawhitehouse.archives.gov/the-press-office/2016/07/01/executive-order-united-states-policy-pre-and-post-strike-measures.

231. See literature on "normal accidents"—ostensibly undesirable consequences flowing from operational design. For example,

Charles Perrow, *Normal Accidents: Living with High-Risk Technologies* (Princeton, NJ: Princeton University Press, 1999).

232. "The other thing with terrorists is that you have to take out their families." Donald Trump on *Fox and Friends*, December 2, 2015.

25. Strikes Through History

233. Richard Berk, "An Introduction to Sample Selection Bias in Sociological Data," *American Sociological Review* 48, no. 3 (June 1983).

234. How? How is getting shot ever intimate? How is violence intimate rather than entropic, destructive, brutal? The acceptance of intimacy in violence is an unoriginal idea, even a craven one, born of inability or fatigue at looking at a bleeding wound, and greed for all the usual lyrical trappings.

235. Although not as undone as one lacking a sense of humor with this voice-of-God rhetoric.

236. *"I'm a color reporter (rose city on the 409) / But the city's been bled white (white city on the yellow line) . . ."* Elliott Smith, "Bled White," *XO* (Dreamworks, 1998).

237. One frequent and early lesson of reporting, usually related with dignity from older correspondents: Your risk is not only your own; it is your fixer's. Most fixers I knew, though, would never take a risk if they didn't really want to.

238. Harry Truman, "Radio Report to the American People on the Potsdam Conference," Harry S. Truman Public Papers, August 9, 1945, Harry S. Truman Presidential Library & Museum, Independence, Missouri, https://www.trumanlibrary.org/publicpapers/?pid=104.

239. "There are voices which assert that the bomb should never have been used at all. I cannot associate myself with such ideas. . . . I am surprised that very worthy people, but people who in most cases had no intention of proceeding to the Japanese front themselves, should adopt the position that rather than throw this

bomb, we should have sacrificed a million American and a quarter of a million British lives." Winston Churchill, address delivered to the House of Commons, August 16, 1945.

240. Hidran Ali Abdullah in her mother's arms (right).

241. Bahiya Hassan Souhail, interview with the author, July 2016, Amiriyat Fallujah.

242. Mark Selden, "A Forgotten Holocaust: U.S. Bombing Strategy, the Destruction of Japanese Cities, and the American Way of War from the Pacific War to Iraq," in *Bombing Civilians: A Twentieth Century History,* ed. Yuki Tanaka and Marilyn Young (New York: New Press, 2010).

243. Via Yuki Tanaka, "British 'Humane Bombing' in Iraq During the Interwar Era," in *Bombing Civilians: A Twentieth Century History*, ed. Yuki Tanaka and Marilyn B. Young (New York: New Press, 2010).

244. British National Archives Document Air 20/8895, "Z Unit Somaliland No. 8, Military Standing and Operation Orders, Corresponding Between C.O.Z. and C.O.S."; Air 5/1315, photos in the file "RAF Somaliland Expedition 1920: Medical Arrangements, Reports and Photographs." Much history in this section was learned from Tanaka in *Bombing Civilians*, and the scholarship of David Omissi, which in turn relies on documents such as this one.

245. David E. Omissi, *Air Power and Colonial Control: The Royal Air Force 1919–1939* (Manchester, England: Manchester University Press, 1990).

246. Via Jonathan Chait, "Five Days That Shaped a Presidency," *New York*, October 2, 2016, http://nymag.com/daily/intelligencer/2016/10/barack-obama-on-5-days-that-shaped-his-presidency.html.

247. David Vine, "Where in the World Is the U.S. Military?," *Politico*, July/August 2015, http://www.politico.com/magazine/story/2015/06/us-military-bases-around-the-world-119321; Emmett Rensin, "The Empire Doesn't Care Who Is President," *The Outline*, September 4, 2017, https://theoutline.com/post/2203/the-empire-doesn-t-care-who-is-president.

26. Origins of This Account

248. Though this does not absolve him of guilt.

249. "For liberal ironists, there is no answer to the question 'Why not be cruel?'—no noncircular theoretical backup for the belief that cruelty is horrible. Nor is there an answer to the question 'How do you decide when to struggle against injustice and when to devote yourself to private projects of self-creation?'. . . or the question 'When may one favor members of one's family, or one's community, over other, randomly chosen, human beings?' Anybody who thinks that there are well-grounded theoretical answers to this sort of question—algorithms for resolving moral dilemmas of this sort—is still, in his heart, a theologian or a metaphysician. He believes in an order beyond time and change which both determines the point of human existence and establishes a hierarchy of responsibilities.

"The ironist intellectuals who do not believe that there is such an order are far outnumbered (even in the lucky, rich, literate democracies) by people who believe that there *must* be one. Most nonintellectuals are still committed either to some form of religious faith or to some form of Enlightenment rationalism. So ironism has often seemed intrinsically hostile not only to democracy but to human solidarity—to solidarity with the mass of mankind, all those people who are convinced that such an order must exist. But it is not."

Richard Rorty, *Contingency, Irony, and Solidarity* (Cambridge, England: Cambridge University Press, 1989).

250. U.S. Government Accountability Office, *The Department of Defense's Use of Solatia and Condolence Payments in Iraq and Afghanistan* (Washington, DC: USGAO, May 2007), p. 13, https://www.gao.gov/new.items/d07699.pdf.

251. Douri, the Agence France Presse office cat, was named for the Ba'athist general Izzat Ibrahim al-Douri, who evaded capture after the overthrow of Saddam Hussein.

252. They gave us vests with their logo for disguise, and I greeted an old colleague whose foot had been blown off in the Iran-Iraq War. On the outskirts of Baghdad security forces stopped one of our convoy, a minivan of Iraqi journalists, ahead of us. Someone apparently had been pointing a camera out the window. My car sped around the checkpoint. At the next cluster of buildings we waited, and my fixer reprimanded me for trying to get out for better view. We speculated on the potential length of our colleagues' detention but there was nothing we could do without jeopardizing ourselves. We left them all behind and followed the lead car, which had also escaped.

253. The army did not want terrorists and refugees coming to the capital but was less concerned with those leaving for the desert, so they weren't rigorous with us.

254. On this drive I was seated beside a young, goateed doctor. On his wrist, an enormous watch caught the sunlight. He'd studied medicine in Kiev and wanted to talk about the beauty of Ukrainian women. My interpreter did, too, joked that he would leave both his wives for a Ukrainian. They spoke about Ukrainian women as though, on landing in Kiev, one simply began having sex, the way one might check into a hotel.

255. In verifying civilian casualties, working quickly was sometimes preferable to the detailed observation of the grim and predominant business of such places, which requires waiting and is necessary to understand them deeply.

256. Hospital documents she provided corroborate this date.

257. +964 07814489385; Rahim Ahmed is the contact.

258. "I am told Outkast no longer appear together. Waiting on team Florence." Eric Simonoff, email correspondence to the author, April 21, 2016. For this, and help throughout the publication process, I'm grateful to Eric Simonoff; likewise John Parsley, Katie Zaborsky, Michelle Daniel, and David Rosenthal, who originally acquired this project. I'm also and especially grateful to early readers, colleagues, and friends Dave Evans, Dr. Tommy Wide, Isabel Buchanan, Azmat Khan, Loveday Morris, Ahmad Mousa, Luke Mogelson, Casey Selwyn, Roopa Gogeneni, John Dempsey, and Karl Taro Greenfeld.

259. Frank Ocean, feat. Andre 3000, "Solo (Reprise)," *Blond*, 2016.

260. Bashir Ahmed Abdullah, collected refugee interviews, Amiriyat Fallujah, July 27, 2016.

27. The Unavoidable Question

261. It was actually her sister's living room, but the spy, Sabrine Abdullah, was living there, too. Some of this story appears in altered form in "The Widow's Network," an article published by Amazon Original Stories in January 2018.

262. When Major Talat received the call from Sabrine, he'd been a member of Iraq's security forces for twenty-five years. Originally, he'd been in the army—like his father, who, in retirement, lived in the big house in Kadisiya Two. Talat had lost his position when the Coalition Provisional Authority disbanded the army in 2003, but he'd been able to get a job with Interior Intelligence. In this capacity, he'd been fighting and spying on insurgents for eleven years by the time ISIS emerged. He'd risen to become an influential colonel—essentially a spymaster for Saladin province, of which Tikrit is the capital. It was his job to know everything, and the sudden assault by ISIS was probably the biggest failure of his

career. He did not, however, see any irony in the request he would make on the basis of Sabrine's intelligence. At forty-eight, driven from his hometown, shrapnel lodged in his thick torso from campaigns gone by, he would request the destruction of his own house.

As Major Talat remembers it, he cried as he made the decision, but never had any doubts.

Major Talat Issa Khalaf, interviews with the author, Baghdad and Tikrit, 2016.

263. Fat Mike received Major Talat's call in Samarra. A city of mosques and shrines about halfway between Tikrit and Baghdad, Samarra

Major Talat Issa Khalaf in front of his destroyed house

plays a key role in Iraq's recent history. The destruction of its golden-domed al-Askari mosque in 2006 is often cited as the spark for the sectarian civil war. It was rebuilt, and a second destruction by insurgents is a nightmare scenario for sectarian relations. Fat Mike's SWAT team was among the assembled security forces that, a few weeks before Major Talat's call, had stopped ISIS's invasion of Samarra less than two kilometers from al-Askari, preventing that catastrophe.

The last time insurgents had swarmed Samarra, in the fall of 2004, American forces had freed the city—among them, the 25th Infantry Division, with whom Fat Mike eventually worked. He started with the Americans in May 2004, when he was sixteen. Employed successively by the contractors L-3 Communications and Global Linguist Solutions, he interpreted for the 82nd and 101st Airborne, as well as the 25th, as all fought for control of Saladin. When the U.S. Army left in 2010, he joined a personal security detail for RTI International, a North Carolina–based nonprofit organization that had a contract with USAID to "foster local governance" in Saladin.

Throughout the war and after, Fat Mike's American colleagues came and went, but one in particular stayed in touch. When they'd met in 2004 he'd been in the U.S. Army, but when he came back in 2006, he seemed to be a civilian. He'd been coming to Iraq ever since. Fat Mike had him saved in his phone as "Marius." He believed Marius worked for the CIA, and regularly passed him information. That summer of 2014, the information was often grid coordinates for ISIS weapons caches, bomb factories, or bases.

The coordinates weren't in standard GPS form. Instead, Fat Mike sent twelve-digit alphanumeric codes associated with a real-time mapping software system called the Android Tactical Assault Kit, or ATAK, developed by the United States Air Force Research Laboratory in Rome, New York. The ATAK icon, on a smartphone, resembles the *Star Wars* robot R2-D2, but holding an assault rifle.

A text containing
ATAK coordinates

Fat Mike's tattoo

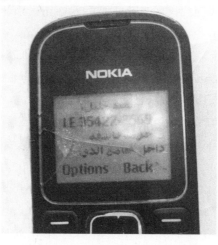

A text from Fat Mike's phone to "Marius"

Once open, the application looks like Google Maps, but with its own coordinate system, and an array of icons indicating the position of various units and targets.

After Major Talat called Fat Mike with Sabrine's information, the two of them confirmed the grid coordinates of Talat's house on ATAK. Then Fat Mike texted them to Marius.

264. From email correspondence with Luke Wilson, A SPC USARMY CENTCOM CJTF OIR, August 29, 2016, after repeated requests:

Here is your query and our response.

Q1. I'm looking for confirmation and/or comment on a Iraqi officer who claims to be running an intelligence network in Saladin and elsewhere which is providing intelligence used in U.S. airstrikes. Can we have a conversation about this, at your earliest convenience? I would like to make sure I get the coalition side of the story properly.

A1. We utilize intelligence from multiple sources on the ground and through ISR in order to validate targets for airstrikes. For operational security we will not release any information in regards to our allies on the ground.

265. The description of this explosion is an old technique—specificity about the mechanisms of death. Sebastian Junger does it for drowning in *The Perfect Storm*. Homer does it for Patroclus's death in *The Iliad*.

266. Usually to the short-term benefit of towns where missiles are manufactured.

267. Iraqi officials said they had no records to check.

268. Colonel Ali Soudani, phone interview with the author, Baghdad, 2016.

269. Major Talat told me so. But in my last interview with him, he also changed his story. Though he had previously produced a notebook in which he claimed to have marked the destruction of his house at the time, though he had told me it occurred definitively on "September 15, 2014," the last time I saw him he said the strike did not occur until the following March, when the Americans began to bomb Tikrit officially. Between our interviews, he had consulted with Fat Mike. I suspect but cannot prove Major Talat decided it was preferable to stick to the official line. I did not press him on the change because at that point in the investigation I did not want to alienate him. I have not had the chance to interview him since, and wish I had confronted him in the moment. I now see no fruit from that compromise, or any compromise I've ever made in the course

of reporting such stories, save that we are safely through them. It is no excuse, but I was treading carefully because another spy had accused Major Talat of collaborating with ISIS. She, however, had boasted to me of her own treachery and cruelty, showed me pictures of herself holding a severed head, and so I was not inclined to believe her. As you can see, there are further leads to follow around this incident. Without the interviews and records I've requested from the Americans, it is impossible to lay this matter fully to rest. I would be eager for clarification and to correct the account should the Americans decide to provide their side of the story. But it is right and I hope some of our politicians, at least, would agree that it is good to begin writing the history and pursue the discussion in a spirit of optimism and collaboration, even if all the players are for the moment unwilling to cooperate.

270. Sara regained consciousness and held on for two months before falling into a coma and succumbing to injuries sustained in the blast. She did not die immediately of blood loss, or decapitation, but her father stated it was the blast that killed her. Major Talat likewise attributed her death to the strike. I could not locate the doctor, but Sara's father reports he blamed the missile for Sara's death as well. Would it be better if she had been killed instantly?

271. Mohanad N. Mohammed, interview with the author, July 19, 2016.

About the Author

Nick McDonell was born in New York City. He is the bestselling author of several books, including the novels *Twelve* and *An Expensive Education*, and a work of political theory on nomadism, *The Civilization of Perpetual Movement*.